Praise for
*100 Places in France Every Woman*

"In this elegant book, Marcia DeSanctis becomes your smartest, most glamorous, generous and insightful friend—your sage, and your guide. *100 Places in France* is a treasure for any woman who wishes to know the country intimately, from its most delectable and stylish surfaces (lingerie! parfum!) to its nuanced and profound depths. Whether traveling by jet, or simply by imagination, you will savor this ride, perhaps along with a glass of fine champagne or the perfect demitasse. I loved it."

—Dani Shapiro, author of *Devotion* and *Still Writing*

"I'm not sure which I would rather do: pack this book and visit all the sublime places Marcia DeSanctis portrays, or curl up in my living room and devour the shimmering language in her 100 beautiful stories. Either way, *100 Places in France* is travel writing at its finest: informative, deep and transporting."

—Ann Leary, author of *The Good House*

"Even if you don't have plans to go to France, Marcia DeSanctis will take you there with her whimsical, encyclopedic guide to Gallic life—from the obvious to the obscure, from her favorite Parisian lingerie shop to her favorite hikes in the Calanques, from the architectural marvels of Le Corbusier to the gardens of Le Notre, from the lavender routes of Provence to the ancient menhirs of Carnac. This book is a necessary indulgence for even the most jaded Francophile."

—Kate Betts, author of *Everyday Icon: Michelle Obama and the Power of Style*

# 100 *Places in France Every Woman Should Go*

MARCIA DESANCTIS

TRAVELERS' TALES
AN IMPRINT OF SOLAS HOUSE, INC.
PALO ALTO

Travelers' Tales and Solas House are trademarks of Solas House, Inc., 2320 Bowdoin Street, Palo Alto, California 94306. www.travelerstales.com

Art direction: Stefan Gutermuth
Cover design: Kimberly Coombs
Cover illustration: Tadahiro Uesugi
Interior design and page layout: Howie Severson
Author photograph: Ron Haviv

Distributed by Publishers Group West, 1700 Fourth Street, Berkeley, CA 94170

Library of Congress Cataloging-in-Publication Data Available Upon Request

ISBN-10: 1-609520-82-3
ISBN-13: 978-1-60952-082-3

First Edition
Printed in the United States
10 9 8 7 6 5 4 3 2 1

*For Mark*

# Table of Contents

# Introduction

WHEN I WAS A GIRL in suburban Boston, I loved to unfurl a certain brand of canned dough and re-furl it into crescent rolls, which I would bake on a cookie sheet. I adored these flaky biscuits, even more so when I learned that they were really called "croissants" and in France, they were eaten at breakfast rather than at dinner alongside beef stew. What eight year-old girl would not become infatuated by a country whose morning tradition was a chunk of melted butter held together with wispy strands of pastry? Sure beat a jelly donut. The food, or the fantasy of it, got me curious about France. But it was the women who held my attention.

For the "Profile in History" I had to write in sixth grade, I chose Marie Antoinette and tried to imagine my 14-year-old sister as the next queen of France. I was transfixed by my junior high French teacher, Mrs. Zack, who tossed a shawl around one shoulder as one might throw a wrap over a lamé gown. Tacked to the wall of another French class was an album cover of the '60s pop singer, Françoise Hardy, whom I believed was, bar none, the most gorgeous woman who had ever existed. I raced through the slim novel *Bonjour Tristesse*, which had two reasons to enthrall me. The author Françoise Sagan was all of eighteen when she wrote it, and the book's main character Cécile, though troubled, was seventeen—same as I was—and steeped in a life of shameless sensuality on the French Riviera. New

England, I concluded, could not produce such a worldly creature (although Jean Seberg, a pixie-haired actress from Iowa, played her in the film version).

Above all, there was Audrey Hepburn, who was not even French, but British and Dutch, and yet her spirit, grace and demeanor came to define Paris for me. I devoured her films on the Boston UHF station, even if I had to fiddle with the antennas. From *Charade* to *Love in the Afternoon*, *How to Steal a Million*, to most of all *Funny Face* and *Sabrina*, with each role Audrey made Paris more enticing and somehow more accessible. The allure was, only partially, a matter of style, although it was hard not to yearn for something besides the rolled-up turtlenecks and worn Levi's cords of my teens. No one had ever accessorized a cherry-red suit with an ice cream cone, but Audrey did, walking the banks of the Seine with Cary Grant.

Paris widened her eyes—she said so in *Sabrina*—and then she opened mine. "I have learned so many things, father," she whispers in voice-over in the film, as she prepares to return to Long Island after two years of culinary school in Paris. It is nighttime, and she is writing a letter at her desk before a window opened to the incomparable vision of Sacré-Cœur on its hill. "Not just how to make vichyssoise and calf's head with sauce vinaigrette. But a much more important recipe. I have learned how to live."

And then I did, too. I arrived in Paris in the summer of 1979 via Italy and the Côte d'Azur. At dawn, I saw the Mediterranean for the first time from the train, and the coming morning was reflected on the silvery sea. At the station in Nice, I waded through the aromas of *tabac brun* and strong coffee, and outdoors was greeted by wide avenues that sizzled in dry, crackling heat, the scent of jasmine and lemon, and glimmering villas with wrought iron balconies overlooking the Baie des Anges.

I spent mornings torched by the sun at the market on the Cours Saleya, where I pressed the rough hides of sweet melons to determine their ripeness, and swooned at the profusion of pastel yellows and corals in the baskets of peaches. I had eaten many straw- berries in my life, but in Nice, I tasted one—a real one—for the first time. As for croissants, there was no comparison between what I had baked at home in Boston and what I tasted in France, especially when served with *chocolat chaud* and fresh apricot jam. Afternoons I stretched out on the beach by the Promenade des Anglais, or took the train to another Riviera sunspot—Èze, Villefranche, Saint Tropez. Eventually, I dared to untie my bikini top.

I knew I could never be French, but I also knew that I belonged in France. I came to realize that most of all when I finally got to Paris that summer, when I counted centimes for a bottle of Badoit at the grocer near my hotel, or ambled through the Jardins des Tuileries in the evening. I was at ease, comfortable, *bien dans ma peau.* I was at home there. That fall, Marianne Faithfull released an album called "Broken English," with her haunting rendition of "The Ballad of Lucy Jordan" in which she sings these devastating words: *At the age of thirty-seven/She realized she'd never ride/Through Paris in a sports car/With the warm wind in her hair.* I listened to it again and again. Its message resonated: Not just me, but every woman belonged in Paris, and to miss out meant missing out on life itself. France was not just my ideal; it was a universal one, a rite of passage, the place we were where we could both escape ourselves and find the power and grace to be ourselves. It was one piffling ocean away, and returning there as soon as possible was the best reason I could think of to squirrel away my paycheck from my job at the faculty club.

Those heightened, instantaneous emotions we feel in the city of Paris hold true for the rest of France. The country opens its arms to us, understands what women love, takes us in and bathes us in starlight that seems to burn brighter over Mont Ventoux or the Pont du Gard than it does at home. It cultivates our sophisticated and sensuous sensibilities and insists we accompany them with champagne. We love the carnal sway of the Eiffel Tower and the stories of France's great queens and mistresses held in the châteaux of Versailles and Chenonceau. Of course, we love the perfume, to scan the market for the best deal on fresh figs, the hollow clack of cobblestones under our heels, the citrusy scent of gorse blowing across a field in Normandy. We love the safety and ease of the Paris Métro and marvel at the sweep of almond blossoms in Haute-Provence. We gasp at the beauty of the bridges over the Seine and always feel at home when we stop in the middle of one to gaze down at the cottony wake of the Bateaux Mouches. We love the mountain air that refreshes us in the Alps, and the nighttime clouds that eat the stars over the Breton coast. We love to slow down, and France requires us to do so.

In France, we find what we are missing. This book contains 100 of those missing things. It was a nearly impossible task to choose just 100, which is why, in some entries, I have included not just one suggestion but two or ten—hikes, gardens, places to shop or landmarks to follow in the path of Joan of Arc. How could I curate France? In my first crack at a list of 100 places, I was barely out of the Marais neighborhood of Paris and already had 50 must-sees. France is diverse, sprawling, magnificent, flush with architecture, culture, style, royalty and religion, soaked in sauce Béarnaise and Bordeaux reds. There are coasts to swim along, mountain ravines to wander, town squares where one can sip coffee all day alone and no one will ever ask you to leave. There are thousands of years of history—from the Celts to the Romans to World War II—all of which are still relevant and resonant. There are dozens of distinct cultures—Normans, Lyonnais and Niçois—and they all exist proudly under the same tricolor banner. There are fashion, gastronomy, and museums full of masterpieces so familiar that they risk cliché. Most importantly—at least for this collection—there are women, and in these pages, I will tell many of their stories. I am in awe of

Eleanor of Aquitaine, George Sand, Catherine de' Medici, Léa Feldblum, Simone de Beauvoir and others, and I hope that like me, you might be inspired to delve deeper into each of them. On the landscape of world history, they are giants, and France keeps their memories vibrantly alive.

This list is for women, but most of us know that men love France just as much as we do. After my first trip to Paris, I returned often, and when I was twenty-nine, my boyfriend convinced me to move there with him. I left my job at ABC News in New York, applied for and received a press fellowship from what is now the European Union, and after a year, returned to my work as a TV producer in Paris. My husband is a sculptor, and he rented a skylit studio near Père Lachaise cemetery. We got married in the *mairie* of the 3rd arrondissement, bought a 7th-floor apartment, and started to build a life together. On some mornings en route to the Métro, or at Christmastime, or when I passed the Eiffel Tower which seemed to be posing for me in the fog, I would say to myself: "I live in Paris. *I live in Paris.*"

Mark and I returned to the United States after four years and regretted it for four years afterwards. Eventually, we relocated from New York City to rural Connecticut. Now, we find Paris to be surprisingly near, once you cross the pond. Shortly after we moved here I switched from television to print journalism, and as the pay was fairly non-existent, a nearby prep school hired me as a French teacher, sort of a permanent substitute for a couple of years. At first, I wanted to refuse the textbooks and teacher's companions that had been handed to me in two towering stacks—and opt to teach the students something more compelling and alive. It seems I've always been on a mission to let people know how France can change you. I wanted to toss them academic bouquets, and give tutorials about Camembert and Brigitte Bardot, in between screenings of *Les Parapluies de Cherbourg* and *Amélie*. We would read

Marie Antoinette's last letter from prison and hope they could get to Versailles one day to visit her tragic, transcendent realm. In April, I would assign them Colette's essay, "Farewell to the Snow," tell them about the sweet blueberries that grow in the mountains, the waves that smash off Biarritz, the sound of gulls at Étretat. We would translate *"Tous les Garçons et les Filles,"* a lilting chanson from 1962 sung by my idol, Françoise Hardy. I would omit the part about champagne buzzing through my veins, but describe the thrill of driving through Paris on a summer evening with a handsome young man named Baudouin at the wheel, which I did long before I was thirty-seven, with the warm wind in my hair.

But they had AP exams to pass and colleges to get accepted to, so I had to restrict my alternative lesson to convey just one kernel of truth. I would tell them what Audrey told me. In France, I learned how to live. I wanted them to have that experience. If you haven't already, I wish that for you too.

MARCIA DESANCTIS
BETHLEHEM, CONNECTICUT

# 1

## A Pink House and a Rose Garden

### THE BAGATELLE, PARIS

American expats in France, and those of us who visit frequently, can sometimes be reluctant to divulge their—okay, *our*—secret haunts. Next thing you know, it's busloads of tourists in baggy shorts and ungainly white sneakers, and soon recherché is an emphatic *démodé*. There is a touch of stinginess in that logic, of course, but mercifully, Parisians themselves do not tend to be quite so turfy about the places they hold dear in their very own city. It was this kind of openness that led me to the Parc de Bagatelle, a place so abundant and airy it should be no secret at all. But to me that day, it was.

I moved to Paris one September, landing with too many duffel bags and a box of blank reporter's notebooks my colleagues at ABC News had given me as a going away present. It was a Winesap-crisp Sunday morning, and I recall the dainty rustle of chestnut trees when I unclasped and threw open the window onto a Paris street for the first time. I was alone; my then-boyfriend (now husband) would be arriving in November. Someone in the building was playing a cello—or maybe it was a recording—and the notes drifted into my new living room. Through a friend's aunt's cousin's brother-in-law or some such, we had secured a one-bedroom sixth-floor rental apartment in a cushy building in the 16th arrondissement. I hadn't yet discovered the buzzy street life on nearby rue de l'Annonciation, or the Marché Couvert de Passy that was right around the corner and is still one of my favorite food markets in Paris. As far as I could tell, everything was closed. I was starving and thirsty, desperate for a liter of Badoit and a two-pack of yogurt or a couple of apples so I could have a nibble and a nap. So I stopped an elderly madame in the foyer, as stately as her neighborhood of mansions and old money dictated, and asked where I could *chercher à manger.*

"The Stella on Avenue Victor Hugo is open and very good, and afterwards of course it's a lovely day for the Jardins de Bagatelle." So much for a chilly Parisian welcome. "It's where we like to go on Sundays."

I thanked her, made sure my trusty red *Plan de Paris par Arrondissement* booklet—left over from my former life as a tourist here—was in my purse, and I walked and walked and walked and in some ways, never looked back.

The park—not to be confused with the Parc Bagatelle amuse-ment park way up in Nord-Pas-de-Calais—is embedded deep within the Bois de Boulogne. It's possible to walk there, as I did, but the Métro stops at Pont de Neuilly nearby. Upon entering, you are struck by the refined grandeur and splendid isolation here on the periphery of Paris. It was built in 1775 on the site of a former *lieu de libertinage*—kind of a grown-up playground—as the result of a wager between Queen Marie Antoinette and her brother-in-law, the Count d'Artois (who, in 1824 would become the reactionary King Charles X of France). The Count had demolished the old hunting lodge and desired a *bagatelle*, from the Italian word for "decorative little trifle," on the property. The Queen bet it would not be ready in the three months the Court was away for the season at Fontainebleau, and she lost. 100,000 pounds worth of lost.

Because he enlisted the expertise of neoclassical architect François-Joseph Bélanger and one of the queen's favorite garden-ers, the Scotsman Thomas Blaikie, the château and gardens were completed in a jaw-dropping 63 days using 800 workers with an expenditure topping 5 million pounds. Later, an *orangerie* was added to the compound, the centerpiece of which is the main château: symmetrical, pink and flawless. The Latin inscription above the doorway reads *Parva sed Apta*—"small but convenient"—which given the luxury and expense, seems the very definition of the humble-brag. The buildings are lovely, but it is the park to which I devoted myself that Sunday morning long ago.

The gardens were designed in the Anglo-Chinese landscape style and contain grottoes and waterfalls, silent pathways, a water lily pond, and a soft blue pagoda that seems to spring straight from the earth. There are fountains and walkways lined with the benches I grew to know and love. Mostly, there are lawns where peacocks mince around making a charming racket and flowers whose blossoms and fragrance change with the seasons. Daffodils and crocus push out in early spring and give way to peonies, irises, wisteria, and a renowned collection of clematis, and the perfume drifts through the park like sighs. And most spectacularly, there is a rose garden with over 10,000 bushes from around 1,200 varieties, where an international competition for new roses takes place every June.

By spring, my boyfriend and I had moved to funkier digs in the Marais and eventually bought the only apartment we could afford, in the Belleville section of the 20th about a decade before it was chic, far from the Bois and the Bagatelle. But I returned to the staid 16th often and I still do, because more than any other park, café, bridge or boulevard, the Bagatelle is my own secret haunt. I'll make my way there on a Sunday, join the dowagers, hipsters and mothers chasing toddlers. There, I seek the memory of the day I arrived to begin a new chapter in France. Only a few hours later, thanks to a kindly neighbor, I already felt like a Parisian.

# 2

# The Artist's Artist

## MUSÉE RODIN AND CAMILLE CLAUDEL, PARIS

Weather permitting, I always begin outdoors in the sculpture garden at the Musée Rodin. It is a silent, green sanctum that doubles as an urban retreat for Parisians, just a few quick steps from the windy sweep of the Boulevard des Invalides. The park is so expansive and yet so soothing, it could be the courtyard behind a dear friend's château—or in one dream, even my own. When I worked in the area, some days I would opt out of the three-course lunch with wine and instead bring a book and a sandwich—and in summer, a tube of sunscreen—to decompress in the company of Rodin's bronzes that are positioned along pristine *allées* and in the center of a large fountain. Often I would wander inside the museum before returning to the office. *Il faut*, they say in French. You must. My friend Beth Kseniak, who has scant downtime directing public relations for *Vanity Fair*, tells me it's the only place she escapes to, religiously, when she is in Paris. "It's such an intimate space," she says. "I feel transported to a different time, as if I had been invited for a private tour. I almost expect Rodin himself to grace us with his presence."

The museum is housed inside the lavish Hôtel Biron, Auguste Rodin's handpicked location for his vast body of work. I come here not simply to admire the artist's brilliance. I can do that elsewhere, too. His house in Meudon on the outskirts of Paris is a vibrant

4

place of pilgrimage and is entirely his. But here, there is a bonus: the chance to pay tribute to Camille Claudel's fierce talent and ponder her extraordinary, tragic life.

Claudel has been depicted in film by two of France's most celebrated actresses, Juliette Binoche and Isabel Adjani, because her heartbreaking story is the very essence of drama—brilliance and madness and marginalization—not least because she was a woman. Until the mid-to-late 20th century, the art world was for the most part an exclusive men's club. This was especially true in the realm of sculpture, the dirtiest, most labor-intensive and least ladylike of the creative disciplines. Claudel, however, was singular in this practice. She was tremendously accomplished, even in the shadow of Rodin, the man for whom she was model, muse, assistant and lover.

Claudel is, perhaps unavoidably, always examined in the context of her master. She was a prodigious artist as a teenager (and already a legendary beauty), and when she was eighteen, a family friend introduced her to Rodin, who was twenty-four years her senior. As his apprentice, she created many of the models for some of his masterpieces, including *The Gates of Hell* and *The Burghers of Calais*, and their love affair was credited with re-energizing Rodin's career. He was living with his common-law wife, and though he promised to break off with her and marry Claudel, he never did. It was a turbulent, erotically-charged love affair full of passion and hard work, but within ten years, the couple separated. Claudel vowed to extricate herself from his influence and forge ahead with her own career, which she did. But work turned out to be scarce when the connection to Rodin dissolved, and she became troubled and erratic. In 1913, her family confined her to a psychiatric hospital near Avignon. The rest is almost unbearable to consider: despite her protestations and the repeated efforts of her doctors to convince Camille's family that she was, in fact, of sound mental health, she remained locked up and alone until her death thirty years later.

During her creative years, Camille Claudel shared Rodin's energy to keep the figurative arts vital at the turn of the 20th century, and she made great contributions to the sustained relevance of statuary. To make revisionist comparisons between them is predictable, but it is clear that spirits meshed between muse and master, and there was a kinetic quality to their approach to modeling clay and in their shared attitude toward drama, which both felt necessary to portray a dynamic figure.

Sadly, she destroyed much of her work, but fortunately upstairs here at the museum, there are seven pieces on permanent display, two of which—*The Wave* and *The Gossips*—are so uniquely Claudel and so heroically executed that they may be two of the most wonderful, quiet moments in the history of sculpture.

*The Wave* is a magnificent onyx (not to be confused with alabaster) carving of a towering crest of water about to overtake three female bathers. The waves themselves morph into human forms that are menacing even on this small scale. It was completed around 1900, while Claudel was getting comfortable with carving this stone, both harder and much less forgiving than marble. The wave is poised as an ominous abstraction while the bathers are preoccupied with each other and oblivious to the looming peril.

 *The Gossips* is another small diorama carved completely out of onyx, which depicts a scene of four female nudes who huddle together at a table within an open architectural setting. Again, I can imagine the dialogue, hear the whispers and marvel at the craftsmanship. I gaze, too, at the translucence of the material and the softness that is evoked in these fleshy little nudes, flecked with veins of iron red. The figures beg to be touched and stroked. *The Gossips* was completed in 1897, and by then Claudel was a master carver who exhibited

those skills even on this scale, minute and most difficult to render. This is a masterpiece—pictorial, spatial, luminescent and fluid with the action of the women engaged in debate. This all-female grouping is also a declaration of Claudel's liberation, as they show complete freedom to express, gossip and argue in the privacy of Camille's fantasy. Private, that is, with the exception of intruding giants like us trying to listen in.

These carvings are symbols of Camille's true power as a craftsman, an expressive force, and—most of all—as an artist and remind us of her gifted, hugely determined voice. I can hear that voice again, in Paris, at 19 quai de Bourbon on the Île Saint-Louis, where she lived until they locked her away for good. "There is always something that is missing that torments me," reads the plaque on the building, taken from a letter to Rodin in 1886. That torment would linger until she finally died in 1943, forgotten by her family but not by history.

❧

# 3

## Homage to La Môme

### THE MUSEUM OF ÉDITH PIAF, PARIS

In October 1963, Édith Piaf died in Grasse at age forty-seven. She was the greatest and most beloved singer France has ever known. She lived an enormous life, which despite her success and acclaim, was ravaged by poverty, tragedy, scandal and eventually the liver disease that killed her. Through her deterioration in her last weeks and months, Piaf still performed, appearing frail those last years, with not much left to her tiny countenance than her great, indestructible voice. Marion Cotillard won an Academy Award in part for her shattering depiction of Piaf's swan song at Paris's Olympia Music Hall in the 2007 film *La Vie en Rose*.

Like the Eiffel Tower, Piaf's music is an emblem of French identity and genius, her voice an indefatigable source of wonderment and awe. Just try not to sprout goose flesh from the pulsating French horn and string introduction of *"Non, je ne regrette rien,"* the same note repeated in a lulling rhythm that starts out loud and grows quieter, paving the way for her immense vocals. When I taught French to high school students, I had them memorize (and translate, of course) the lyrics of this song, rather than those of the equally iconic *"La Vie en rose,"* not just for the straightforward grammar in its construction, but for the philosophy Piaf seems to espouse from the depths of her being. As a poem of inspiration, one could and should recite its verses every day. Live your life without clinging to the past—both the good and the bad—and don't waste emotions on regret. "*C'est payé, balayé, oublié, je me fous du passé*"—"It's paid for, swept away, forgotten, I don't care about the past," she sings. It must have raised the roof back in the day, and it elevates us today.

Just hours after Piaf's demise, her great friend and fellow artist Jean Cocteau died from broken heart syndrome, or so the story goes—a sudden coronary from news of her passing. It is one of the great coincidences in the annals of art and friendship. They both towered over the French cultural landscape, but where Cocteau has museums, retrospectives, and most recently, an exhibition in the Palais-Royal dedicated to him, there is precious little in France that celebrates the life of "La Môme"—the Kid—Piaf's nickname. Maybe it's because her voice was her instrument, something you can't exactly frame and hang on the wall. Maybe it's because she grew up on the streets and in brothels, in the rough quartiers of Belleville, Barbès, and Ménilmontant and, unlike Rimbaud, Renoir, or Balzac, there is no childhood home where memories of her can be assembled. Which is why I urge you to visit the Musée Edith Piaf at 5, rue Crespin du Gast right off the rue Oberkampf in the 11th arrondissement. Fittingly, the museum is on a residential block in the once-gritty neighborhood (now full of artisanal fromageries and farm-to-table cafés) that she wandered as a child named Édith Giovanna Gassion before she was discovered on a street corner at age nineteen.

The private "museum" is an oddity, starting with the oversized and hardly pristine stuffed bear, a gift from her last husband, the Greek hairdresser Théo Sarapo, that occupies an entire upholstered chair near the entrance of the fourth-floor apartment. Next to it is a life-sized cutout of Piaf, who stood a mere 4'8". The space has the feeling of a cluttered attic, but you've got to hand it to Bernard Marchois, the obsessive archivist of the pieces of Piaf's life, who was driven by devotion to open the museum in 1977 and whose passion is contagious. Visits are by appointment only on Monday-Wednesday afternoons and Thursday morning, and as it is in a residential building, Bernard has to give you the door and intercom codes. The day I was there, the place was packed, which left scant room for us with all the furniture, knickknacks and memorabilia. It was satisfying to see a crowd turn out to pay their respects to Piaf's valiant life, and on a Wednesday afternoon no less. Do not try to sneak a photo, as you will suffer a stern rebuke by Bernard!

The two rooms display her clocks and carpets, letters, photographs and objects both marvelous—pairs of her miniscule size 34 shoes (US 4), handbags and a black stage dress complete with the cross she wore around her neck—and touching—a pair of boxing gloves that belonged to her prizefighter husband and great love Marcel Cerdan, who died in a plane crash. There is a leather-bound volume, *La Cuisine de Bourgogne,* from her friend Colette and a worn couch from her last apartment in Paris, as well as candlesticks, urns, and an old Victrola record player.

To complete the homage, I crossed the Boulevard de Ménilmontant to the entrance of Père Lachaise Cemetery, one of the wonders of Paris (see Chapter 13), where Piaf is buried in a modest grave alongside her daughter who died at two of meningitis, her father Louis-Alphonse Gassion and Théo Sarapo. It is a proper resting place for Piaf, to be in the company of such a constellation of luminaries (French and otherwise), among them Molière, Balzac, Proust, Sarah Bernhardt, Jim Morrison, Oscar Wilde, Apollinaire, Chopin and Delacroix. Piaf's funeral *cortège* in Paris brought the entire city to a standstill; more than forty thousand people walked the route to attend her burial, a throng of the curious and the grieving who mourned the loss of the French icon who had the most heavenly of human voices. I should think at least that many would be interested in visiting an official museum in her honor. In the meantime, you can capture the story of her huge life with a visit to this tiny but compelling shrine to the great Édith Piaf.

※

# 4 Bring a Big Shopping Bag

## LA GRANDE ÉPICERIE AT LE BON MARCHÉ, PARIS

Of all the cathedrals in Paris, the one where you may linger longest is La Grande Épicerie at Le Bon Marché department store on the corner of rue du Bac and rue de Sèvres. The religion here exalts the god of food and with that, style, abundance, and quality. You will marvel and wonder, gawk shamelessly, be stunned into a stupor, and feel propelled to spin around in a lose-your-senses euphoria. And then, it can't be helped: you will spend money, perhaps even too much, and you will still leave contented.

I learned about the revamped market—one of the few that really deserves the prefix "super"—and the risks to your wallet at a dinner party in Paris. The host prepared a lasagna that was tasty enough, but we all marveled at the noodles—their density and unusual smooth texture. Provenance, of course: La Grande Épicerie. After dinner, he brandished a simple 8" square of black chocolate, which turned out to be a shell. He raised it and unsheathed the cake beneath, paper-thin layers piled between jam, ganache and cream. He had gone to the store to buy lunch, but he emerged with treasures, several of them. He was delighted, and so were his guests.

Le Bon Marché opened its doors in 1852, and is the oldest department store in France and some say the first in the world. The food hall was created in 1978, but in December 2013, it reopened after an eighteen-month renovation. And it is a dizzying 38,000 square feet of extravagance. Have a hankering for Argentinian bottled water? There's a section for that. Plain old chestnut honey from Les Mées in the Alpes Provençales or Fossier rose biscuits from Reims? Sure thing. How about marshmallow fluff or artisanal maple syrup from Vermont? Done. The truffle department alone is larger than most charcuteries in France, and there is an elegant lunch counter (there are several in the store, as well as wine bars) for whatever you are craving: ravioli with parmesan truffle cream, or scrambled eggs with grated truffles. There are wire baskets of fresh eggs and jellybean-hued crates for you to put them in. There are bakeries, wine caves, a produce department distinguished by a vintage  Citroën truck feigning to spill its contents of just-picked vegetables. And the cheese, the dairy, the butter—there are stacks and stacks of it, including piles of the legendary Beurre Bordier and Pascal Beillevaire brands, both in simple paper wrapping.

Around Paris, people are engaging in spirited debates about the merits of this place, the excess and the decadence. After all, doesn't every quartier have its local fresh market to buy Jambon de Bayonne and seasonal produce, like soft Mirabelle plums from Lorraine? Yes, it's true; nothing can replace a morning at Marché d'Aligre near the Bastille or scooping up handfuls of cherries at Marché La Chapelle in the 18th. But I believe La Grande Épicerie does not herald civilization's decay, but rather an expansion of it. If not in Paris, where then? The place is so stunning and the offerings so sweeping that it screams "innovation" down to the stage-lit cuts of grass-fed beef in the butcher's glass refrigerator. And hey, no one is forcing you to buy anything. But I know you will.

❧

# 5 The Patroness of Paris

## SAINTE GENEVIÈVE AND L'ÉGLISE SAINT-ÉTIENNE-DU-MONT, PARIS

If there is a place I consider to be the heart of Paris—I mean its true, spiritual, pulsating heart—it is the Église Saint-Étienne-du-Mont, deep within the Latin Quarter, which holds the filigreed tomb and relics (or what is left of them) of Paris's patroness and savior, Sainte Geneviève. It is one of the loveliest churches—make that places—in all of Paris, and it's devoted to a colossal figure of faith and magnetism, whose ability to rally the citizenry in prayer spared the city from the ravages of Attila the Hun in A.D. 451. In this sanctum, beauty and female fortitude combine, as they so often do. And yet its greatness lies in not what is visible but in a more rare and unseen *je ne sais quoi,* the kind that makes gazing skyward in a perfectly-calibrated cathedral similar to standing at the edge of a canyon or near a pounding surf at daybreak. In such gently over-powering places we are able to ride the exuberance and vanish in the stillness, all in the space of a couple of breaths.

I discovered it like I did most of the things I love in Paris: by accident. I was meandering home to the Marais after a typically light Parisian lunch of lamb, *gratin dauphinois* and *mousse au chocolat* at Brasserie Balzar on rue des Écoles, when the rolling swells of organ music beckoned me hypnotically toward this small church. Owen Wilson, too, was drawn to the stone steps of this very place in the film *Midnight in Paris*, and along came a carload of partygoers from the 1920s. Within the hour, he was carousing with Hemingway and the Fitzgeralds. In Paris, it's important to allow yourself to be lured—by instinct, a spectacular sound, or by any kind of hunger. You will never regret it.

The church is dwarfed by the massive Panthéon next door, with which it is closely connected and without which the story of Geneviève is incomplete. In the 1740s, King Louis XV was stricken with a mysterious illness and pledged that if he survived, he would build a church for St. Geneviève to house and honor her remains on the site of a basilica and abbey founded by King Clovis in 507, and where in 512 the revered patroness had been buried. Her bones became rather itinerant in the ensuing centuries, stored and paraded around Paris in times of need, and returned to the crypt as a place of pilgrimage, where miracles were sought (and frequently found).

L'Abbaye Sainte-Geneviève took almost four decades to realize and was completed just in time for the French Revolution, whose incendiaries rejected churches, Catholicism and all of its saints. So they opened the tomb, burned the contents and threw the ashes into the Seine. In 1802, the stone slab was found, authenticated and moved over to Sainte-Étienne-du-Mont, where it and the tiny quantity of undestroyed relics are today. The British writer Edward Verrall Lucas put it succinctly in his 1909 book, *A Wanderer in Paris*, "They are sufficient, however, still to cure the halt and the lame and enable them to leave their crutches behind."

After the Revolution, Louis XV's architectural tribute to St. Geneviève became the Panthéon—a shrine to the (mostly) male heroes of France. Strange, isn't it, that a church built in reverence of the woman who saved Paris from invasion and later, famine, should bear the ironic inscription, "To the great men, the grateful homeland"? But the lady is everywhere within. Beyond the mesmerizing Foucault's Pendulum, the Greek and Gothic interior and the stately dome, there are a series of frescoes depicting, from her rustic beginnings, the eventful life of Geneviève, painted from 1875-1877 by Pierre Puvis de Chavannes. Her story is not unlike that of her eventual soul sister, St. Joan of Arc—both young girls, portrayed as shepherdesses with pastoral roots, divinely endowed with the drive, charisma and humility to change the course of history. My favorite is the painting of her at age seven, a waif in a simple white dress with a crown of flaxen hair, being singled out as marked by God by the Bishop St. Germain of Auxerre, who is easily twice her size.

Though named for St. Étienne, whose relics were also within the former abbey, the church in the shadow of the Panthéon belongs to Geneviève. It took 130 years to complete, during which Gothic style began to bleed into Renaissance, but the effect is one of unusual harmony and calm, even daintiness, despite the flamboyant vaults that spring skyward inside the church. The delicately-carved, lacy white structure that crosses the nave symmetrically is called a rood screen. It is the only one left in Paris and considered one of the rarest of its kind in the world. These were built to separate the clergy from the laity, and this one, carved of pale stone, gives the appearance of a wedding cake.

The gold tomb on the stone foundation has detail that is unmistakably Gothic, illuminated by candles that perpetually burn around it and the reliquary. Most moving, however, are a series of marble engravings inlaid into the panel walls, testimonials to faith, and gratitude to the Patroness. "I prayed to St. Geneviève and I was answered. C.L. 1859," reads one.

No matter what your beliefs, there is peace within this sanctuary, and that sensation has not changed since the first time I was enticed inside by the booming sounds of an organ. The hymn was ending as I entered, and when the amen cadence ceased reverberating, it was the hush that seemed to bounce off the stone. You, too, can find this in Paris, here or wherever you happen to find yourself when you follow the music.

# 6 *Always Pack a Bathing Suit*

## POOLS, THE SEINE BEACHES, AQUABIKING AND HAMMAM, PARIS

Paris is a watery city, not Venice or Bruges wet, but coursing with the streams of hundreds of fountains, from the stately reflecting pool at the Louvre Pyramid to the Second Empire monument at the Jardin de l'Observatoire. The Seine flows under the bridges, past the quai booksellers, and just below the feet of a rotating cast of sweethearts who for centuries have sought out the banks of the great river to magnify their senses and pacify their chaos. And then, there is the rain. Audrey Hepburn lovably enthused about a good soaking in *Sabrina*, one of her many films that featured Paris as an equally illuminating character and co-star. "The rain's very important," says Sabrina. "Because that's when Paris smells its sweetest."

The sky in winter can switch from pale violet to flannel gray to nearly black over the course of an hour, and I'm sorry to say that the skies often weep—as Edith Piaf sang in "*Sous le Ciel de Paris*"—"because they are sad and jealous of the city's millions of lovers." A spring cloudburst can be refreshing as it taps the leaves of chestnut trees, but the winter downpours can turn on you like a faucet, sneak down the neck and infuriate you, drench your spine and ruin your perfectly good hair.

And yet, many women in Paris carry on a love affair with water, not just those sweet April showers or a bottle of Vittel, but a good therapeutic dousing, the kind that won't drench your good suede ankle boots. I often noticed, while living there, how so many women brought a bathing suit and towel to work each day. My dermatologist, whom I visited frequently, always had wet hair from doing her laps. "I do all my thinking in the water," she told me. With that in mind, whether you hope to find your equilibrium, get exercise or wash clean your body and soul, here are four ways to take the waters, Paris style.

First, a swimming pool. The sparkling Piscine Joséphine Baker, on the Quai François Mauriac in the 13th, is a pinnacle of modern engineering. It floats on a barge in the Seine, creating the zen sen-

sation of water upon water, and the steel and glass roof retracts in summer. At night, the pool lights mingle with the glow of the city, and both are reflected in the river, which creates a lustrous tableau. My other favorite is the Piscine de la Butte aux Cailles, at 5 place Paul Verlaine in the 13th, set in a neighborhood with an enchanting maze of streets. The pool recently refurbished to its brightly-hued Art Nouveau glory—so authentic you can almost imagine Scott and Zelda stopping by for a dip. The indoor pool (there are two outdoors in the summer) sits under high concrete arches and over a naturally-occurring sulphurous spring, which heats the water to a toasty 28°C all year round.

For the workout of your life that will not leave your clothes damp or your forehead dripping sweat, aquabiking has been all the rage in Paris in recent years. It is like a spin class in a pool, instructor-led with a rousing beat, on a simple steel bike that leaves your legs and part of your arms submerged while your head, back and shoulders are above the water. My favorites are the super clean Atelier Mood at 9, rue d'Aboukir near the Place des Victoires in the 2nd and the glamorous L'Entrepôt at 21, rue du Faubourg Saint Antoine in the Bastille. After a forty-minute class, I have never felt so fit, so restored. And frankly, so blissfully exhausted.

When I asked Paris-based writer Dana Thomas what was meaningful to her in Paris these days, she mentioned her love of Hammam Pacha, a North African-style day spa at 17, rue Mayet in the 6th arrondissement near Montparnasse. Water! Thomas is the author of *Deluxe: How Luxury Lost Its Luster*, a fascinating bestseller about the rising price and declining quality of many designer goods. For her, the gleaming space, the steam room, plunge pool, and massages by skilled hands add up to something wonderfully transformative. "It's in the heart of the city but once you've stepped in, you feel like you have traveled to Morocco," she says about the hammam, which can be almost too popular (and should best be avoided) on weekends. "There's a nice restaurant too, so you can spend the entire day there and come out a new person."

Lastly, though you may not see many locals hanging out on the Paris Plages—the artificial sandy beaches that extend along the Seine from mid July to mid August—they are a singular feat of urban ingenuity. Every year, the city unloads 5,000 tons of sand and 100 or more giant potted palms along two miles of the riverbank, placing chaises, blue umbrellas, cafés and ice cream stands along three different stretches of ersatz Caribbean beaches. Topless sunbathing isn't an option, but it's also too hot to be terribly modest. The misting stations offer a cool respite, and the dousing showers keep you from hallucinating from the blistering city heat, jumping into the Seine and getting tossed about in the wake of a Bateau Mouche. And when it gets too stifling, you can always pray for rain.

❧

# 7 *Unmentionables Never More*

## THE PERFECT LINGERIE, PARIS

It is widely accepted that French women are born with knowledge that the rest of us just have to learn. One of the most universal truths, even if it may not actually be universally true, is that they are the standard-bearers in the ways of seduction. It is a curious alchemy of coquetry, grace, humor, intuition and just enough vulnerability that makes even the toughest Frenchwoman a temptress without equal. She doesn't even have to try. But she does, and the proof is in the lingerie.

 If you have ever been in the common changing room at a gym, spa or public pool in France, you have probably noticed that where it concerns her undergarments, a French woman is always perfectly turned out. Her lingerie is her sweet secret beneath the impeccably-tailored suit or the skinny jeans. Whether they will go home alone or steal off to meet a lover, the art of wearing fine lingerie is a statement: femininity always matters. Her skivvies would never include anything as butch as your faded bra and wash-and-wear cotton briefs from a three-pack. What's more impressive is the two-part harmony that in France is a matter of principle. "A French woman cannot imagine having a mismatched top and bottom," says Heather Stimmler-Hall, a Paris-based

journalist, author of *Naughty Paris: A Lady's Guide to the Sexy City*, and creator of the indispensable *Secrets of Paris* website.

The French did not invent underwear, but they may have perfected it as it evolved from ankle-length drawers, worn under the Grecian-style muslin dresses of the post-revolutionary era, to the silky little whispers they are today. But it was the fashion designer Paul Poiret who sought to liberate womens' breasts from their corsets, while Herminie Cadolle, a Parisian woman who owned a lingerie workshop on the Chaussée d'Antin, introduced the world's first bra in 1889. Ironically, today Maison Cadolle creates luxurious corsets, including those for the dancers at Paris's Crazy Horse nightclub.

Lingerie boutiques are part of the fabric of every block in Paris, like the neighborhood pâtisserie and pharmacy. These shops, often staffed by an elegant woman named Annick or Odile, will almost always carry French brands such as the exquisitely sexy Lise Charmel or lacy Aubade or sleek, minimalist Eres. Frequently, the smaller and more intimate the shop, the more helpful and personal is the service. The saleswoman wants to fit you perfectly, so will not be shy to whip out the tape and measure your bare breasts. She will be concerned about the color and style. Balconette or demi-lune? Satin or lace? Toile or mousseline? Blush pink or deep blue? These decisions are critical.

Almost never will you see the exaggerated push-ups so prevalent in the U.S. French lingerie creates a more natural, clean line, and if there is padding, it's subtle (and tasteful). "It's not supposed to make you look huge," says Stimmler-Hall. "It's supposed to make you look great." In fact, French lingerie is ideal for women who may be considered small-breasted in America, those with A and B cups, though rest assured there's something glorious for every shape.

You need not be rich to emulate Catherine Deneuve, catlike on the sheets in a bedroom scene from *Belle de Jour*. In France, even inexpensive stores like Etam and Monoprix have lingerie departments that dispense risqué bra and underwear sets. But if you are going to shop for lingerie in Paris, my advice is to go big or go home.

When you go to one of the boutiques, plan on taking some time, even spending all day. And most of your money. Try also to fend off your feelings of intimidation or modesty. The salespeople are helpful and will serve you a cup of tea. In addition, be prepared to see a man or a couple whiling away the hours doing the same thing. Some lingerie is not meant to be worn under anything but rather as an accessory to the seduction, and a man will have a strong opinion about his wife or lover's attire in the bedroom. Whatever the occasion, really fine Parisian lingerie, especially when it fits perfectly, will feel like nothing you have ever known. Remember that unlike other attire, lingerie de luxe is almost always designed by women for women, in women-owned businesses. So if you dare (and you should), here are some of suggestions of where to find your subtler, sexier self:

* Fifi Chachnil: There are three Paris locations of these pink-hued, ultra-feminine boutiques (that smell divine), which sell soft, frilly babydolls and silk bikinis adorned with tiny rosettes.

* Daniela in Love: Everything in this store is extra-daring, beautiful and dainty—bedroom wear, negligees and bathing suits as well.

* Cadolle: Run by Poupie, a 6th generation Cadolle, the boutique sells expertly-cut ready-to-wear lingerie and yes, the sexiest of corsets. But for true perfection and personalization, make an appointment for a custom fitting.

* Chantal Thomass: This lingerie magnate's cozy boudoir sells feminine, comfortable, seductive stockings and lingerie with a drop of what the designer calls "impertinence." It's also great for accessories such as eye masks, fans and even umbrellas.

❋ Sabbia Rosa: A warm, beautifully-lit, celebrity-favorite boutique on the Left Bank that uses only lace from Calais and Lyonnais silk for ensembles in a palette of lush jewel tones. According to legend, in 1976, after a visit to Sabbia Rosa for some intimate garments for his then wife, actress and style icon Jane Birkin, the poet and singer Serge Gainsbourg was inspired to write his classic song "Les Dessous Chics"—or "Chic Undergarments."

❋ Mise en Cage: You need to make an appointment for this private showroom in the 15th arrondissement, for very high-end and very erotic lingerie and if it's your thing, the subtlest of fetish wear.

I discovered Odile de Changy on the street where I lived for years in Paris, rue du Pont aux Choux in the Marais, and she creates beautifully-designed, body-hugging bras and underwear out of stretch lace that feel like a second skin.

If you're wondering how to take care of such finery, that's easy. Go to the grocery store and pick up a hot-pink bottle of Mir—France's answer to Woolite—that has a clean, freesia scent. I never leave Paris without stocking up for myself and for an equally addicted friend.

If ultimately you opt out of the afternoon splurge at a personalized boutique, the revamped lingerie department at Le Bon Marché department store is unmatched for its selection and setting. What's best is the manicure bar set right amongst the Stella McCartney lace thongs and stretchy Monette Paris bras. You can get a *pose vernis*—a simple application of polish—for only fifteen euros. Nothing says seduction quite like nails that are perfectly groomed in indigo, scarlet, pale pink, or whatever matches your sexy new underthings.

❧

# 8 *You Can Hear Heaven*

## CHURCH MUSIC AND CONCERTS,
## INCLUDING AT SAINTE-CHAPELLE, PARIS

Many of the limestone basilicas and ancient cathedrals in France are not simply museums, but still-working parishes where devout Catholics celebrate the liturgy every Sunday, receive First Communion, get baptized or married and raise money for youth groups. Stone-cold edifices in winter, these buildings remain living, breathing entities that were constructed to praise the Almighty, and hundreds of years later, their pews still fill up with the faithful. After all, these buildings were built for worship. Or were they? Sometimes, I think they were built for music.

It is possible—and probable if you visit on a Sunday morning—to hear music in one of Paris's churches. You can do so by chance or you can do it on purpose, because many of them have concert series and performances throughout the year, from gospel choirs to string ensembles playing secular pieces such as Mozart's *"Eine Kleine Nachtmusik"* or Vivaldi's *"The Four Seasons."* As a venue, a medieval or renaissance church has a powerful added value. It is profound—a counterpoint to all the shopping and eating. It is soothing, to dovetail with the nonstop pace. But most of all, it is the kind of experience and balance we seek when we travel to Paris, the double sweep of lightness and meaning.

Music works to silence the noisy head, and I contend that a great
and effective comfort is celestial sounds witnessed in a sacred place.
You can be a believer in God or a skeptic; Catholic, non-Catholic
or non-anything; but because you are human, you can't help but
be moved when the melody begins and unleashes its magic within
the stone enclosure. You may find your gaze drifting inward in
contemplation; you may even find it lifting up towards heaven.

I urge the traveler to experience a celebrated religious monument as more than a museum, and when on the street, to seek
out the sounds. Be listening for the refrains of "Hallelujah" when
the music wafts out of the church. Wander in and stand on the
side. The rapturous vibrations of an organ or the harmonies of a
parish choir can touch something primal in us, an emotion that
transcends time and bridges the centuries. Even for a moment,
the strains of music can unpack our sorrows or free our joys, cause
us to examine the extent of our faith if that's what surfaces, or just
transport us through the force of its simple beauty. Most enthrall-
ing of all is to hear mass sung in Gregorian chant, as it is done every
Sunday at 10 A.M. at Notre-Dame Cathedral. It begs to be listened
to with eyes squeezed tight, and it catches you in the throat.

And then, there are the concerts, offered by nearly all of Paris's
churches, including Église St. Germain des Prés and La Madeleine,
both of which have packed and diverse schedules. Most lovely, for
its intimacy, accessibility and sheer, devastating beauty is the concert series at Sainte-Chapelle on Île de la Cité in Paris, which, with
music, transforms from resplendent to transcendent. Here, you
are enveloped in one of the most unique concert halls in the world.
It has been years since mass was celebrated in the chapel (the church
is on the property of the Ministry of Justice, hence the added security), so there is no chance of running across someone who has just
attended confession. Today the church exerts its vibrancy through

music, both sacred and secular, offered twice nightly from March to November and again at the holidays.

Sainte-Chapelle is a high Gothic masterpiece, built from 1242–1248 by King Louis IX to hold the relics of Christ's passion, the most precious of which was believed to be the Crown of Thorns. It was the private chapel of the French kings and, along with the Conciergerie, was housed in the Palais de la Cité, which from the 6th century was the royal residence and seat of power.

The concerts—for the most part small orchestras, chamber music, and string quartets playing Bach, Vivaldi or Gounod's "Ave Maria"—are held in the upper chapel, which is one of Paris's unrivaled treasures and is known for its superb acoustics. You would need a lifetime to study the 1,113 biblical scenes masterfully depicted in 15 stained-glass windows, through which the light of Paris enters and illuminates the chapel. The lone rose window at the western end shows the Apocalypse of St. John and is a swirl of kinetic luster and color. Often there are two concerts per night, which begin at 7 or 8:30 P.M., and for which—like many of Paris's rarest attractions—it helps to buy a ticket beforehand.

Depending on the time of year, the lowering sun will pierce the stained-glass windows, creating blazes of light that shift by the moment. The music soars up to the blue and gold vaults in the ceiling and expands grandly, majestically to work its way into your bones. Once, I attended a concert of a solo cellist playing Bach—just a man, the music and this astonishing room. The instrument's rich tones must have penetrated every one of us, because when he finished, the audience stayed hushed, still rapt. We were all carried away to somewhere we were reluctant to return from. Finally, we caught our breath and applauded. Only then did I collect my spirit, which had taken flight and was floating somewhere among the candlelight.

# 9 *A Food Itinerary*

## MY RESTAURANTS, PÂTISSERIES
## AND TEA SALONS, PARIS

When you travel to Paris, it's essential to have a *carnet*—a notepad—whose blank pages are ready to receive your jottings and scribbles, places you happen upon, connect with, grow attached to, and finally call your own. I recommend the brand Field Notes. No, this is not a paid endorsement, but there is nothing so efficient as these plain, palm-sized paper notebooks, your retractable pen clipped over the pages.

Moments of ecstasy are made of happenstance, and Paris would just be a pretty place if not punctuated with serendipitous food discovery. When you stumble upon a warmly-lit café or find yourself dining at a place that reveals itself to you at the day's pinnacle of hunger, fatigue and curiosity, take a moment and write it down. It was here, on the corner of such-and-such, that I lit upon this perfect spot and ordered a *café crème* and *tarte aux cerises* and had one of the purest moments of my life.

And this trip or the next, you will reacquaint yourself with this refuge of yours, as Ernest Hemingway does in *A Moveable Feast*. The writer walks in the rain, past the Place du Panthéon, the Cluny and the Boulevard St-Germain, to a place he knows well. "It was a pleasant café, warm and clean and friendly," he writes, and orders a café au lait and soon, a rum St. James.

What is inevitable is that when you are back from Paris, some friend will be traveling there soon and will ply you for tidbits, and so on. And then, you will return again, notes in hand, ready to visit your old familiar haunts. Sometimes, things change, and it can feel like losing an old friend. My last trip to Paris, I discovered that the boulangerie where I had many times bought *allumettes au fromage*—soft breadsticks laced with gruyère—had closed its doors. I was despondent.

But never mind. You move on. There are others, and I am forever adding to the list. Before leaving for Paris I always peruse the magazine blogs and the many wonderful (and addicting) websites devoted to Paris food: *The Paris Kitchen, Chocolate and Zucchini, Dorie Greenspan, David Lebovitz, Adrian Moore* and *Paris by Mouth*. But mostly, I discover places on my own by ducking in on a windy afternoon, or my friends share with me their favorite food addresses, which, in turn, become my own.

My first day of each visit to Paris, I lunch at the celebrated and always-packed Yard at 6, rue Mont-Louis in the 11th. The owner (and occasionally, the chef) is a young woman named Jane Drotter, and the fact that she is my goddaughter only makes the stick-to-your-bones, beautifully prepared bistro food—*gigot d'agneau* with mint confit, and *pot-au-feu* with marrow—more delicious. If I could start my meal with the "Kate" chocolate mousse, I would. I have yet to meet its match in Paris.

On the way across town, I'll visit the Marché des Enfants Rouges on rue de Bretagne. This was my neighborhood market when I lived in Paris, and I will always believe that clementines, sold by the kilo with their shiny leaves still attached, are sweeter and juicier when they come from here.

In the afternoon, I may head to À Priori Thé, a tea salon located in one of Paris's most elegant covered passages, the Galerie Vivienne, in the 2nd. I have been known to spend a whole afternoon among the topiaries, or beneath the opulent glass ceiling, around heated tables resting on 19th-century mosaic floors, with a cup of hot chocolate and a plate of creamy scones with jam. I love to stop at Le Valentin, a favorite for years, at 30-32 Passage Jouffroy, a covered gallery in the 9th just off the Boulevard Montmartre. Everything here is made on the premises, even their jars of melon-thyme jam, and I crave the tangy lemon meringue tart, a refined cousin to its coarse American counterpart. I will drink a pot of Dammann Frères tea, usually Soleil Vert, perfumed with blood oranges.

A word about teatime, one of the best ways to spend a day. In fact, to understand Paris, it's important to stand still for a few hours. We tend to cram as much as possible into our time there, but all-day tea is a great way to commune with the essence of the city. I could spend a year at Un Dimanche à Paris, a concept store at 4-6-8 cour du Commerce Saint-André in the 6th, that has a sumptuous tea room and chocolate bar. It's impossible to leave this muted gold and gray space  empty-handed, so I'll grab a jar of miniature crispy chocolate balls to pop into my mouth all day long. I believe in the big splurge once in a great while, and there is no better place to experience Paris than a polished afternoon tea at a grand hotel—the Bristol, George V, Meurice or Plaza Athénée. The waiters will spoil you to death and let you sit as long as you like. A good thing, since the more I can't afford it, the longer I tend to while away the hours in daydream.

End of the day, cocktail hour, I'll meet a friend on the terrace or in the gilded mirrored room of Carette on Place du Trocadéro in the 16th. It's an institution, and I don't think there is anything like it in Paris, or perhaps that's just my devotion speaking. Anyone can walk in at any time—the Channel 1 newscaster, the politician who was just indicted, the lady with the big sunglasses toting a

chihuahua in her bag—but it's not trendy, hip or suffocatingly anything, and the waiters are as solicitous to a solo woman as to a table
of big shots. And though Ladurée seems to have the brand recognition lock on macarons, those from Carette—the caramel *au beurre
salé* and the blackcurrant-violet variety in heart-breaking shades of
purple—are, for my money, the best in Paris.

I am very attached to Chez Georges on 1, rue du Mail in the
2nd, and in all the years I've been coming to Paris, it has never
changed. It is where I always go for a traditional Parisian dinner—the best lentil salad anywhere and a beef filet—a *pavé*—always
followed by profiteroles, hot, cold, swimming in bitter chocolate
sauce. Something about this place strikes my heart. The bright
white linens, brass rails and clean lighting. I know I'll be back.

It is customary that my friend Françoise and I meet for a drink
at Le Fumoir at 6, rue de l'Amiral Coligny in the 1st, on my first
night in Paris. It occupies the prime corner across from the Louvre,
and after dinner hours, the place sizzles in subdued glamour.

Most mornings I will stop for a warm pain au chocolat at my
neighborhood (the one I usually stay in) pâtisserie/boulangerie,
Comptoir Gana, an artisanal shop on rue Oberkampf in the 11th,
where you can see the bakers up to their elbows in flour through
the window. But I also like to cross over to the Left Bank, to La
Pâtisserie des Rêves on the rue du Bac in the 7th. The pastries are
displayed like jewels in stylized arrangements under glass domes.
The Tarte Tatin is laid out in a photogenic still life, with a heaping pot of crème fraîche. Over on the side is homier fare—just as
elegant. I'll always buy a *chausson aux pommes*—a sweet apple turnover,
for breakfast.

Lunch sometimes is at Au Sauvignon located on a strategic Left
Bank intersection at 80, rue des Saints-Pères in the 6th. Here, I will
eat little *tartine* sandwiches on sourdough *pain* Poilâne, with foie gras,
thick slices of *saucisson sec,* or Cantal cheese, with a glass of Beaujolais.

If I'm in my old neighborhood of the Marais, I unfailingly stop at the casually elegant La Briciola for a gorgeous individual wood-fired pizza, Napoletana style.

Often I will detour to Michael Chaudun's tantalizing shrine to chocolate—with that intoxicating aroma—at 149, rue de l'Université in the 7th arrondissement, that is always bathed in a sensuous mocha glow. I pick up a box of *pavés*, little squares of ganache dusted in cocoa, for whomever deserves them when I get home—usually, my children. You too will find your perfect Paris chocolatier—perhaps it is Debauve & Gallais at 33, rue Vivienne in the 2nd, that looks and feels more like the royal jeweler than a purveyor of something creamy and rich.

Another afternoon favorite is Le Café Littéraire by Noura at l'Institut du Monde Arabe, at 1, rue des Fossés Saint-Bernard in the 5th. The tearoom is on the ground floor of the museum dedicated to Arab art and culture, in a building designed by architect Jean Nouvel. The edifice itself is a marvel of ingenuity, where the photosensitive portals expand or contract according to the light outside. I love the Lebanese pastries flavored with honey and pistachios, but mostly, I could sip the mint tea the whole rest of the day, and often do.

These are my familiar refuges, my own slices of Paris, my old friends. What are yours?

# 10 *Peace in the City*

## THE CANAL SAINT-MARTIN, PARIS

One of the most beguiling sequences in *Amélie*, a quintessentially Parisian film, is when the title character, played by Audrey Tautou, is shown partaking in her favorite small pleasures—running her hands through a sack of lentils, cracking the caramelized crust of a crème brûlée, and finally, skipping stones on the Canal Saint-Martin. The last shot pans up from a waterfall and pulls out to focus on Amélie in her red dress, kneeling on the bridge, with a muted green background from the reflected plane trees that frame the canal. Like the other Audrey before her—Hepburn—you can't help but want to emulate her worldly naiveté, to be able to float along the streets of Paris with the same ease with which she can peer into the depths of another person's soul. It's all embodied in this painterly vision of Amélie, so focused on the trajectory of the stones, as if to shove the big, troubled world aside for a moment. In other words, taking delight in small pleasures.

It's a good lesson, actually, and one you put into practice, oddly enough, right there at the Canal Saint-Martin where it runs through the 10th arrondissement. Sometimes, the inner part of Paris, the parts that hug the Seine and hold its glittering monuments, can be overwhelming for us visitors and can feel like an enormous museum you'll never be able to grasp, let alone conquer. Even when strolling around the Left Bank, to wander and absorb it all, you are bombarded by history, plaques and countless repositories of culture, which, if you ignore or walk past, leaves you feeling like an indifferent heel. This book notwithstanding, Paris can put pressure on you to always be curious, always be starved for another heaping ladle of knowledge. Down by the canal, the pressure dissipates. I walk there alone sometimes, or with my husband, hold his hand, and enjoy the respite from Paris's sometimes overwhelming gifts.

The French call it a *balade*—a stroll—and the canal lends itself perfectly to the charms of the aimless afternoon. As always, there is history involved. In 1802, Napoleon I  ordered the construction of inner-city waterways to provide fresh drinking water to a growing population of Parisians. In addition, it would be a needed alternative to the Seine for all manner of supplies to reach the city. It took twenty-three years to complete the project, financed by a tax on wine, and today the canal runs almost three miles from the Seine to the Canal d'Orucq, running through the Bassin de la Villette, Paris's largest artificial lake. But you'll want to stay in *Amélie* territory, cross the blue ferrous footbridges, pass clusters of ancient foliage and quiet grassy paths.

The area has gradually been sprucing up in recent years, as once-neglected districts often do, but though it's hip, it's almost always understated. That goes for the area's most distinguished landmark, the Hôtel du Nord on the Quai de Jemmapes, where the French director Marcel Carné filmed his masterpiece of the same name. It is now a stylish restaurant and bar whose exterior remains as it was in the 1938 movie.

You'll need some vittles if you're going to sit by the water, and at the corner of rue Yves Toudic and rue de Marseille is Du Pain et des Idées, a glorious shop that creates some of the most celebrated bread in Paris. We'll buy a loaf of ginger walnut sourdough bread and tear off little chunks of crust, or buy a *cassis escargot* pastry, full of butter and shaped like a snail. Then we'll mosey to La Fabrique à Gâteaux on rue des Vinaigriers, a little gem of a pâtisserie owned by a pair of young women, for raspberry macarons and financiers, a staple of fine Parisian pâtisseries for over a century. Then, we'll find a bench on the Quai de Valmy. A random tour boat will pass on the water, but that may be the only reminder of all the sights that await you in this great city. Tomorrow.

❧

# 11 *Slip into the Shadows*

## ARTHOUSE CINEMAS, PARIS

On December 28, 1895, an announcement at the Salon Indien du Grand Café on 14 Boulevard des Capucines near Place de l'Opéra in Paris read as follows:

> ### Cinématograph
> This device, invented by Monsieurs Auguste and Louis Lumière, allows, by a series of instantaneous prints, the collection of all movements that occurred before the lens during a given time and then to reproduce these movements by projecting their images on screen before an entire room.

The Lumière brothers were sons of a wealthy Lyon entrepreneur who had recently witnessed a demonstration of Thomas Edison's much-ballyhooed Kinetoscope. He believed his clever sons could make a lighter device that would combine a printer with a projector, thus enabling the images to be shown outside the camera. That day in Paris, the brothers debuted ten short films, starting with a 51-second movie of workers passing through the gate of their factory in

Lyon. With that, cinema was born and so, logically, was the movie theater, albeit without popcorn or Twizzlers.

France remains justifiably proud of this contribution to the planet's cultural heritage, and Parisians are insatiable for all manner of moving images, from a Hollywood blockbuster to a first-run Icelandic thriller to obscure black-and-white classics. A 2012 World Cities Culture Report survey revealed that Paris has 302 cinemas and 1,003 movie screens—significantly more than any other city in the world. Because they are shrines to France's collective obsession, I'm hard-pressed to name a better place on earth to watch a movie— even one in a language I don't understand—Kurdish, Persian, Yoruba, what have you (American films here are usually left in English with subtitles). When I'm in Paris alone, I'll see what's playing, wander in off the blustery streets, and take in a flick, cocooned away in solitude. It's the perfect vanishing act, when the theater lights dim, to be all snug in a ridiculously comfy seat with no one on earth knowing where you are. Also, there is no afternoon more intimate than the one spent curled up in the crook of someone's arm under those moody lights. Especially at one of the arthouses, whose velvety adornments uphold as Parisian dogma that a day at the movies is something special and to be savored in luxury.

La Pagode at 57 bis, rue de Babylone in the 7th arrondissement, may be one of the most unusual theaters in the world, and, I have always thought, one of Paris's most remarkable buildings. It is a Japanese temple that was disassembled, shipped and rebuilt as a ballroom in 1896 by one of the owners of Le Bon Marché. In 1931, it became a cinema and today shows largely first-run American films. It is hard for any movie to live up to the ornate backdrop of the screening room—perhaps *The Last Emperor* or Sofia Coppola's *Marie Antoinette* would be stylistic fits, layered as they are with texture and opulence. Most atmospheric of all is to repair to the theater's quiet Japanese garden for tea after the movie.

The Cinéma du Panthéon at 13, rue Victor Cousin in the 5th arrondissement dates to 1907 and is the oldest movie house in Paris and one of the first to show the films of Jean-Luc Godard and François Truffaut, which ushered in the Nouvelle Vague era of French cinema. The theater seats are newly-restored in chocolate-and-ochre chenille, softer and more comfortable than my couch at home. Upstairs, though, is pure Parisian glamour: Le Salon du Panthéon, a casually chic lounge and restaurant designed by the movie star and one of the great French fashion icons, Catherine Deneuve. It feels like the most stylish of living rooms, a sleek mid-century hangout that caters to film types and just plain movie-lovers. I could languish in a corner by the window forever, switching from Earl Gray tea to an aperitif just as the light dwindles on the street below.

Also on the Left Bank, across from the Relais Christine hotel, is Action Christine, which shows almost exclusively vintage American films. It's a cozy little place, and one of my favorite detour-hideaways-escape hatches in all of Paris, a place to disappear for two delicious hours. Recently, I slipped inside on a freezing February day just as William Wellman's *Yellow Sky* (1948), with Gregory Peck and Ann Baxter, was about to roll. I love this place.

You can't get much cushier than the cherry velvet seats at Studio des Ursulines at 10, rue des Ursulines, also in the 5th. This cinema, too, has been around since the dawn of the motion picture era and has held the premieres of several tours de force, among them Marlene Dietrich's *The Blue Angel* (1930) and Luis Buñuel's *Un Chien Andalou* (1929). I remember being entranced there, a lifetime ago, by *The Lovers on the Bridge*, which was filmed around the Pont Neuf.

It makes sense for a historic (1928) arthouse cinema to be located in Montmartre, which because of its altitude and quirky but leafy streets, make it one of Paris's most popular film locations for both French and foreign filmmakers. Cinéma Studio 28, too, is super-plush, with a surprisingly generous screen. The entrance wall bears a quote from Jean Cocteau: *"La salle des chefs-d'oeuvre, le chef-d'oeuvre des salles"*—"The theater of masterpieces, the masterpiece of theaters"—who also decorated the screening room with curvy multi-colored wall chandeliers in his signature playful, pointy lampshade style. Those same lights flicker behind the heroine in a scene from *Amélie*, who frequents this cinema alone on Friday nights.

The Louxor Palais du Cinéma is close to the elevated Métro in Barbès Rochechouart, the area in the 19th arrondissement with a large African and Arab population. A movie theater since 1921 (and not technically an arthouse), the Louxor fell into decline and, with the intervention of concerned citizens and Paris City Hall, merci-fully was spared from demolition. In 2013, the Louxor burst again to life, coming back as a high-polish temple to Egyptian-inspired Art Deco, with friezes, gold-hued walls, floral mosaics, and a little alcove bar on the third floor with potted palms, crisp stained-glass windows and a killer view of Sacré-Cœur. While visiting Paris recently, my husband and I found ourselves at an II A.M. showing of the Japanese animated movie, *The Wind Rises*, and were the lone spectators in the gorgeous 340-seat theater. We scampered up for a gander from the balcony, swooned at the Egyptian motifs, glass skylight, and Sphinx heads. Is there any cooler feeling than having the run of a movie theater? It felt like our private screening room, but one of many we might contrive to find in any neighborhood, on any wintry day in Paris.

❧

# 12 *Fragrant City*

## FIND YOUR SCENT, PARIS

If, as Christian Dior once declared, a woman's perfume reveals more about her than her handwriting, then my feminine identity was like a text message: barely there, void of substance, gone in a second. It has been years since I've gotten dressed with perfume, dabbed my neck (or knees) as a matter of routine. In college I spritzed myself with girlish Miss Dior, a bouquet of lily of the valley and jasmine I brought to the classroom every day. In my twenties, I went for a stronger statement: Amazone by Hermès, woodsy and thick with vetiver and green flowers. Then in my thirties I took to Issey Miyake's L'eau for an unfussy sillage—the scented trail that lingers—of clean, fresh water. Recently, I felt the void where my perfume had once been, so on a recent trip to Paris, I decided to search high and low for my signature scent: the one that would give clarity to my elusive identity and fill up the empty space around me with the waft of flowers or citrus fruit, pungent spices or the woodsy wild.

A new perfume can transform a woman instantly and entirely, even more so than a facelift. It can change the way she feels about herself and the way the world responds to her. The woman who greets you with a pale scent of mimosa will leave a very different impression than the one who's drifting in myrrh and patchouli. I needed to decide who this woman would be—the impression my scent, and therefore I, would both give and leave in my wake.

My quest confirmed that Parisiennes still take their perfume very seriously. As a business, it's booming, and as an essential, to accessorize the outfit and complete the woman, perfume is an unrivaled, unquestioned necessity. I resolved to narrow my search to the profusion of small or niche boutiques scattered throughout Paris, high-concept architectural temples of olfactory innovation…with one exception. Many friends insisted I begin with Guerlain at 68 Avenue des Champs-Élysées, an institution since Eau de Cologne Impériale was created in 1853 for Empress Eugénie, the wife of Napoleon III. I feared it would feel stodgy or stale, and I was completely mistaken. The spiral staircase leads to a shimmering gold room, which has the aspect of an elegant perfume museum, modern as tomorrow but grounded in the history of women and of scent. Sheet music stands hold fans infused with fragrance including old favorites Shalimar (1925) and Jicky, which, despite being created in 1889, felt fresh as new-cut lavender. Guerlain's offerings were tempting, but I couldn't let my hunt come to an end so quickly.

There is a cluster of perfume boutiques on the right bank near the Place Vendôme, including IUNX, a minimalist black-and-red hideaway on 239, rue Saint-Honoré. Here, you smell the perfumes on crepe paper strips, which emerge from motion-activated aromatic tubes attached to the wall. Nearby, at 21, rue de Mont Thabor, is the right bank outpost of Parfums Frédéric Malle (its flagship is across the river at 37, rue de Grenelle), complete with space age yellow glass "smelling columns." The world's most distinguished noses create for this chic perfume house, and I was surprised to fall hard for the not-at-all-wispy Portrait of a Lady by Dominique Ropion, thick with Turkish rose and musk.

At 5, rue d'Alger is an intimate jewelry box of a shop where Francis Kurkdjian, one of the world's most celebrated and sought-after perfumers, sells his exquisite creations, including scented blowing bubbles—Les Bulles d'Agathe, which smell of violet, pear, cut grass and mint. My favorite there was Aqua Universalis, a heady blend of citrus and bergamot.

Over on the Left Bank, I paid a visit to Parfums Lubin, a sensuous boutique with a deep aubergine and black storefront at 21, rue des Canettes; inside, it wafts with the smell of desire and luxury. Lubin was an apprentice to Marie Antoinette's personal perfumer, Jean-Louis Fargeon and founded the house bearing his name in 1798. In 2011, they unveiled Black Jade, rich with flowers and spice, named after the perfume flask the last French queen always kept close at hand. The scent fits a monarch, and I'm not quite ready to smell of such opulence (though maybe someday I will), so reluctantly I give it a pass and move on.

The Marais has become a mecca for a perfume pilgrimage, packed with lots of high-end smaller brands, all with diverse philosophies and cutting edge store design. Parfums Nicolaï, Annick Goutal and Fragonard, whose updated Provençal orange flower, lavender and rose perfumes are lovely and not at all cloying, have stores in the Marais. The staff was particularly helpful in the marvelous color-coded world of L'Artisan Parfumeur on the rue du Bourg Tibourg. I'm torn between the delicious Verte Violette and La Chasse aux Papillons, which promises me a game of hide-and-seek among the lime blossoms.

Over on the Place des Vosges, I dip into Christian Louis, a *maître parfumeur*, whose fragrances are inspired by the Basque region of France. Biarritz is one of the most addictive scents of the day, with crisp notes of Turkish rose, cassis and iris, and back on the sidewalk, I keep pulling the aroma-swabbed stick from my pocket.

Whenever I'm in the Marais, I love nothing more than to stop into Mariage Frères and linger for an hour or so over a steaming pot of vanilla Bal Masqué or one of their other aromatic teas. Today,

I'm afraid that trying to select my brew there would be too similar to my hunt for a new perfume and equally confusing. So I make a break for Le Sévigné on the Parc Royal for a croque-monsieur—the creamiest and crunchiest in Paris. From there, I walk to État Libre d'Orange on the rue des Archives. It is an edgy enclave for Paris's most intriguing collection of unisex perfumes including Like This, created by the actress Tilda Swinton, whose notes of neroli, tangerine and Moroccan heliotrope have me in a swoon. The Different Company on rue Ferdinand Duval is a pale, airy branch of the luxury house, which commissions well-known designers to fabricate perfumes. There, I am taken in by the outdoorsy Sublime Balkiss. I wonder: can my sillage be of pines and cypress?

Fortified with a glass of Beaujolais from La Trinquette on the rue des Gravilliers, my feet carry me to Serge Lutens at the Palais-Royal. The store is the most sensual of all, an exquisite emporium of black, purples, and gold that is reflected in a perimeter of smoky mirrors. It is a place where the 18th century mixes decadently with 21st-century design. I'm almost ready to declare a winner with the delicious, tropical Fleurs d'Oranger, but I hold off for the final stop, a few yards along the colonnade.

My quest ends when the day does, at Les Parfums de Rosine, a tiny store that's pink, gold, and womanly, like the most delicious dressing room—that dispenses twenty or so perfumes all based on the rose. What more do I want? Right here I make a crucial decision: if my scent lingers, I want it (and me) to be remembered as clean and fresh, not dark and oppressive. My choice is Un Zeste de Rose. There are notes of lemon and notes of tea, but in the end, it smells like a rose. And so do I.

❧

# 13 *Homage to Lovers*

## HÉLOÏSE AND ABÉLARD, PARIS

Paris is for lovers. It is also for their graves. The dead certainly outnumber the living by now in the city's two-thousand-year-old ether. And unlike in Hollywood, the city's celebrated couples are not hiding behind alarmed gates, but are entirely approachable under their tombstones in Père Lachaise, Cimetière Montparnasse and Basilica St. Denis.

Rather than some sort of morbid pseudo-stalking, an outing to one of Paris's cemeteries and the burial sites of her great men or women—or great man and woman together—is far from grim. Père Lachaise is a vibrant city-within-a-city, full of cobblestone streets, dynamic sculptures, and gleaming stone temples, where architectural style is as paramount as it is on any Paris boulevard. An excursion here is joyous and quite normal, as is evident by people picnicking and strolling their babies along the avenues. It also is a foray into reverence, rumination, innocent fandom and romance. After all, the whole fabric of the city is its history, and its history is its people, especially the royals and poets and those they loved, from which emanate all the great legends of France—the true and the exaggerated.

A queen in her grave is one thing. A queen in her grave beside her husband is another. Their marbleized images give allowance to speculate, empathize, compare our smaller loves, and even judge. Royal likenesses starting from King Clovis are stretched out on crypts and under effigies at Basilica St. Denis in a suburb of Paris. The formidable Catherine de' Medici, looking miserable, lies forever next to her husband Henry II, who loved another woman, Diane de Poitiers, all his life. Queen Marie Antoinette and King Louis XVI are there as well, magnificently rendered in their sadness and dignity.

At Cimetière de Montparnasse, Simone de Beauvoir is buried alongside Jean-Paul Sartre, their brilliant, incendiary minds melded forever on the Left Bank, where they were the intellectual leaders of their time, and memories of them are still kindled around the tables of the Café de Flore.

The actors Simone Signoret and Yves Montand had an often scandalous but enduring thirty-four-year marriage, which they lived out visibly as residents of the Place Dauphine, the charming triangular square at the end of Île de la Cité. Their union is honored in a simple sepulchre at Père Lachaise, under a burst of foliage.

But the most potent place of romantic pilgrimage is where France's greatest love story is remembered, one that has endured for 900 years. Forbidden affair! A baby boy named Astrolabe! To the nunnery! Castration! Known simply as Héloïse and Abélard, theirs was a mad whirl of a medieval love story, whose themes are as contemporary as the *Twilight* saga and can be swooned over at their ornate mini-mansion of a final resting place at Père Lachaise.

Abélard was a brilliant philosopher who rose to fame as one of the keenest intellects in 12th-century Paris, a teacher at the cathedral school of Notre-Dame, where his lectures drew followers by the thousands. He fell madly in love with a gifted student, Héloïse d'Argenteuil, the niece (and pride and joy) of the Canon of Notre-Dame on Île de la Cité. Desperate to be close to her, he approached Héloïse's uncle and offered himself as a private tutor to the beautiful fifteen-year-old intellectual prodigy (twenty years his junior). The epic *amour fou* that quickly entangled the lovers living under her uncle's roof was the very archetype of passion over reason. "Under the pretext of study, we spent our hours in the happiness of love, and learning held out to us the secret opportunities that our passion craved," wrote Abélard in his memoir. His verses to her went viral and their illicit affair became well-known to all but her uncle.

Uncle Fulbert finally caught on. Héloïse got pregnant and Abélard spirited her off to Brittany, where she gave birth to a son named Astrolabe, whom she left to be raised by his family there. Upon their return to Paris, Héloïse refused to be wed, believing matrimony to be a form of bondage, and that her love of Abélard and their erotic connection soared above the triviality of convention. "I despised the name of wife that I might live happy with that of mistress," she wrote in one of her later letters, "and took a secret pleasure in being admired by a man who, when he pleased, could raise his mistress to the character of a goddess."

The uncle prevailed upon them to wed in secret, but, opposed to being a martyr to marriage (and to protect Abélard's teaching career), Héloïse continued to live as a single woman. To quiet the scandal over their affair once and for all, Abélard convinced Héloïse to retire to a convent. Uncle Fulbert took violent revenge when he sent thugs to castrate Abélard while he slept. Abélard became a Benedictine monk and carried on with teaching and scholarly pursuits. The lovers were apart and out of contact, but still in love.

The intervening years only served to deepen the erotic spell under which Héloïse had fallen. Her words, written from within the walls of the abbey, cry boldly, recklessly and impiously of the power of desire and the destructive hold of obsessive, fruitless longing. They resound with guilt that his injury was at the hands of her relative, and mostly, with declarations of her undiminished love for Abélard. "This cloister has resounded with my cries, and, like a wretch condemned to eternal slavery, I have worn out my days with grief," she writes from the abyss. Nine centuries later, the letters seem to surpass their own truth about the eternal conflict between what society expects of women and what we want, need, and dream about for ourselves. How frequently these things are at odds.

Héloïse and Abélard were to meet again many years later, at which time Abélard told her to forget the trauma of the past. Though she never stopped yearning for him, she became one of the most important abbesses of her day.

The couple's remains were moved to Père Lachaise by Empress Josephine, wife of Napoleon I. Perhaps the doomed romance resonated with her, or perhaps it was Héloïse's courage in defying both her family and God. Their lavish Gothic tomb still draws the lovelorn, the fascinated, and me. They lie parallel to each other, their marble hands raised in prayer. I can't help but wish they had been carved otherwise, with Héloïse reaching out—defiantly and forever—to the man she desired.

≈⟨

# 14 The View from Elsewhere

## PLACES TO VIEW THE EIFFEL TOWER (INCLUDING THE EIFFEL TOWER), PARIS

There are several reasons to ascend the Eiffel Tower, either by the elevators that go all the way to the third and top level, or via the stairwell to the first or second decks (328 steps and 340 steps, respectively—you can't walk to the top). In winter, there is ice skating on the first level. The rink, big enough to accommodate 80 skaters at a time, is 188 feet above the Champ de Mars and was opened in 2004 as part of Paris's (failed) bid for the 2012 Olympics. To skate in the breast of Gustave Eiffel's masterpiece, under the intricate steel lattice work, is about as mystical an experience as I could imagine, imbued with just enough magic to wake up the next morning and believe you dreamt it.

The second reason is the tiny bar on the third level that serves miniature flutes of champagne. I once took a friend there, who had feared it would be too touristy. Instead, our toast there over Paris was a poignant celebration of our friendship. Third, of course, is the view. Unlike other tall buildings around the world that are surrounded by other equally-tall buildings, the Eiffel Tower is

Paris's lone giant (well, except for the dark shadow of the Tour Montparnasse in the distance that forever marred a certain scan of the skyline), so it affords an unobstructed 360-degree view of the city and beyond. From the top, Paris spreads out before you topographically, like a map.

Then there is the most obvious reason: to be astonished by the intricate handiwork up close, some of the 18,038 pieces of iron and 2,500,000 rivets that hold it together. Prepare yourself for the enormity of it, as it's monumental in scale and grander than it seems from afar. Prepare yourself, as well, for the contradiction you will experience. Though it is massive, it is skeletal, airy, and ethereal.

Like the *Mona Lisa*, there is so much more behind this structure than the trinket it has become—the emblem on the t-shirt, the charm on the bracelet. It may be the sexiest building in the world and the most photogenic—it can't take a bad picture, regardless of the weather, time of year or day—but it is crucial to remember the Eiffel Tower's role in the history of architecture and engineering, and marvel at its creation. It represents one of the first conspicuous achievements of the modern age of steel, the material that transformed society in the 19th century. At the time of its construction, a "skyscraper" was a ten-story Louis Sullivan building in Chicago. The Eiffel Tower was eight times higher than that. (The Statue of Liberty, whose inner framework was also engineered by Gustave Eiffel, is a third the size of the tower, a mere 305 feet.) In 1889, there was no man-made structure 986-feet high or even close to it. To get so high, you had to take a ride in one of Montgolfier's balloons.

The tower was designed as the entrance of the 1889 World's Fair—the Exposition Universelle—and was meant to be demolished twenty years later. In 1909, it was saved by virtue of its technological operations, in particular its efficacy as a radio tower, which Eiffel himself had encouraged. At the top you can see his little apartment, preserved, wax figures and all, as the scene of a visit from Thomas Edison during the World's Fair. The scientific purpose should not be diminished, perhaps, but I would argue that the Eiffel Tower's real function is its beauty, and its duty is to be an icon to Paris and the world. And as an icon, its impact has only grown over time, with new technologies like light, pyrotechnics and lasers, which now allow it to be celebrated day and night.

You do not need to be in the belly of the tower to feel that power; there are also good reasons *not* to voyage to the top—acrophobia, long lines, maybe you have a bum knee or your shoes hurt. For me, it's simpler. When you are inside the Eiffel Tower, you can't see the whole of it. You can't marvel at the swoops, or celebrate the verticality and suggestion of flight, years before the Wright Brothers made aviation history.

In Paris, the Eiffel Tower is a locator and a touchstone, and it almost cannot be helped—you will gasp every time you see it, and even lifelong Parisians never tire of its grace. If you are like me, you will seek it out like a trusted friend or a secret love and forever make a detour just to cast a longing glance. So here I offer you my best places to see the Eiffel Tower from without:

1. Climb to the top of the Basilica of the Sacré-Cœur in Montmartre. The stairs are narrow, torturous and slippery when raining, but it is perhaps the most comprehensive view of Paris, and in the morning, the most beautiful.

2. The Parc de Belleville in the 20th is the highest park in Paris and is also one of the city's loveliest green spaces, made more so by the spectacular view. Just overlooking the park, on the rue des Envierges, is the O'Paris restaurant, which has an outdoor dining terrace with one of the most expansive vistas in the city.

3. If you go to the beginning of Avenue de Camoëns in the 16th (around number 2), you will see the entrance to a beautiful stone staircase. From the top, you can see the curves of the Eiffel Tower, regal between the staid apartment buildings.

4. Also in the 16th, the outdoor café at the statuesque Musée d'Art Moderne next to the Palais de Tokyo has great coffee and is an ideal vantage point. On a wet morning, the tower is dark and aloof through the fog.

5. Rather than a spin on the Eiffel Tower's rink, try night skating nearby at the Trocadéro at holiday time. The tower is across the Seine, the ultimate Christmas tree that illuminates the winter night.

6. The restaurant Les Ombres is on the roof of the Musée du Quai Branly, a museum for primitive art in one of the most architecturally daring and original buildings in Paris. The tower is right there, almost close enough to touch. Pricey, but unforgettable.

7. The chic outdoor space at "The 7th," a restaurant at the Terrass Hôtel on rue Joseph-de-Maistre in the 18th, is open from April to the end of September. On a spring evening, the tower seems like a distant blaze down on the flat plains of Paris.

8. Follow your guide on the dizzying, 206-step walk to the colonnade beneath the dome of the Panthéon. The former church sits on one of the highest points in Paris and has a perfect view of the Eiffel Tower, though it's only open in the warmer months.

9. See the Eiffel Tower from everywhere, in its nighttime spangles, over 20,000 lights strong. Photographer Barbara Vaughn has this memory of a "Paris at Night" Fat Tire Bike Tour of Paris's landmarks, which includes a boat ride down the Seine in darkness. "Unquestionably, the most spectacular viewing of the Eiffel Tower is at night, during the five minutes an hour when it sparkles," she says. "This is even more dramatic from the perspective along the Seine, where its reflection in the moving water creates a shimmering double of this display."

10. Lastly, see it in the movies, most winningly in the 1957 musical *Funny Face*, when Audrey Hepburn, Kay Thompson and Fred Astaire converge there for the final verse of their number "Bonjour, Paris!" Nothing can upstage her, but the Eiffel Tower is the only co-star ever to have come close to matching Audrey's glamour, allure and timelessness.

☙

# 15 Shop Well

## STORES FOR BUYING AND BROWSING, PARIS

Back when the currency in France was the franc and there were seven of them to a dollar, we visitors would scour the city for everything we could cram into our suitcase, and when the zipper on it threatened to pop, we'd go buy another one. I could load up on Fauchon's Solliès fig jam or a couple bottles of Armagnac for my guy at home. Yes, there was a time when we could haul these things in our airplane carry ons. Once it was so easy, and incredibly, you could pick up a pair of Robert Clergerie boots or agnès b.'s incomparable leather trousers for a song.

But the strong euro seemed to conspire against us, as did airplane restrictions and the fact that some French products were so cheap at home (and much more available—you can get the superb La Roche-Posay skincare line at CVS, and you can even find minty Marvis toothpaste stateside). But Paris remains full of earthly wonders, and there is still too, too much to buy.

Instead of spending all your time in Paris on the hunt, comparison shopping or just stocking up on stuff because it's there, I suggest the targeted spree spread out over several days. Have your list: of places you want to discover, presents you want to bring home, something special—a scarf, a pair of sandals—for yourself. I recommend, as well, to shop on days when you will not be sightseeing too much. It's burdensome to lug bags to museums and monuments, and if you plan to climb something—Notre-Dame, say—forget it. Lastly, when planning a shopping whirl, I shelve the snappy sensible shoes I wear when logging in a museum binge and opt for a more refined outfit, so as not to look like I tumbled off the tour bus. Women no longer wear white gloves and carry parasols to shop in Paris, but the city still has its formality, and it is satisfying to feel as though you've respected that de facto dress code. Remember that "comfort" is a concept that is not always understood by Parisian shopkeepers. Style, on the other hand, is.

That goes for both high-end and basic shops, both of which you should include on your list. There's a lot of daylight between Monoprix, which is everywhere, and the Hermès store on the rue de Sèvres, which is extraordinary, but they are both required stops for me. Monoprix is akin to Target or Kmart, and it's where I find sundresses and long, crinkled cotton scarves and stock up on little Mavala nail polishes, for about four euros each. Hermès is another story, an architectural dreamscape of flowing blonde wood structures and rippling light, built on the former site of the swimming pool of the Hôtel Lutétia. Fortunately, looking is free. Also for browsing, and even a once-in-a-lifetime indulgence, the Dries Van Noten boutique on the Quai Malaquais feels like the apartment of a fabulous Parisian woman, chic to the bone, and I have stopped in here on occasion to admire the décor and ponder a little chiffon blouse.

My daughter and I always seem to need bathing suits, and my stop for that is Princesse Tam-Tam—there are many in the city—for the brand's great quality and crisp, classic cuts. I'll also stop for the super-inexpensive sweaters in every shade of sorbet at George Hogg, at 78, rue de Grenelle. The concept store was born in Paris—Colette on the rue Saint-Honoré is still the high priestess of the genre, and a stop at the water bar there is a lark. My friend Judith Friedman, who has a brilliant eye when she travels, recommended another concept store with which I duly fell in love: Sept Cinq at 54, rue Notre-Dame de Lorette in the 9th. It sells handbags, scarves, and books all made by Parisians, and also has a spot for tea in the back.

Merci is the concept store where I can (and do) spend hours—there is a café attached, located inside a bookstall/library. I browse the three cavernous floors and recently found an Étoile Isabel Marant blazer on sale there. I always bring back Merci's waffle dishtowels and signature tie bracelets. Not far away on the Boulevard Beaumarchais is Rougier & Plé, my one-stop for incredible art supplies—inks and paper, as well as wooden stamps and cool, very Parisian sticker sets for kids. Also for children, Pain d'Épices, tucked away in the Passage Jouffroy, is the place for real wooden toys, mini-cooking sets and French play food that includes Président butter, pots of yogurt and Nutella.

I'm not sure why I like to shop for bedding in Paris, but I do, and Liberty's, a tiny shop at 75, rue Oberkampf (with an outpost in Deauville), sells inexpensive and incredibly soft, real linen sheets. There are fancier florists in Paris, but L'Arrosoir also on rue Oberkampf is a jungle of scent and color. The sidewalk display recently included a flowering lime tree, voluptuous armloads of cut mimosas and little birchbark flowerpots with sprouting bulbs. And, from a display behind the vintage wooden counter, they sell rosé champagne to pair with your bouquet. French merchants are so smart.

I like to look my best in Paris, and all the walking and eating and oohing and aahing (and often, raindrops) can exhaust my poor face. So, I make an appointment at one of the most charming spots I know: Houppette et Compagnie at 120, rue Amelot for a twenty euro make-up application. It's a lovely, quiet half-hour, and last time I went, Blandine made me feel like a cover girl—and was not trying to hustle products, either.

It's my tradition to have a look around BHV on rue de Rivoli, which is undergoing a facelift, making some locals long for the good old days when it was more of a giant hardware store than another outpost for designer fashions. When I was renovating my Marais apartment, mostly by hand, this is where I came for everything, my washing machine, curtain rods, and the contraption that steamed off my thousand-year old wallpaper. But I still love the place, for unique office supplies, fabric, curtain panels, notions and a dizzying cosmetics department, where you can buy small luxury brands like Absolution and Erborian as well as classics like Chanel.

Back then, I was doing a lot of reupholstering, stitching the slipcovers myself, and was frequently at Dreyfus, at the Marché Saint-Pierre just below Sacré-Cœur. I always make a pilgrimage to this massive, comprehensive fabric emporium and leave with a few meters of something I love, even just plain white muslin to use as a table cover.

The simple leather sandals from Liwan at 8, rue Saint-Sulpice are so chic they should be expensive, and there is much more in this bright Left Bank store, whose products come from Lebanon. Also for shoes, I go directly to Bensimon for the French version of Converse sneakers, and its store at 12, rue des Francs Bourgeois has housewares, notebooks and all kinds of gift ideas, not to mention comfy, inexpensive sweaters. Nearby in the Marais is Repetto, one of several locations in Paris for the iconic ballet flat with the little tie. If there is one pair of shoes to bring home with you, one stylish present to offer yourself that will help you reminisce of your time in France (and Louboutin is out of the question), treat yourself with a pair of ballerines—they come in every color.

Lastly, I always make a weekend pilgrimage to one of *les puces*—the flea markets. My Paris friends love Saint-Ouen, because it has everything—from retro jewelry to Belle Époque marble fireplaces and a few great restaurants now, too. But my sentimental and actual favorite is Sunday at Porte de Vanves, where at one time, I bargained for vases, torchères and faded photographs that still decorate my home today. The last time I was in Paris, I bought an antique three-way vanity mirror there, the kind I've always wanted, for forty euros. It even fit in my carry on.

# 16

*The First Lady of Science*

## INSTITUT CURIE, PARIS

It is impossible to overstate the reverence aroused by a visit to the Curie Museum, located on the ground floor of the Curie Institute on the Left Bank, not far from the academic throngs of the Sorbonne. It was surprisingly stirring to find myself in Paris paying tribute to a female icon who achieved greatness not through beauty, marriage, or birthright, but through the indomitable force of her brain. More moving was to see a toddler in a pink snowsuit with her palms and nose pressed to the glass case containing scientific instruments, and wobbling up a stool to fiddle with a touch-screen timeline of Marie and Pierre Curie's lives and scientific discoveries.

For this reason, this little museum shakes me up. It's an inflection point and an occasion to ponder why there are still so few "Madame" Curies, as I was taught to call her in grade school. She accomplished the unimaginable, more than most male scientists have done in any century. Curie was the first woman to win a Nobel Prize—for Physics in 1903, shared with her husband—and then another, in Chemistry, in 1911, also making her the only Nobel Laureate to have ever won in two different disciplines. She coined the word "radioactivity," and invented radiation therapy for the treatment of cancer. Her research helped usher in the atomic age, paving the way for Albert Einstein and Edward Teller.

Even to this day, she has no equal. Her influence on humanity and on women is immeasurable, and in these times when academia and society are crying out for more female scientists, Marie Curie is  an everlasting symbol of what is possible. "She served as a role model—starting from my preteen years—of a woman who could work independently to explore her dreams and ambitions of doing science," says Anna Balazs, Distinguished Professor of Chemical Engineering and Robert von der Luft Professor at the University of Pittsburgh. "That seemed very glamorous to me."

Curie broke through during a golden age of science, and the few women in the field could scarcely compete with the big male names of the day. In 1891 at age 24, Marie Sklodowska arrived from her native Poland, where she was a governess, to study in Paris, barely able to speak a word of French. Two years later, she received a Masters in Physics, finishing first in her class. She married Professor Pierre Curie in 1895, and soon he shelved his own promising research in support of his wife's at a time when such reverse gender self-sacrifice was unthinkable. She, with Pierre, built hand-held devices that recorded radioactivity. They identified that matter was the source of radiation, discovering two new radioactive elements—polonium (named after Poland) and radium. This was an important discovery, because many formidable scientists of the time thought that atoms were indivisible; this discovery presaged the slicing and dicing of the atom that continues to this day.

As for life-work balance, she wrote her own rulebook on that, too. When Pierre died in 1906 in a tragic accident, Marie was 38 and became a single mother of their two young daughters while looking after her elderly father-in-law. In 1912, they moved to 36 Quai de Béthune where she lived until her death in 1934. As a widow, she was tainted by scandal from the revelation of her affair with a married physicist. Through it all, her work never faltered, and as improbable as it was for the time, her star continued to rise in the male-dominated international scientific establishment. She was the first female Professor of Physics at the Sorbonne, she launched and ran two research institutes, and in 1995 became the first woman honored at the Panthéon, Paris's temple to the mortal gods of France. (Two more women, at last, will be inducted and buried there in 2015, Resistance fighters Germaine Tillion and Geneviève de Gaulle-Anthonioz).

The entrance at the Musée Curie reads: "Institut du Radium, Pavilion Curie," and is part of the facility that was built for her in 1911, which still serves as a teaching and research center for physics and chemistry. Inside, the museum is compact, modern and well-organized. The walls are filled with photos, original hand-written documents, notes and letters, and of course many scientific objects the Curies used in their prolific investigations.

The chemistry laboratory is a perfect reproduction of the original, which had to be replaced in 1981 because of radiation contamination. Curie worked here for twenty years and later shared the space with her daughter and son-in-law (who, together in 1935, won the Nobel Prize in Chemistry). There is the ghost of a resolute will in this room, permeating the lab equipment and bottles of chemicals. Here was a woman whose work mattered.

Curie had toughness and savvy that enabled her success. She knew that to compete with the giants in her field, she had to publish quickly and keep discoveries quiet until she did. She also knew that her methods could benefit society. She worked in mobile X-ray units during World War I to diagnose battle wounds. At 66, she died of radiation exposure, the dark side of her discoveries the world had yet to learn.

What is still difficult to grasp are the enormous challenges that Marie Curie had to face almost a hundred years ago and how much she achieved simply by overcoming them. "Part of her legacy is her tenacity, dedication and intellectual drive," says Professor Balazs. "These are valuable attributes in pursing science, and it is important for young girls interested in the sciences to know that."

Such a degree of success is still not easy for women to attain. But for those of us who were girls long ago, for my own teenage daughter, and for little cherubs in snowsuits just starting to explore the world around them, Marie Curie and the museum dedicated to her achievements delivers a message about women that is both emphatic and clear. With hard work, the possibilities are endless.

❧

# 17 The Walls of Memory

## MÉMORIAL DES MARTYRS DE LA DÉPORTATION, SHOAH MEMORIAL AND THE DRANCY SHOAH MEMORIAL, PARIS & DRANCY

On July 16, 1995, at a memorial to the 13,000 Jewish men, women and children who in 1942 were rounded up by French police and crammed into the Vel d'Hiv, an indoor cycling arena, the newly-elected president Jacques Chirac spoke the words the world had waited fifty years to hear. "Yes, the criminal folly of the occupiers was seconded by the French, by the French state," he said. "France, the homeland of the Enlightenment and of the rights of man, a land of welcome and asylum, on that day committed the irreparable. Breaking its word, it handed those who were under its protection over to its executioners."

With this speech, Chirac broke ranks with his predecessors who, incredibly, had refused to acknowledge the French state's complicity in the Holocaust, placing blame squarely on the collaborationist Vichy government of Marshal Pétain. The distinction, which may at first seem minor, was not, and was of deep significance. Since the war, France has been at pains to face its own culpability in its deplorable treatment of the country's Jewish population during World War II. There was the lingering shame of the collaborators and the equally malignant legacy of those who looked the other way while horrors were perpetrated on their fellow citizens. But France has made strides addressing this collective history at three remarkable memorials in Paris (in addition to many throughout France), which honor those killed in the Holocaust, acknowledge the enduring reality of anti-semitism, and confront this unfathomable and all-too-recent past. They can be considered, in the spirit of Chirac, an apology of sorts for the country's role in this black chapter of its ownhistory.

The first is somewhat overlooked in one of Paris's busiest tourist areas, on the Île de la Cité, not far from Notre-Dame, Sainte-Chapelle and the Conciergerie prison. Just on the tip of the island, at a fork in the Seine, between the Pont Saint-Louis and the Pont de l'Archevêché is the Mémorial des Martyrs de la Déportation. Admission is free, and it is extraordinary. The monument was designed by the modernist architect Georges-Henri Pingusson and unveiled by President de Gaulle in 1962 to commemorate the 200,000 people arrested and deported from France to concentration camps between 1940-1945. Though the memorial wasn't built specifically for Jewish victims, here we remember that 76,000 of those deported were Jews (11,000 of them children), and that only 2,500 returned home.

You descend into the memorial through a narrow staircase between high concrete walls, designed to mimic the claustrophobia, darkness and menace in the concentration camps. The image of the triangle, used to mark inmates in the death camps, is pervasive in the crypt. Urns with names of the main camps hold earth and human ashes from each one, and there is a Tomb of the Unknown Deportee. Most breathtaking is the long, narrow gallery horizontally lined with thousands of luminous rods, one for each deportee.

In the Marais, the neighborhood that has been at the center of Jewish life in Paris for 900 years, the Mémorial de la Shoah is a second point of remembrance—stirring, powerful and profoundly moving. It requires a day, and it will be an emotional one. The museum opened in 2005 on the 60th anniversary of the liberation of Auschwitz. At the Memorial's entrance, the names of the 76,000 French Jews who were deported between 1942-1944 are engraved on the Wall of Names. The Memorial is also the repository for the "Jewish files" compiled by the Vichy government on Jews who were arrested, deported, released and wanted during this time. All now digitized, they are part of the National Archives and are among the extensive resources that make this the largest information center in Europe on the Shoah.

With the help of these records, six full-time researchers over two years were able to compile the Wall of Names. The result is nothing less than a tragic indictment of France's official collaboration with the Nazis. The wounds are still fresh, and one applauds France's head-on confrontation with its own remorse. But the museum also recognizes 3,376 people in France who were known to have risked their lives to help, save, or shelter Jews during that time. Their names are engraved on the Wall of the Righteous—*Le Mur des Justes*—in tribute to their acts of courage as well as to reaffirm what remains of our faith in humanity.

The permanent exhibition tells the history of Jewish persecution during World War II both in France and in Europe at large, detailing the rise of Nazism, ghettos, and then, mass slaughter. It does so using ingenious multi-level displays that show both collective and individual life stories. Dispersed throughout are films and windows that contain the possessions, photographs and biographies of victims. The last exhibit is the Memorial to Children, where we ponder the imponderable in a room lined with photographs of 3,000 children deported from France—smiling, beautiful faces, stripped of everything, gone from the world.

When a Jew was arrested, he or she was herded into a transit site before being sent by train to one of the death camps in occupied

Poland: Majdanek, Auschwitz, Treblinka, Sobibór, Chelmno, or Belzec. For 63,000 out of the 76,000 arrested Jews, Drancy was their final stopping place in France. Conditions there were so squalid and desperate that an estimated 3,000 died before deportation. The first convoy (destined for Auschwitz) was on March 27, 1942, and out of 1,112 people on the train, only 22 survived. Drancy was a key link in the Nazi's strategy for extermination, and in 2012, a memorial affiliated with the Shoah Museum was inaugurated here, about 30 minutes from Paris. It contains both a research facility and a permanent exhibition on the history of this infamous site, including displays on the life of the prisoners and how the convoys were organized. Most harrowing is the windowless boxcar, the Güterwagen, that forms a centerpiece of horror, standing on what remains of the railroad tracks.

The story of the French collaboration with the Third Reich is a truly tragic and disgraceful one, but the country remains justifiably proud of the brave actions of members of the Resistance who risked their lives and died during the war. In February 2014, President François Hollande named four members of the Resistance to be interred as national heroes in the Panthéon. This includes two women, Geneviève de Gaulle-Anthonioz and Germaine Tillion, whose first act of solidarity was to give her family's identity papers to a Jewish family. Both women were deported to Ravensbrück concentration camp and survived. By 2015, we will be able to pay tribute to these four people, in addition to the 76,000 French Jews who suffered or perished in the Holocaust. The more we confront these memories, the more powerful they become, which is precisely the point at these three—unforgettable—memorials.

❧

# 18 *More than Sunday Strolls*

## LUXEMBOURG GARDENS AND
## TUILERIES GARDENS, PARIS

When we visit Paris, we tend to overstuff our days there, which can leave our head spinning, limbs whirling and the rest of us, exhausted. It's odd the paces we put ourselves through, because an onerous schedule may actually defeat the purpose of a trip there in the first place. To understand the city, and to be lulled into its mythical aura, it's crucial to slow down, forget the schedule, park yourself and observe. I hope you will make time—and take it—to explore one of Paris's many public parks or gardens. A woman can slip into almost any neighborhood via its green spaces, and it is the best way to access the genuine pulse of life and inhabit Paris as locals do, whether they're grandparents shuffling along with canes, the chic woman *d'un certain âge* taking her terrier for a walk, or a young mother gulping a bite of fresh air with a napping baby. Parisians have been doing this in one form or another for hundreds of years, and now, there is much to do in the city's outdoor expanses, especially if it is not idle time you crave.

Some of the liveliest descriptions I have ever read of life in the French capital are from the letters of Abigail Adams, a practical and unfussy woman, who joined her husband in Paris in 1784, where he had been serving as a diplomat under Ambassador Benjamin

Franklin on and off since 1778. A prolific correspondent, Mrs. Adams wrote with a gimlet eye on the dress and rituals of French ladies, much of which resonates—sometimes brilliantly—to this day. Being an earthy type of solid New England stock who greatly missed her gardens back home in Boston, Abigail had real appreciation for the parks in France and their role in Parisian life. "...I proposed to your uncle to stop at the Tuileries and walk in the garden, which we did for an hour," she writes her niece, Lucy Cranch, on May 7, 1785. "There was, as usual, a collection of four or five thousand persons in the walks. This garden is the most celebrated public walk in Paris."

In Adams's day, the Tuileries was still a royal residence, as it had been since Catherine de' Medici first envisioned it in 1564, but it was burned in 1871 and was destroyed altogether in 1883. Fortunately, we were left with the park, which occupies the most stunning, 63-acre stretch of real estate in Paris, and one could argue, the world. The gardens lie grandly between the Louvre, the rue de Rivoli, the Place de la Concorde and to the south, the Seine. All day, all year, the wide pathways here vibrate with life and hum with conversation, sometimes hushed and private, sometimes exuberant.

You can spend an entire day just observing from one of the iconic green metal chairs or wander over to l'Orangerie and bow down to Monet's *Water Lilies*. Another way to enjoy the Tuileries is how many Parisians do these days: as the world's most glamorous outdoor track. When writer and lifestyle expert Martha McCully gets to her hotel room in Paris, instead of dozing away her first day, she throws on her running gear and heads straight for a spin up and down the shaded *allées* here. "I love the nearness to history and all that beauty, with the river right there," she says. "For me, it is the quintessential Paris morning."

Indeed, some of Paris's parks are more than the simple prom-enades they were in pre-Revolutionary France, and are necessary refuges for urban athletes. My friend, Jessica Stedman Guff, who often stays in the 6th arrondissement, will spend a free afternoon in fine weather playing tennis at the outdoor courts of the nearby Jardin du Luxembourg. In all my years living here, I had never known about these courts; when I walked across the park to investi-gate, I was cheered by the thwack of tennis balls in one of the most otherworldly settings imaginable. "You have to be sure you sign up on the posted sheet," says Jessica about the system, which is best not left to chance. "But once you're on the court, it's one of the most gorgeous places in the world to play tennis."

The (Jardin du) Luxembourg stuns with the graceful unfolding of its parterres, gravel pathways, and grassy lanes. All of it reveals itself beyond the Luxembourg Palace, built  by Marie de' Medici, the Italian wife of King Henry IV of France, and now the seat of the French Senate. In warm weather, the octagonal pond in front of the palace is thronged with children setting sail to miniature model boats. Surrounding this area is something quite enlightening: a series of twenty marble statues of females, "Queens, Saints or Illustrious Women," as the plaque describes them, commissioned between 1843 and 1846. Some of them are magnificent sculptures, with clothing carved in ornate detail: the Mademoiselle de Montpensier's rope belt and upraised skirt, and Anne of Austria, who was a Queen of France, with her fitted bodice and lace epaulettes. Some of these women are unknown to me, such as Clémence Isaure, a poetry muse in medieval legend, but I see she was beautiful, as is her body-hugging dress. Most heartbreaking is the statue of Marguerite d'Anjou, who was

Queen of England, forced to rule in place of her occasionally insane husband Henry VI, who lost her only son in war. "If you don't respect a proscribed queen, respect an unhappy mother," reads the inscription, the only one in the circle.

Some green spaces, like the Parc des Buttes-Chaumont, are enormous mini-worlds in which to run or get lost, with carousels, hideaways and plenty of lawn on which to spread a picnic blanket. Others, such as the Place des Vosges, perhaps the most elegant park in Paris, are more intimate refuges, where you may assume that coveted vantage point of Parisian insider. Of course, you can (and one day should) visit Maison de Victor Hugo, the writer's house, now a museum on the southeast corner of this beloved sanctuary in the Marais. But if the weather is warm, take an hour to find stillness under the linden trees here. I have no doubt that is what a Parisian, even one pressed for time, would do.

# 19 *A Portfolio of 12+1*

## JUST FOR WOMEN:
## HIGHLIGHTS OF THE LOUVRE, PARIS

This much is certain. You will go to the Louvre because the truth is, you have not really been to Paris until you have. It is the world's largest museum, built as a medieval fortress, transformed into a royal palace and residence of the Sun King, Louis XIV, before he moved to Versailles, updated to modern glory by President François Mitterand in the 1980s. The facts are intimidating: over 650,000 square feet of galleries exhibiting 35,000 paintings, sculpture, *objets d'art*, and antiquities in 403 rooms over nine miles of corridors. Intimidating, yes, and it would be easier to keep walking down the rue Rivoli for hot chocolate at Angelina. But 10 million people visit the Louvre annually, and with a good map and an audio-guide—a godsend and antidote to museum overdose—you can too, and you won't break a sweat.

I'll assume you will join the throngs in catching a glance of Leonardo DaVinci's *Mona Lisa* and the ancient Greek statue of *Venus de Milo*. It is hard to recall what the fuss is about in either of these contexts, but see these ladies you must, and do so with good cheer. There are thousands of other women in the Louvre, and I've singled out twelve of them, thirteen actually, one for extra credit. At times, sifting through the choices felt, admittedly, like a fool's errand, so varied and diverse were the possibilities, especially when I was not judging the contestants on beauty alone. In choosing them, I've leaned towards portraits, not because of their glamour, but because of the narratives of female swagger—self-confidence, progressive thought, and strength.

1. *Portrait of Madame Récamier* by Jacques-Louis David, was painted in 1800. This could have been a *Vogue* shoot introducing the latest neoclassical style both in fashion, with her plain Empire dress, and in furniture, with the carved chaise lounge. Though much of David's borrowing of classicism includes mythological themes and Greek flavors, his rendering of Juliette Récamier is far more naturalistic and candid. She shows real flesh rather than the colored-in statuary often found in retro-classical worship. Her sideways glance seems to summon the viewer and adds a fetching quality to her reclined but not so vulnerable figure. Récamier was a social and political force in Paris, with a salon that was a premier venue for literary and political dialogue and heady contemporary thought. She had married a man thirty years her senior and was a virgin well beyond child-bearing years. However, her life was not to be completely devoid of passion, as we know from her long affair with writer-historian Châteaubriand. Ultimately she became a tastemaker in earnest when the chaise on which she reclined in the painting became known as a récamier.

2. *The Marie de' Medici Cycle* by Peter Paul Rubens includes twenty-four cinematic freeze frames that glorify the events in the life of Marie de' Medici. Instead of a Super 8 format, however, each frame is a monumental painting placed around the perimeter of a gallery room in the Louvre. This is as close to an IMAX presentation of a life that a painter could pro-

duce. In 1621, the project was commissioned for the powerful Florentine, who became Queen of France by her marriage to Henry IV (who was assassinated the day after her coronation). As her son Louis XIII's regent, she was absolute ruler of France for seven years. The cycle speaks in allegorical terms about a life of trials based on the actions of others, but the paintings themselves are a triumph of self-aggrandizement and with it, female power.

3. The *Nike* or *Winged Victory of Samothrace*, has the key position at the top of the Louvre's grand staircase, and the scale itself is heroic, as it stands over eighteen feet tall. It was immortalized in cinema by Audrey Hepburn who, clad in a red Givenchy sheath, vamped alongside it in *Funny Face*, and it is still the most accessible piece in the museum. Carved from Parian marble, she has been described by many historians as a true masterpiece of Hellenistic sculpture. As a portrait, the messenger goddess braced against the wind is a symbol of courage and triumph, freedom and force. Headless, as many marble sculptures are, her female form has been paraphrased and quoted by artists in all media. Her drapery is full of movement, which accents her own fluid body, and its close fit and style is dramatic and yes, even sexy.

4. *Sleeping Hermaphroditos* is a spectacular ancient marble figure reclined on a soft, sensual-looking bed, also marble, carved by the great Baroque master Gian Lorenzo Bernini in 1620, when he was 22. You are mesmerized by the figure's lovely derrière, which can make you forget where she ends and the cushions begin—such was Bernini's affinity with his material. A typical experience with this piece often ends in surprise if the title is unknown. After admiring the figure from the back, you

walk around to the front and find that this beautiful woman is endowed with a set of family jewels.

5. *Liberty Leading the People* by Eugène Delacroix was painted in 1830 as a two-dimensional monument to the July Revolution of that same year. The muscular female figure holds a bayonet in one hand and the Tricolor flag in the other. If ever there was an early feminist rendering, it would be this fierce protagonist whose pedestal is the battlefield strewn with fallen bodies, as she leads the citizens to the ousting of King Charles X. She is Marianne, symbol of the French Republic and figurative ancestor of famed World War II icon, Rosie the Riveter. The painting was not only seen as an inspiration to future French upheavals, but signaled the end of romanticism and the Age of Enlightenment.

6. *La Grande Odalisque*, Jean-Auguste-Dominique Ingres's masterpiece, was painted in 1814 and marks his transition from neoclassicism to a more romantic treatment of his subjects. Depicting a confident, heroic nude female in recline, it has its place in a long tradition of idealized women whose social strength, self-assurance and sexuality were evolving. Aside from the obvious pose, which dates back to antiquity, the figure has conceptual ancestry that includes any number of Venuses and more recently, David's Madame Récamier.

7. Rembrandt's *Bathsheba at Her Bath*, also known as *Bathsheba with King David's Letter*, was painted in 1654. The model is often said to be his live-in lover Hendrickje Stoffels, and most historians agree that this is the Dutch master's most compelling nude. Rembrandt approached this biblical narrative from a different angle than most previous artists. The strict Dutch Reformation had endangered the nude as a subject matter, but Rembrandt

zoomed in on this one and filled the canvas completely. As such, he has even eliminated the male in the story—King David, one of the Bible's great voyeurs, who from his balcony saw Bathsheba bathing, seduced and impregnated her, and then sent her husband to battle and certain death. Here the dia-

logue between Bathsheba and the king is represented by her contemplative pose while holding a letter from him.

8. *Gypsy Girl*, also called *Bohemian*, was painted by Franz Hals around 1630. The unique use of thick paints and brushwork set Hals apart from his contemporaries, but many artists followed his quest for a painterly realism—the use of paint as a material to give more life to the subjects of his portraiture. This was in conjunction with the people he used as sitters, or models. Though he made his living in portraiture of the upper classes, he did not ignore the compelling characters in the lower eche-lons of life. The gypsy girl, no doubt a prostitute, shows a vigor and confidence that none of his high-class subjects could ever radiate. It is Hals at his best and one of the most vital depic-tions of female energy ever imparted by a painting.

9. Elisabeth Vigée-Lebrun's *Portrait of Madame Lebrun and her Daughter* by the pre-Revolutionary female court painter is a "selfie" masterpiece that is subversive on many levels. The date of this painting is significant: 1789. This portraitist of Marie Antoinette has begun to transition into a style that abandons the frilly Rococo ether of the royals. The narrative moves into empathy and reality, in complete contrast to the idealization of kings and queens. Even more universally subversive is her

format of mother and child, taking the most celebrated biblical narrative and replacing the son with a little girl. The result is a relationship that is truly intimate, especially since the happy child embraces her mother back. With these subtle tweaks, the artist has questioned a style, an autocrat and a religion.

10. Madame Lebrun's pupil, Marie-Guillemine Benoist, had a similar progressive character to her master. Her *Portrait of a Negress* from 1800 was iconic in both its beauty as well as its timing six years after the abolition of slavery in France and its colonies. Unlike much of the so-called Exoticism of the time, such as Delacroix's studies of Algerians, this woman gives a direct gaze bravely, with no bow of the head. Here she may be equating womanhood with slavery and the impending emancipation of both. Both dialogues were reaching maturity during the Age of Enlightenment, and Benoist was in the center of these debates with her teacher and circle of intellectual friends.

11. The *Pastoral Concert* by Titian has also been attributed to his master, Giorgione. Painted around 1509, it is generally thought to be a portrait of muses inspiring music and poetry, with fine arts implicit as well. The voluptuous nude women are perhaps invisible and exist only as inspiration in the minds of the men. This piece is clearly a predecessor of Manet's *Le Déjeuner sur l'Herbe* where dandies serenade two nymph-muses. Like many significant paintings, it shows a convergence of two separate worlds, where refined men from the upper classes indulge themselves while shepherds labor in the raw landscape. The contemporary world contemplates an Arcadian past while the female muses inspire.

12. *Magdalen With the Smoking Flame* was painted circa 1640 by Georges de La Tour at the height of French Baroque experimentation

with light. This French master took cues from Caravaggio about the use of chiaroscuro—great contrasts of light and dark for the sake of meaning and drama. Whereas the earlier Italian master used chiaroscuro to stage violent biblical acts or divine intervention, his successor, de La Tour, typically used an unhidden light source to create a contemplative and mystical setting for his subjects. Here he has given Christ's lover a sublime stage for meditation and reflection. She can be repentant, or lost in love and memory.

13. The presumed portrait of *Gabrielle d'Estrées and One of Her Sisters* was painted circa 1594 by an unknown artist from the School of Fontainebleau, established by Italian Mannerists invited by King François I to decorate the Château de Fontainebleau some sixty years earlier. Gabrielle d'Estrées was the favored mistress and great love of Henry IV, the first Bourbon king of France, who had been childless with his wife Marguerite de Valois. Theirs was a very public affair that grew into national legitimacy, as the monarch tried to normalize their relationship in the eyes of the church as well the nobles. This portrait shows the two sisters sitting up in a bath, Gabrielle holding what is presumed to be Henry's coronation ring while her sister softly pinches her nipple. Based on the time of the painting, the gesture is most probably pointing out a pregnancy—she bore Henry three children, whom he legitimized—reinforced by a woman sewing in the background, preparing an infant's layette. The beauty and love of a woman had inspired a king to restructure social mores and make hugely unorthodox requests of his country and the Catholic Church. It also inspired a tender, erotic painting that confronts these institutions without shame.

# 20 *A Portfolio of 12+1*

## JUST FOR WOMEN:
## HIGHLIGHTS OF THE MUSÉE D'ORSAY, PARIS

The Musée d'Orsay sits grandly by the Seine on the Quai Anatole France, and when you sail past on the water, from a Bateau Mouche or one of the glamorous evening dinner cruises, it looks every inch the Beaux-Arts train station it used to be. The towering clocks on the façade bracketing a row of arched windows form an emblem of symmetry that represents quintessential Parisian grandeur. But naturally it is the content that matters, and nothing, not even the immaculate architecture inside and out at the Musée d'Orsay, can overshadow its collection of art from 1848 to 1915, arguably one of the most aesthetically pleasing eras of painting in history.

Socially, politically and artistically, the second half of the 19th century was a time of great and rapid progress. Fortunately, there was painting and sculpture to embody these changes. So how did I decide what to include on this very unscientific list? These thirteen—out of an average of 3,000 exhibited at any given time—were chosen not specifically for being in the artist's mainstream body of work, but because they are either portraits or images that represent some of the great changes of this time. The women depicted in these works were not necessarily empowered by wealth, but were in the process of being included in universal social, post-revolutionary thought. Though some are endowed with beauty, they were not selected for this, rather for the degree of pathos the artist was able to render and the strength that could be found in a simple narrative during the periods of Realism and Impressionism.

1. *Olympia* by Edouard Manet was painted in 1863, almost two decades before his famous *Bar at the Folies-Bergère*, and is considered by many to be the Impressionist point of departure. Olympia represents the last link in the evolution of the confident, confrontational, reclined female figure. One can see the borrowed attitude from the  Venetians Giorgione and Titian, and even David's *Madame Récamier* taken to a bold extreme.

   When this painting was presented to the Paris Salon two years later, it caused unprecedented outrage and scandal. The woman is nude, imperious, and bears many clues that she is a prostitute: the loosely worn slipper, black ribbon around her neck, the orchid in her hair, and the bouquet being delivered by her servant. In the long tradition of reclining nudes, Olympia is thoroughly and bravely modern, as represented by the frankness of her expression and the openness of her body language.

2. Berthe Morisot, along with Marie Bracquemond and American Mary Cassatt, was one of the leading ladies of the Impressionist movement. *The Cradle* of 1872 is a portrait of the artist's sister Edma, also a painter, and her infant daughter. Morisot had developed close collegial ties with Camille Corot and Edouard Manet; this same year Manet painted one of the most sensual and candid portraits ever rendered of a woman, *Berthe Morisot*

*with a Bouquet of Violets* (also in the d'Orsay). She eventually married Manet's brother and had a daughter with him. But *The Cradle* demonstrates a purity of empathy between mother and child that perhaps only a woman could render. Her sister's undistilled tenderness is the very essence of motherhood. Also, although most mother/child portraits can't escape their biblical origins, this one bears no religious baggage, which represents a facet of female liberation.

3. Gustave Courbet's *L'Origine du Monde* was painted in 1866. Here, the artist took female portraiture to an erotic and bold extreme by zooming in on her torso and genitals, almost as if the body were a sculptural cropping. But there is nothing stone-like about this form—it is soft, warm human flesh. She is examined from a clinical, gynecological angle, which is consistent with how Courbet represented genre scenes and landscapes: to cut straight to the truth of the subject. Courbet rejected the idealization of figures in paint and regarded the frivolous soft nudity of mythological characters as a sterilized version of pornography. If ever a female figure represented a landscape or the architecture upon it, it is the one in this painting. She embodies everything: an entrance, an exit, an abyss and a source—all within the extreme close-up of an anatomically authentic rendering.

4. Edouard Manet's *Le Déjeuner sur l'Herbe* of 1863 was denied acceptance to the Paris Salon of that year and shown instead at the notorious Salon des Refusés, causing enough controversy that would soften the reaction to the even more risqué *Olympia*, painted later that year. Like *Olympia*, this earlier painting is a thoroughly modern quotation from Titian/Giorgione's *The Pastoral Concert* (see Chapter 19 on the Louvre) carried to an even more obvious degree. The women seem to occupy a

different realm from the men, who are chatting. They exist separate and aloof, embracing their nudity and free spirit and their own more liberated consciousness.

5. *La Capresse des Colonies* is a multimedia sculpture of an African woman completed in 1861 by Charles Cordier, some thirteen years after the second abolition of slavery in France and many of its colonies. The sculpture used anthropological studies and ethnography to find the universal beauty in the human figure. Sublime artistry is not only evident in her face and form, but also in the materials the sculptor assembled. Her flesh is rendered in a luscious patinated bronze, and the drapery she wears is from an onyx Cordier discovered in Algeria. While the subject bears her own ethnicity, so do her materials, and the public fascination for the polychromatic is satisfied on many levels. This sculpture does away with the cultural condescension of earlier periods of Exoticism. There is instead an idealization of natural beauty and the strength of the recently emancipated.

6. The original model for *La Petite Danseuse de 14 Ans* by Edgar Degas was begun in the 1860s, and the piece was completed just before the Impressionist exhibition of 1881. Until the time of his death, it was considered the only significant sculpture by Degas, known mostly for his in-depth investigations of movement and light through his paintings of dancers. This was a time when artists were exploring the vast physical possibilities of material, and on a quest to learn the limits of paint and light, Degas was a huge protagonist in this discovery.

His paintings are not invisible to us if they are not included on this list—there are more than a few on permanent display at the Musée d'Orsay. But the degree of naturalism of this rare sculpture makes it one of the most accomplished of its time, no matter when the final bronze was cast. This piece defies the "academic" boldly enough to render it the three-dimensional icon for this period.

7. *Arearea* by Paul Gauguin, painted in 1892, is a quiet depiction of a pastoral scene—lightly dressed women, with animals, plants and sacred ritual. It is also one of the most important works of its time. Gauguin himself reinforced this by buying it back from its original purchaser right before he left France forever in 1895. The year before this painting, he had begun his sojourns to Tahiti, searching for simplicity and the primitive, and *Arearea* depicts a certain enchantment with life at its most elemental. The women are the embodiment of uncomplicated contentedness and comfort in their surroundings, as represented by one woman's ease as she sits on the ground in her clean white dress.

   Gauguin, in his disconnected way, began the modern experiment with reduced form, narratives and compositions. He could be credited for igniting the European envy for the primitive existence, while the dreaminess of his canvasses certainly serves as a precursor to surrealism.

8. Gustave Courbet's *The Artist's Studio of 1854-55* was also known as *A Real Allegory Summing up Seven Years of My Artistic and Moral Life*. As a painting that celebrates painting, it is certainly one of the grand prizes of the Musée d'Orsay. It is also a manifesto on the reality of the life of an artist. The largely unself-conscious female figure is not just his model but his essential muse and accomplice. There are politicians and writers, Baudelaire amongst them, lurking in the background. He celebrates himself as a painter as well, leaning back in an arrogant gesture while laying brush to canvas. It is a self-portrait of a king in his domain.

It is also filled with contradictions starting with the title—this is no allegory, but a summary of real life. Though academically it is flawless, the painting could not be less academic because of its greater earthy realism. Though the model, his muse, stands next to him, she is not what he paints. He paints a landscape—perhaps his memory of childhood in the Jura? In an ever more urbanized Paris, the idea of untouched nature became a notion of refuge.

9. *The Gleaners* by Jean-François Millet, painted in 1857, was presented at the Paris Salon that same year and drew criticism, as might be expected, from the upper classes. Following the revolution of 1848, and recognizing the recent writings of Karl Marx, the wealthy found this painting to be a glorification of labor and lower classes. It was certainly not about the vanity of women.

    The three muses—the gleaners—bend at the waist to harvest wheat, not as laborers but as scroungers who essentially pick up the scraps of the real harvest that has occurred in the background. The overseer pays them no mind—they are doing what needs to be done. These are powerfully built women obviously capable of executing man's work. This covert feminism and the labor potential of women has always been an ingredient of socialism. Though Millet received little recognition during his lifetime, this painting remains a forceful reminder of the struggles in rural France and the notion that everyone could benefit from women in the workforce.

10. *The Snake Charmer* by Henri Rousseau was painted in 1907, over a decade after Gauguin left France to live out his days in Tahiti. An autodidact, Rousseau's reduced and honed images take primitivism to another level. However, he has rendered a

biblical narrative in a primal and seductive context. His work, though linear and flattened, produces feelings of hallucination and dreamscape as much as the ethereal Impressionists before him. He has cloaked his female protagonist in a mystery where her entire form is but a frontal silhouette. One sees only her eyes and the form of a flute. It is clearly an Eden where the African Eve form has taken charge, resisted the serpent and charmed it.

11. Mary Cassatt's *Girl in the Garden* was painted in the early 1880s. Cassatt was a Pittsburgh-born American who moved to Paris as a young woman and was largely responsible for awakening the American consciousness to Impressionism. She was part of a group of influential female artists, writers and intellectuals so vital to Parisian culture at the time.

    This painting belongs to the strong tradition in women's portraiture where the subject would be involved in some manual activity, avoiding idle hands. Perhaps Cassatt had taken cues from the many portraits of upper class women in the Louvre whose hands are occupied for the sake of self-esteem and purpose. In this almost ethereal painting, the woman sews, but her activity emerges as a snapshot of daily life, unposed, unaffected, focused, content. With all the earmarks of a developed Impressionist, the accomplishment lies in the degree of empathy for the anonymous subject as expressed in paint, light and the resulting quietude.

12. As the patron saint of the Barbizon school, Camille Corot is usually associated with an entire approach to landscape painting. His muted palette and earth tones result in a gorgeous mix of romance and mystery in his canvases. But the real surprises with Corot are in his sensitive, thoughtful portraits of women.

(There is a particularly luminous one at the Louvre: *Woman in Blue*, from 1874). There are so many, it is hard to favor any single one, but *Une Matinée. La Danse des Nymphes* from 1850 demonstrates a joyous expression of freedom—of paint, long before the Impressionist movement, and mostly, of the female spirit. His depiction of carefree women dancing in a voluptuous landscape is Corot at his most complete, both empathetic and visionary. This painting is a prognosis of great change in the arts, culture, and in society, with the landscape and the backlit female figures rendered from the same earthy paint.

13. Pierre-Auguste Renoir painted the *Bal du Moulin de la Galette* in 1876 and as one of the earliest Impressionist masterpieces, it is also one of the most revered. It includes just about every major element that was valued at the time, both in art and in life. Within the realm of painting, the date tells us of Renoir's pioneer status as an Impressionist, while the achievements with light, color, the swooping movement of the people and the experimentation with the brush make him the absolute painter's painter. He elevated his medium with this work.

The narrative speaks distinctly of Paris reborn in the mid 1870s. Only a few years after the 1871 revolution, it is about pleasure, gaiety, leisure time and romance. The activities of dancing, drinking and eating allow the artist to luxuriate in the paint by rendering an ether of glasses, light fixtures, liquid, lace, flesh and cloth. He is able to flex his painting muscles within a scene of relaxed motion and activity that demonstrates his own flirtation with paint and the possibilities of excess.

This may well sum up a day at the Musée d'Orsay. Excess and beauty, and in this context, too much is still never enough.

# 21 Day of Glory

## BASTILLE DAY, PARIS

One of the most gooseflesh-inducing scenes in *Casablanca*, and maybe even in the entire history of cinema, takes place in Rick's Café when Nazi officers belt out a carefree round of "*Die Wacht am Rhein,*" to the disgust of all, especially resistance fighter Victor Laszlo—husband of Ingrid Bergman's Ilsa. Laszlo orders the band to play "*La Marseillaise,*" and, with a nod from Bogart, they do. Just try to quell the lump in your throat when one by one, the crowd rises to its feet and joins in singing the French national anthem, thus drowning out the vile Germans. "*Vive la France!*" cries Rick's jilted lover Yvonne, face streaked with tears, and played by an actress who, like many others in the movie, had fled Europe and the Nazis. *Casablanca* was filmed in California in 1942, soon after the Americans entered World War II, so the emotion in this scene was genuine and contained real fear, real uncertainty and absolute truth.

"*La Marseillaise*" is that kind of stirring song, and it is the perfect anthem for a country that manages to make its nationalistic slogan "Long Live France!" sound charming and passionate rather than jingoistic. Both the song and the battle cry ring out across the country on July 14, the holiday known as La Fête Nationale, the anniversary of the Storming of the Bastille Prison by a revolutionary mob on that date in 1789. Bastille Day is a countrywide party, but I love to celebrate in Paris. Yes, it's crowded and can be very hot, but by the time the fireworks erupt over the Eiffel Tower at day's end, I am moved to reverence by this display of France's glory, symbolizing the victorious uprising of the French citizenry against the despotic rule of kings.

The prison was an emblem of the *ancien régime* and the absolute power of the Bourbon monarchs, both as a jail for those who had displeased the government and as a weapons storage facility. By the end of July 14, 1789, the revolutionaries had overcome resistance, and when the military commander of the Bastille opened the doors as a gesture of capitulation to the mob, it signaled the beginning of the end of the monarchy. Later that summer, France would issue the "Declaration of the Rights of Man and of the Citizen," drafted by the Marquis de Lafayette with lots of input from his American friend Thomas Jefferson, who was the Ambassador in Paris at the time. The French Revolution was in full swing. The country would have many struggles and many enemies to guillotine before emerging as a full constitutional democracy in 1871.

Bastille Day gained greater significance after the defeat of Adolf Hitler in 1945, and it seems the annual military parade down the Champs-Élysées echoes General de Gaulle's triumphant march to rekindle the eternal flame at the Arc de Triomphe on August 26, 1944. Just as it did then, the French flag—the Tricolor—waves in the center of the arch, big enough to be visible even at the other end of the avenue. The parade begins at about 10 A.M. on Bastille Day, but it's best to arrive early, wear a hat, and use the bathroom beforehand. The crowds are thick, lining up for the impressive military parade and the show of fighter planes from the French Air Force, whose formation above the Champs-Élysées leaves blue, white and red ribbons of smoke. The street becomes a living embodiment of French pride, with divisions of Army, Navy, Air Force and Gendarmerie both marching and mixing with the crowd.

It's thrilling, and then you spend the day as Parisians do: you picnic in the Parc des Buttes Chaumont or eat French-red raspberry tart at an outdoor café. The last time I was in Paris for Bastille Day, I was lucky to get a sidewalk seat at Café des Musées on rue de Turenne in the 3rd arrondisement. There is an added bonus to eating in the Marais on July 14 if homage is on your mind. After lunch, walk north on rue de Turenne towards République, and you will come to Place Olympe de Gouges, named for the 18th-century activist-thinker. There is popular movement in France to get her *panthéonisée*—honored in the Panthéon—but this is the only place that commemorates de Gouges, who courageously campaigned to change the destiny of women. Many people consider her the first great feminist. She campaigned against the institution of marriage, believing it to be the "tomb of love and trust," and in support of civil partnerships. Her efforts advocated for complete equality of the sexes in all institutions and of all people; she was also an abolitionist who wrote against slavery in the French colonies, and for the rights of prostitutes and widows. Her treatise, "The Declaration of the Rights of Women," is an exhortation to her sisters not to tolerate the status quo. "Women, wake up," she writes, "Recognize your rights." Olympe de Gouges, whose views and outspokenness threatened the men in post-Revolutionary power, was guillotined in 1793.

Bastille Day is the time to remember her and all the other hard-won battles, all over the world, that brought freedom and equality to men and women. Bring a tissue for the spectacle of the bombs bursting in air over the Eiffel Tower. Bring another one for the moment the last notes of "*La Marseillaise*" fade into the summer night.

☙

# 22 *Colonnades and Colette*

## THE PALAIS-ROYAL, PARIS

The writer Sidonie-Gabrielle Colette, known simply as Colette, died in 1954 at an apartment overlooking the Jardins du Palais-Royal, where she had lived for sixteen years. She was eighty-one. Colette was beloved by the French, a novelist, essayist, journalist, observer, author of articles, memoirs, chroniques, and fifty-some-thing books, from her early Claudine novels to *The Vagabond*, to *Gigi*, published in 1945. No one wrote with such knowingness about the raw emotion of love. But she was equally adored for her style that was as exuberant as the Burgundian landscape of her childhood, full of commas, exclamation points, and lush descriptive detail about flowers, women, soil, creatures and sky. As an exercise, open *Earthly Paradise* to any page and point. "Cold and rushing waters, naked woods threaded with sunlight, strewn with mauve-veined anemones, seas of violets," she writes on a page I randomly choose. One stunning sentence after another, passage after passage, in book after book.

Colette was also revered by intellectuals of the day—Marcel Proust, André Gide, Simone de Beauvoir, who wrote copiously about her in *The Second Sex*, and her great friend and neighbor on the Palais-Royal, Jean Cocteau. At her funeral, held at the opposite end of the garden, she was offered the highest honors ever accorded to a

French woman writer. Perhaps they raised a glass to her at Le Grand Véfour, one of Paris's most glamorous restaurants that was just

below her suite of rooms. Towards the end, when she was overweight and nearly immobile with arthritis, she was helped downstairs, perhaps by Cocteau, to dine in her own banquette in the crimson and gilded room where Napoleon and Josephine, Victor Hugo and George Sand had supped years before her in the royal opulence of the storied restaurant.

Colette is the draw of the Jardins du Palais-Royal, but so is Le Grand Véfour. In fact, I was married there one September afternoon. Arriving guests were handed flutes of champagne on the terrace by the statuesque gates, and we celebrated in the sunlight, under the colonnades, and drifted out into the gardens, one of Paris's most elegant enclosures, before dinner.

The Palais-Royal remains much as it looked centuries ago, with one major stylistic interruption on one end: the black-and-white Daniel Van Buren sculptures from 1986 that most Parisians seem to revile but tolerate just the same. On the actual garden side, the space redeems itself in glorious symmetry and quiet. There are beautiful shops—Parfums de Rosine, Serge Lutens, and Didier Ludot's vintage boutiques—and it is my favorite spot in Paris for a weekday picnic (on a bench, rather than the more elaborate weekend version, on a blanket). But mostly, there is Colette, who grew old and truly great here, and breathed the air that blew in among the rows of blunt-cut chestnut and linden trees. Here, we bow down to her.

Colette's success had been triumphant, her writing genre-defying, and her life both original and extraordinary. She was full of paradoxes, a sensualist with a honed eye for sharp detail, who disliked feminism while unconsciously and defiantly forging an image of how women could be. Though raised a strict Catholic in pastoral Burgundy (in her hometown of Saint-Sauveur-en-Puisaye, there is a wonderful museum dedicated to her life), she divorced twice, worked as a music hall showgirl at the Moulin Rouge, lived as a lesbian for a decade, and had a daughter whom she couldn't be bothered much with raising. She wrote a sexual autobiography called *The Pure and the Impure* and had an affair with her sixteen year-old stepson that lasted into her fifties and, in a perfect example of art imitating life imitating art, her 1920 novel *Chéri* had a similar plotline. Shortly after that—in the 1920s—she had a facelift, and in 1932 (when she was already a literary giant), she opened a beauty salon in Paris, Colette's Institut de Beauté, where she worked as a make-up artist and seemed to cement her philosophy about female resilience: "The harder the times are for women, the more determined women become, and proudly so, to hide the suffering it inflicts on them," she writes. Amen.

In 1938, just before the outbreak of World War II, Colette moved to 9, rue de Beaujolais, and her imagination explored what preceded her in this outdoorsy place above the lollipop trees, especially the mezzanine, or entresol, which she fancied bore a colorful past. "A gambling-den, worse maybe? I really don't know, they're just stories I tell myself," she writes. "It may be that the entresol where I hollowed out my nest had in fact been the dwelling, the observation post, of those ladies of pleasure."

The Palais-Royal is a bucolic island in the center of Paris, but as Colette knew, it swarms with myth and memory. Of all the places in Paris that would be a great setting for a juicy 18th-century *Melrose Place* meets *The Tudors* mini-series—and there are quite a few contenders—this would get my vote. Politics and society have enjoyed a lively intermingling here—most famously when the politician Camille Desmoulins stood on a café table and gave an impassioned call to arms two days before the Bastille was stormed on July 14, 1789.

The Palais-Royal was constructed for Cardinal Richelieu in 1629 and despite its name, was never actually a royal palace like the Louvre and the Tuileries. The biggest changes we still see today came in the 1780s courtesy of Louis-Philippe II, duc d'Orléans. He refashioned the Palais-Royal into a haven for commere, gastronomy, shopping and entertainment, with gardens framed by arcades housing small shops called *galeries,* lined by stately limestone colonnades, and two grand theaters that are still in use today. In 1784, Le Grand Véfour (originally the Café de Chartres) opened at the northwest corner of the Palais-Royal.

At that time, the Palais-Royal became the center of the center of Paris, pulsing with the beat and thrum of all human nature, a place where class distinctions seemed to evaporate, the center of the mad urban debauch. Often the layer of decadence lay just under the prim veneer of society here. "It is well-known that the new Palais-Royal is the general rendezvous for all the passions and enterprises of vice, prostitution, gambling, swindling, crime, and hence has become the center of all observation," wrote the novelist Rétif de la Bretonne in his novel about the Palais-Royal. It was where countesses might mingle with courtesans, shopgirls and prostitutes. A place of commerce until 5 P.M., afterwards it became a place for respectable people to dabble in the pleasures of the flesh with girls svelte or voluptuous, according to de la Bretonne.

Alas, it was Colette who would define the Palais-Royal for a new era and forever. She moved there just before the German occupation of Paris, and though it was a prolific time for her, she worried about her third and last husband and great love, Maurice Goudeket, who was Jewish and was interned briefly, only to be released through the efforts of a German official's wife, a fan of Colette's. In *Paris from my Window,* which she wrote during the war, she documents the mundane and the unchanging nature of humanity during perilous times. Above everything is her great love for France. "The worship I offer to my country is a slow-burning fire deep inside me," writes Colette. "We were spoiled when young by the succulence and the grace of the French earth, warm in its every fold from having provided shelter to the human race."

So it was also appropriate for Colette to settle in the most rural of settings in Paris, to return to the countryside she loved right in the center of the city. There is astonishment in her language of rivers, flowers, wildlife and landscapes. I could faint for the beauty of her images of rushing streams, cherries honeyed by the summer sun, the clean scent of earth, and all the wonders of the natural world. Even on a Paris balcony. "If I don't have the top of a tree in front of my eyes, then I must have the length of a moiré sky," she writes. Unfurled, of course, over the Palais-Royal.

❧

# 23 The Hidden Places

## UNIQUE MUSEUMS, PARIS

"You haven't been to the Musée Nissim de Camondo?"

I'm at a friend's house for dinner on rue de Bagnolet in Paris, and five French women and two French men are staring at me, stunned. Yes, I am writing a book on France, and No, I haven't been there...yet. One of them brandishes an iPhone and scrolls through photos from a recent visit, offering me a virtual guided tour. This is what Parisians do. They just happen to have visited a beautiful little museum recently, and just happen to have pictures handy. It's an incredible country.

Suffering this type of chagrin from well-meaning friends is how I have gathered most of what I know about France over three decades. The scenario has unfolded in a similar manner, more times than I can count. A passing mention of a place, my head tilts blankly, the reproach followed by encouragement, and off I march as soon as possible to discover a new, uncharted (by me, at least) spot.

More than shoe stores or the latest champagne bar, it is the museums that spur the greatest rapture from Parisians. You could say that Paris is a museum of museums. There are dozens, some estimates put the number at 200, and the range of this cultural banquet can seem almost infinite. There are places to honor the life and work of painters (Musée Marmottan Monet), the history of currency

(Musée de la Monnaie), or collections of Asian art that span centuries (Musée Guimet). Museum design also runs the gamut, from edgy (La Maison Rouge, a contemporary exhibition space) to drop-dead opulent (the Petit Palais, a traditional art museum, where the portrait hangs of Sarah Bernhardt with her borzoi) to raw and literally underground (the Sewer Museum—it exists).

Sixty are covered on the Museum pass, which costs sixty-nine euros, but many of the more intimate or less-trafficked places will cost about eight euros at most and are often free. Either way it's a steal. If you don't like the permanent collection, you can move on to a temporary exhibit, and if either of those fail to spark, you'll admire the setting, or the architecture, and often, a little *buvette* snack bar on premises. Lastly, some of Paris's best shopping is in museum gift shops, for the most part well-curated boutiques selling high-quality stuff. The Maritime Museum (Musée de la Marine) has sailor shirts that could have been designed by John Paul Gaultier.

One of my favorite shops is at the Musée des Lettres et Manuscrits on the Boulevard Saint-Germain. I pass by the museum frequently on my way to Café de Flore and occasionally detour into this shrine to the written word. Christina Henry de Tessan tells me it's a critical stop when touring in the footsteps of many historical figures. She is the author of *Forever Paris*, an impeccable book detailing twenty-five walks around the city focused on some of its greatest personages (Colette, Victor Hugo, Audrey Hepburn, Simone de Beauvoir and Jean-Paul Sartre, among others). "It's right in the literary and intellectual center of the city," she says. "It's dazzling to see the notes and scribblings of people like Balzac or Hemingway. It gives so much insight into their creative lives in Paris."

One of the loveliest places to live vicariously is at the Musée Jacquemart-André, a splendid *hôtel particulier* right on Boulevard Haussmann. The villa houses the private art collection of the couple that lived there, including portraits by court painters Elisabeth Vigée-Lebrun and Jean-Marc Nattier. For me the real draw is the sigh-worthy *belle époque* café in the mansion's dining room, a highly civilized spot for afternoon tea or Sunday lunch.

The Musée Baccarat, showcasing the famous crystal, is housed in the exquisite former home of Vicomtesse Marie-Laure de Noailles. Everything here literally sparkles, especially when reflected in the many mirrors. Recently, this small temple to all that glitters underwent a redesign by Philippe Starck, so it's as chic as it is shiny.

If you would be bothered by stuffed hunting trophies, including a kind of cute upright polar bear, skip the Musée de la Chasse et de la Nature. If not, and you are moseying through the Marais, this weird and wonderful world dedicated to the history of the hunt is strangely, perhaps disturbingly, beautiful. It's as if a Museum of Natural History were dismantled and reassembled in a sumptuous townhouse.

The fashion-oriented Musée Galliera is a neo-Renaissance palace with soaring windows and sweeping gardens from which you can take in the open expanses of the 16th arrondissement where it abuts the Seine. This vast building is entirely dedicated to *la mode* from the 18th century to the present day. Though its permanent collection is not on public display, there are frequent temporary expositions with works that are enhanced by the glamorous setting. In the spring of 2014, it hosted, "A Century of Fashion Photography from Condé Nast," which was like visual sorbet, artful and refreshing.

I often have dreamed away an hour or two in the courtyard strewn with rambling roses at the Musée de la Vie Romantique, the former house of 19th-century painter Ary Scheffer. Here, in his studio, he entertained Frédéric Chopin, Eugène Delacroix, Pauline Viardot, Franz Liszt and others, most memorably George Sand, whose artifacts—jewels, pens and seals initialed "G.S."—are displayed in a setting that is both grand and homey, with lots of different fabrics and wall coverings. "It's not at all your typical museum," says my Paris-savvy friend Judith Friedman. "It tweaks all of your aesthetic sensibilities."

Along these lines—for both intimacy and the scope of history— is the Musée de Montmartre, a calm enclave set apart from the crowded neighborhood. Montmartre's artistic past is celebrated here; the dancers, the Lapin Agile and Moulin Rouge Cabarets, and the Can-can itself. Most beautiful on a spring day are Renoir's flowering gardens that compose a green frame for the museum; it is here the artist lived and painted *Bal de Moulin de la Galette* and other iconic works.

And finally, the Musée Nissim de Camondo, located right on the Parc Monceau. My friends' enthusiasm was not exaggerated. It is the former home, brilliantly preserved, of a wealthy early 20th-century banker, Moïse de Camondo, built to match the magnificence of his art collection and other rare treasures and promised to the city following his son's death in World War I. The modern bathroom must have been groundbreaking in its day, and 100 years later, retains its clean, chic lines, as does the kitchen with its rows of lustrous copper cooking pots and massive, still gleaming state-of-the-art stove. But this museum has a sadder layer of historical context, and it is palpable within the lush décor. Eight years after his death in 1935, de Camondo's daughter, her husband and their two children were all deported and killed at Auschwitz. The legacy of this man is his marvelous house, empty of any descendents, but full of passion and his towering spirit.

❧

# 24 *All Around the Pompidou*

## BRANCUSI'S STUDIO AND NIKI DE SAINT PHALLE'S FOUNTAIN, PARIS

There are two spectacular destinations near the Centre Georges Pompidou besides the building itself and the Musée National d'Art Moderne, housed within. Both are on the Place Beaubourg, just outside the museum. One is the *Stravinsky Fountain* by Niki de Saint Phalle and Jean Tinguely and the other is the Atelier Brancusi, as serene and monochromatic as the other is (literally) splashy and playful.

When I used to live in this neighborhood, I confess I found de Saint Phalle's sculpture, with its lips, hearts and loud palette, a tad frivolous. It took my teenage daughter, who decided it was among her favorite sites in Paris, for me to take another serious look. Not surprisingly, my child urged me to see the joy as more than superficial and to discover this artist as a feminist and a feminine icon. One of the best places to get an eyeful is from above at Le Georges, the ultra-modern restaurant on the top floor of the Centre Pompidou. From a bird's eye view, the fountain sculpture is a unified whole, not merely the piecemeal backdrop for the crowds that gather on the plaza for brunch and cocktails.

Niki de Saint Phalle was born near Paris to a wealthy, aristocratic French father and American mother and raised in New York, where she was a model, appearing on the covers of *Vogue* and *Elle*. When she moved back to Paris, she began to flourish as an artist and was a contemporary of her future (second) husband, the Swiss kinetic artist Jean Tinguely. They both fit neatly into the movement of Nouveau Réalisme, a term coined in 1960. Her earliest work explored women and childbirth, themes she returned to often in her career.

The mechanical-minded Tinguely and the Gaudi-inspired de Saint Phalle had completely autonomous careers, studio practices, and aesthetics. But unlike the turbulent relationship between Auguste Rodin and Camille Claudel, Tinguely and de Saint Phalle were mutually supportive, and they collaborated on many projects during their 20-year marriage. This includes the fountain on the Place Beaubourg, where Tinguely shared authorship with his wife's brightly colored cartoon forms.

Tinguely had been selected for this commission based on the success of a recently completed fountain in Basel, Switzerland. He requested the addition of de Saint Phalle to contribute her signature shapes and color to the focal points of the fountain, which would be right next to the recently completed, groundbreaking Centre Pompidou. This made sense, as nothing could be too over-the-top next to Renzo Piano's brightly painted steel-ducted building in what had been one of the most architecturally homogenous cities on earth.

She was no stranger to kinetic qualities in the arts, having been involved in film and even more radical demonstrations of performance art, including using firearms on sculpture in the early '60s, predating similar gimmickry by others such as William Burroughs. When she was in her thirties, she began work on her large-scale concrete constructions, bold-colored rotund female figures termed *Les Nanas (the Chicks)*, whose girth and architectural-scaled presence show woman as a vessel and the nucleus of fertility and energy. Later, she expanded these further, making playground environments of her giant, bulbous forms, which were both avant-garde and childishly playful. As pop and psychedelic as they seem aesthetically, there are heroic qualities in the female protagonists in her sculptures.

With the placement of her multicolored fiberglass (for the ease of movement) pieces upon the Paris fountain's completion in 1983, public art was transformed. Loosely basing it on Igor Stravinsky's *The Rite of Spring*, she created an exuberant celebration of fertility, modernity and unabashed femininity—all this in the context of Tinguely's dark, metal, dynamic framework. To add to the frenetic movement of shape and color, the piece spews water from various orifices and anatomical points of interest at unpredictable intervals. To gaze at this is always rousing, and unlike the tranquil waters of most public fountains, this one keeps the senses busy instead of lulling them to sleep.

As easy as it is for the *Stravinsky Fountain* to catch your eye, it is equally possible to miss the anonymous-looking outbuilding nearby that houses the Atelier Brancusi. When you enter here, you enter a rarified universe. I've often voyaged to this serene islet with my husband, a sculptor, who believes it to be the world's finest collection of early 20th-century sculpture and objects. It all belongs to one artist: Constantin Brancusi, who in 1904 walked across Europe to Paris from his native Hobita, Romania, arriving with the bloody feet of a pilgrim.

The Atelier Brancusi is an exact duplicate of his studio, based primarily on photographs from his original space in the 15th arrondissement where he spent more than fifty years until his death in 1957. He left it and all of its contents to the French state, and forty years later it was reconstructed, also by Renzo Piano, outside the Pompidou. The atelier houses many of his masterpieces, as well as tools and simple objects he collected. It is reassembled as he left it, with no changes to the room's composition, as he believed his work was best viewed collectively and better understood in context with one another in his own chosen arrangement, rather than alone.

The space is enhanced by light from above the plaza and is a sea of calm in this frenzied part of Paris. Here, you can see many of his iconic sculptures, or studies for them, including *Bird in Space, Endless Column,* and *Sleeping Muse,* of earthy-soft stone, plaster, wood and polished bronze. It is a private view of a great artist's working process and a candid setting for the magic that he made.

Considered by many historians as the father of modern sculpture, depending on where we start with that notion, Brancusi was the master of reducing human and organic renderings to their essential honed forms. His aesthetic was not the hard-edge masculine constructivism we associate with most modern sculpture. Rather, his reduction of form was sensual, feminine and almost maternal. He was clearly the creative ancestor of Jean Arp, Henry Moore, and Isamu Noguchi who had been an apprentice for a short period.

His early muses and female portraits show deep understanding and investigation of the essential figure of a woman. This, as a woman, is perhaps what makes the pieces in this space so sensuous and tactile to me: Brancusi's demonstration of a will to understand, and not just recreate, our universal form.

❧

# 25 The New French Revolution

## LA JEUNE RUE, PARIS

Something extraordinary is afoot in the culinary world in Paris at an epicurean utopia called La Jeune Rue, whose shops and restaurants began to open—one by one, door by cutting-edge door—in a northern corner of the Marais in autumn 2014. Despite its high and quite glamorous concept, the mission is deceptively, deliciously simple: to recognize and showcase ranchers, farmers, and food producers from all over the country and have their expertise—marginalized in the quest for over-the-top cuisine—become implicit in what we eat and how we cook. And to do it in the highest possible international style. It is beyond organic, beyond farm-to-table even. Rather, it strives to be a fully integrated movement, even involving great chefs, some of whom have begun to recognize that without the people in the fields raising food the old-fashioned way, they are nothing but empty toques.

Enter La Jeune Rue, which broadens this philosophy to the public, and offers it in an architecturally daring 21st-century set piece, consisting of thirty-six shops and restaurants. It is the brainchild of Cédric Naudon, a wealthy financier and owner of Le Sergent Recruteur, a very *du moment* restaurant on Île Saint-Louis. His passion for design as well as gastronomy anticipated this slow-burning revolution in how people—especially urbanites—consume and understand food.

Jean-François Gaillard has taken a keen interest in La Jeune Rue since the project's inception and helps explain what at root is a return to quality as embodied in a one-stop culinary wonderland. "For a long time, people have not really known good ingredients, because many of the restaurants dressed up food to where the quality of the product was unrecognizable," says Gaillard, a Parisian businessman now gentleman farmer in the Pyrénées, provenance of many of the farmers represented so far in Le Jeune Rue. "When the chefs take the lead, start with an incredible product and just maximize the taste, people will want to duplicate that in their own kitchens."

At La Jeune Rue, these values are embraced and promoted in refined, ultra-modern settings. Naudon invited several leading architects and design stars from Europe and the world—the UK's Tom Dixon and Jasper Morrison, Italy's Paola Navone and Michele De Lucchi, among many others—to create his or her bold, minimalist space in which to house the various markets. This includes a butcher, dairy, produce, ice cream, bakeries among many others—as well as concept stores, a tapas bar, a Korean restaurant and several bistros. Lest you think this is a gimmicky twist on another high-end urban mall, think again. La Jeune Rue defiantly stays on theme, even behind the scenes. For example, whole stalks of wheat grown in the Pyrénées from the farmer's own ancient seeds in a 12th-century mill will be trucked into La Jeune Rue's processing facility outside of Paris, ground into fresh flour every day and made into the bread sold at one of the two stunning bakeries, that are anything but old school.

The idea is to promote enthusiasm—hunger if you will—for knowledge about what we eat. As any proponent of conscious eating is aware, this itself is a civic act, as it validates a farmer who treats the earth and the animals with care. When we know where our meat comes from, who the producer was, how the cow was fed and where, we are connected to the earth, which gives complete transparency to what we are actually feeding ourselves. This extends down to minute details, even incorporating the idea of *terroir*—the composition of the soil and other geographical factors that is usually used in the context of winegrowing—into what we consume. "La Jeune Rue shows the public that each region of France has different grass, different flowers, different weather, that can affect the taste of milk, cheese, even meat," says Gaillard. One can envision a dairy connoisseur, who can taste the difference between Auvergnat and Alsatian cow's milk.

Of everything La Jeune Rue represents, from style to quality to purity in all its interpretations, like all revolutions, it has elements of the rebellious, and even the subversive. Eliminating the middleman, for one, which keeps prices low. Messing with the status quo. It is telling that the endeavor blossomed in a neighborhood of empty 18th-century storefronts, which La Jeune Rue has preserved. This means that this historic area will remain uninfected by those deadening scenes of urban blandness—chain stores and fast food outlets—that are as prevalent in Paris as in any other city on earth. So of everything La Jeune Rue is offering, it is most resolutely a move to reassemble the story of this great food-obsessed city, when the boulangerie, pâtisserie, épicerie and charcuterie thrived together on one happy block. All of us are crying out for the real thing, and the Parisians are getting it at La Jeune Rue. And when all of it comes in a beautiful, architecturally audacious package, it's a win-win, all around.

# 26 *Follow the Philosopher*

## THE NIETZSCHE PATH, ÈZE-SUR-MER

In the summertime, the scent of geranium and rose drifts up the cliff from the beach to Èze Village, known as the Eagle's Nest, one of Provence's most dramatic perched villages—towns built as fortresses that rise on the edge of mountains, which are plentiful throughout the region. The village is crested by a botanical garden blooming with cacti and succulents, from which you can see the Mediterranean in wrinkles of blue, violet and white, as well as a perfect view of the corniches—the Riviera highways that hug the cliffs on three different elevations. In such a tranquil spot, it strains the imagination to know that Èze rarely saw peace from the moment it fell under control of the House of Savoy in 1388. Moors, Turks, Italians, the plague and King Louis XIV all laid siege to Èze until 1860 when the town became, at last, a part of France.

Since then, all manner of celebrity arrives to lose themselves in one of Èze's two landmark hotels whose rooms and outer doors, illuminated by gas lanterns at nightfall, are tucked into the village's cobblestone streets—which are impossible, by the way, to negotiate in stilettos. Until 1953, Prince William of Sweden summered in a medieval castle that is now a luxury hotel, Château Eza. And celebrities from Beyoncé to Barbra Streisand have cooled their heels at the Château de la Chèvre d'Or, some of whose rooms seem to be carved, glamorously and discreetly—into the mountainside itself.

It is just to the left of the gate of the Chèvre d'Or where transcendence trumps luxury. The entrance to the Chemin de  Nietzsche—The Nietzsche Path—is marked by a small sign with an arrow pointing down to Èze Bord-de-Mer. The receptionist at the hotel says the round-trip trek of the 427-meter-high former mule path will take about three hours, and at moments it is rocky and quite strenuous, though not for a reasonably fit person. But what really leaves you breathless is the emotional sweep that seems to carry and lift you, especially on the descent, when the coast reveals itself and leaps straight up from the limestone rock formations.

"And when he had reached the top of the mountain-ridge, behold, there lay the other sea spread out before him: and he stood still and was long silent," wrote Friedrich Nietzsche in *The Wanderer*, the beginning of Part III of his masterpiece *Thus Spoke Zarathustra*, which the German philosopher conceived on the trail in Èze that now bears his name. It was the early 1880s, and for a time he was ensconced on the sunny coast between Nice and Genoa, suffering from failing eyesight, melancholy, and burgeoning madness. If he had been able to find joy at all in his tormented life, he found it here. If it all sounds too cumbersome with this weight of genius, it's not. He simply led the way for the rest of us. Later, his words were left on plaques along the path, encoded with meaning for the solo, lonesome or searching traveler. "I await friends, ready day and night," reads one, from *Beyond Good and Evil*. "Where are you friends? Come! It's time! It's time!"

The first part of the trail through Le Vallon du Duc—the Duke's Valley—has remnants of paving, and without the correct footwear, the loose gravel renders this the most perilous part of the journey (you can do the walk in sturdy sneakers, but I always bring hiking shoes when traveling). The trail soon becomes stone and dirt, and as you descend, the path plays tricks, turning sharply and vanishing, while a seemingly new one opens to expose a fresh slice of sky and a sliver of the Mediterranean. The air is a perfume of rosemary, rock rose blossoms, olive trees, and myrtle, all of which cluster here and there near the path. Butterflies flit about as they have for thousands of years.

And then there are the crags that rear and loom to form the twisted walls of the valleys, some of which also disappear sideways. At times, the sheer grandeur of the rock faces seems almost on the scale of Yosemite, and some hover almost protectively. Soon, the sea appears in full, jutting out from the valley in a perfect V, and the trail extends to the main road, crossing over to a white stretch of sand. You may also do this walk in reverse; start at the beach and work your way up, but if you're not feeling adventurous enough for a round-trip, you can catch a bus in either direction from Èze Village back to the train station and the coast.

If you've walked down, it's a good idea at least in summer to wear a bathing suit, because you'll want to cool off in the gentle surf. The trek back up is steep in parts, and the cliffs that seemed like friendly giants on the way down now seem a tad forbidding. Remember to look up, because the stone façades of Èze Village begin to emerge like characters out of a fairy tale through the leaf cover. The path zigs and zags, and soon, the bell tower of Notre-Dame de l'Assomption seems to rise straight out of a giant spur. Behind you, and off to the right, is the sea again, a soothing wash of blue.

This walk may inspire you to bone up on your Nietzsche. Maybe you skipped most of your Philosophy 101 lectures or never quite

got acquainted with the man most famously known (and misun-
derstood) for the declaration that "God is dead." It's worth it. *Thus
Spoke Zarathustra* is about a prophet who descends from a mountain to
offer his wisdom to the world, and it's not a stretch to see how this
climb, these boulders, this ascent from the sea to the Eagle's Nest
inspired the philosopher to produce his greatest work. "My muscle tone was always greatest when my creative energies flowed most
abundantly," he wrote about his daily uphill jaunts from the train
station. "The body is spirited—let us leave the 'soul' out of play...
One could often have spotted me dancing." Or, just stopping to
smell the rosemary.

❧

# 27

## *Detox and Retox*

### LES SOURCES DE CAUDALIE AND
### CHÂTEAU SMITH HAUT LAFITTE, MARTILLAC

There are countless luxury hotels in France, so many places with 1,000-thread cotton sheets on which to bask and swish your vacationing body (some, like the Grand Hôtel du Cap-Ferrat actually have a bar to select the qualities you desire in a pillow and voilà!— one will appear at your door). And many of them build spas of such grandeur that well-being hardly seems worth pursuing anymore without four-foot orchids in the bathroom and indoor infinity pools. Sometimes, you have to wonder how high the bar can go.

What distinguishes the Vinothérapie Spa at Les Sources de Caudalie in Martillac, however, is the concept itself—something that could only have taken root twenty minutes from the city of Bordeaux in the heart of Aquitaine's wine country. From this stretch of land, bottles of deep, rich Graves depart for the finest tables in London or Beijing. On an autumn day, the damp smell of earth floats among the 250 acres of forest and Cabernet Franc, Cabernet Sauvignon, Sauvignon Blanc 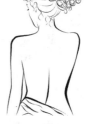 and Merlot vines, whose edges are just beginning to yellow. When the taxi pulls away, new desires sweep in, as will happen at posh places in magical settings: to stroll upon the vineyard's soil and stones, to feel the thick flow of red wine down the throat. *To sell an app to Google or another high-tech giant and never have to leave this place.*

Across the way is the *domaine* of one of the area's great Bordeaux, Château Smith Haut Lafitte, which was bought in 1990 by the current owners (and former French Olympic skiers) Daniel and Florence Cathiard, whose daughter and son-in-law run the hotel and spa. Another daughter heads up the international cosmetics business for the Caudalie brand, with its tubes of luscious concoctions all created from one of nature's true bonanzas: the grape.

Outside the spa, the décor has more in common with a traditional tobacco drying barn than a marble temple, but it turns out the weathered wood isn't just construction dunnage but rather, lumber from the cellar of Château Lafite Rothschild. The smooth interior is all luster and gleam, with a clean scent of flowers and fruit, but what is most intriguing is what's being done in the treatment rooms. In 1993, or so legend has it, a professor and researcher from the University of Bordeaux revealed to the Cathiards that the seeds and skins of grapes—all the supposedly useless stuff that remained after wine was produced—contained a mother lode of chemicals called polyphenols that were loaded with antioxidants and anti-aging properties. We all know what resveratrol is now and how good it is for the heart. Some of us even nibble on the little chews that taste like bitter Starburst, a vitamin on-the-go to keep us from dropping dead prematurely of old age. Caudalie was one of the first companies to recognize the benefits of resveratrol on the skin to help boost elasticity and fight free radicals. Because whatever free radicals are, they are bad and have no place on a woman's one and only face.

As it happens, the spa has naturally warm spring water from a well 1,800 feet deep. The beneficial minerals of the water, combined with the extracts of wines and grapes, is the essence of *vinothérapie*, a word trademarked by Caudalie. It is clear what this neologism means from the spa menu: Crushed Cabernet Scrub, a massage that exfoliates with grapeseeds. The Vinopure Facial, which incorporates a polyphenol derived from the discarded stalks and sap of Sauvignon Blanc grapes. The spa incorporates every part of the grape in its treatments except for the juice, which has better things to do than keep your skin soft. You will find that across the way.

As with most of the wine producers in the region around Bordeaux that includes St. Èmilion, Médoc, Pauillac, and Pomerol, the vineyards of Smith Haut Lafitte surround the château, which sits in the middle of the rows of vines. You will need to make a reservation for a tour and degustation, especially if you are not booked as a guest at the hotel. Wander across the road refreshed, buffed, slathered head-to-toe in wonderful grapey potions, along the dirt path, past one of sculptor Barry Flanagan's giant bronze rabbits towards the château, whose watchtower is concealed in ivy. The guide will take you inside the woodshop from another century, where a cooper turns barrels—450 of them a year—out of perfectly toasted oak. This is one of the few estates in Bordeaux that fabricates its own casks. Marvel in the underground cave, where two of the vintages are stored in a chilly vaulted chamber, lit to perfection, as orderly and peaceful as a church. Savor the Grand Cru Classé in the tasting room. Make reservations in advance for a tasting that pairs four vintages with dried fruit and dark chocolate from the Basque country. Remind yourself what they say about wine and women.

Remember one more thing: Whatever science is behind keeping us youthful, it may not ever compete with the intangibles of keeping us happy. Here in Bordeaux, there is comfort in gazing out at the vines from an indoor, poolside chaise. There is vigor in getting polished and worked over with expert hands and tiny shards of grape seeds. And nothing can really beat sipping Bordeaux in Bordeaux. If that isn't wine therapy, I'm not sure what is.

☙

# 28 The Green Muse

## ABSINTHE BAR, ANTIBES

> My glory is only a humble ephemeral absinthe
> Taken stealthily, fearful of treasons,
> And if I drink no more, I have my reasons.
> —Paul Verlaine

It's part of France's fickle charm that there is no market more perfect than the one you are strolling through at that very moment.
There is always the fear that you will never see raspberries such a
deep fuchsia again or catch the very same scent of *saucissons* laced with
garlic, fennel or Comté cheese. But Antibes's daily *marché* on the
Cour Massena is, by any standard, singular. Like most Provençal
markets, this is the kind of place that makes you wonder how you
will ever darken the doorstep of a big box store back home again.
Here, you gaze at towering rows of pastel-colored jasmine, lavender
and rose petal jams, pass by bins groaning with flavored sea salts,
alongside terracotta bowls of briny olives and lemon confit, towards
baskets of purple artichokes dwarfed by their still-attached leaves.
This morning, I buy a small loaf of bread and the tiniest chunk
of chèvre infused with herbs, tucking them into my bag for later.
I may need to nurse a midday hunger after a visit to the Absinthe
Bar, an underground shrine to the mythical and highly alcoholic

(110 to 140 proof) drink distilled from wormwood, bitter anise and fennel.

The bar is cocooned underneath a storefront next to the market's busy thrum. It is a dizzying setting for this museum-like hideaway, which celebrates one of the world's headiest spirits. There is a slight whiff of tourist-treaded steps, but lower your nose, dear reader, and revel in the history.

Upstairs is a shop lined floor-to-ceiling with Provençal fare—honey, biscuits and fruity pastilles—as well as row upon row of the real point of the place: bottles of absinthe. The owner shows me a gorgeous little paperback book, *L'Absinthe au Féminin* by Marie-Claude Delahaye, that illustrates in detail the mysterious and romantic connection of women with absinthe, and it is staggering. Because drinking absinthe was believed to induce creativity, it played an enormous role in France's cultural history in the late nineteenth and early 20th century. The A-list of artists who famously consumed—and were consumed by—absinthe, including poet Paul Verlaine, painter Vincent van Gogh and writer Charles Baudelaire, explains why the drink was known as the "green fairy" and the "green muse." Absinthe drinkers were some of Picasso's favorite subjects during his Blue Period. Like a muse, it was imbued with those same feminine qualities that were used to sell it. Advertising posters, some of which are displayed on the Absinthe Bar's antique walls (and many of which can be seen at the Musée de l'Absinthe in Auvers-sur-Oise, about twenty miles from Paris), depict the chicest of *belle époque* women as they seduce, tempt, tantalize and cast a spell while sipping bright green liquid from a glass. Others show tight clusters of stylish women whispering about the medicinal wonders of absinthe, which was thought to cure maladies from indigestion to menstrual cramps. "I enjoy it with my husband," one lady tells another in an ad for Absinthe Terminus. "My doctor won't drink anything else."

Where once it was a drink of the upper class, by the late 1880s it was five times cheaper than wine and embraced by the masses; bohemians notoriously short on cash made it their unofficial liba-

*Absinthe*

tion and helped cement its romantic mystique. But absinthe developed a notorious reputation.

The wormwood used in its distillation con-tained a substance known as thujone, which was believed to have mind-altering properties that could induce insanity, epilepsy or hallucinations. But the side effects and erratic behavior that absinthe induced may have been accentuated by the quantities imbibed. Van Gogh was known to drink three liters a day. Even though it was one of the few alcoholic drinks to be con-sidered ladylike, Degas's famous portrait of a downcast woman star-ing blankly behind a glass of pale green liquid shows the unlovely and isolating side of absinthe addiction. Because it was considered a powerful, psychotropic narcotic (or perhaps because it was killing the wine industry), France outlawed absinthe in 1915. In 2011, the country lifted the ban, following the lead of other European Union countries. Since then, distilleries have sprung up all over France and absinthe has enjoyed a modern revival.

It is too early for the "green hour"—the absinthe equivalent of happy hour—but the owner leads me to the bar in the basement, an arched ancient Roman tunnel which, usually, is a nightspot. Behind a zinc bar, over fifty different absinthes are on display, from large producers like Pernod to an array of small-batch bou-tique brands. On the other side of the room, beyond the small tables, is a collection of vintage water fountains—crystal samovars affixed with a spigot—that are used in the absinthe ritual. At the table, the owner hands me a glass with about two fingers of liquid, atop of which sits a perforated spoon and cube of sugar. I release the tap and allow water to drip onto the sugar through the spoon, and soon my glass clouds up. The famous green color, it turns out, comes from fresh wormwood leaves, but here, mine is pure white. I intersperse sips with slices of baguette and tapenade the owner has procured from the market outside.

I wait for the sledgehammer...it descends slowly, even gently, after about five swallows of the diluted liquid, sweet and warming. It's easy to comprehend why absinthe had a chokehold on those who fell under its spell. I ask for coffee—it's only noon. I add more water, more sugar, finish up and head outside to lunchtime in Antibes. The vendors are breaking down their stalls, packing up their langoustines, persimmons, and beeswax candles. I buy the last container of raspberries that seem an entirely deeper shade of red than they were an hour ago. Maybe it is the angle of the sun. Maybe it is the absinthe.

֍

# 29
# The Red City of
# Toulouse-Lautrec

## ALBI, MIDI-PYRÉNÉES

Some cities come alive by night, but Albi needs to be savored in the daylight hours when, depending on the position of the sun and the

time of year, it smolders, explodes, or simply luxuriates in its rose-hued glory. It's known as the "Red City" because of the buildings fashioned out of fired Languedoc brick, but the soft Midi-Pyrénées light gives Albi a palette more resembling tiered icing on an autumn birthday cake: pink, peach, coral, pomegranate. When you see it, try not to whip out your iPhone. Many vistas in France deserve a higher honor than Instagram: the snapshot of memory. Seen from the banks of the Tarn River, Albi is one of them.

The red buildings that tower over the riverside gardens are their own mighty draw to Albi, as are the tales of ancient bloodshed that inspired them. But the city has a second, equally fascinating legacy as the birthplace of Henri de Toulouse-Lautrec, one of history's most empathetic painters of women. The narratives wound together neatly when in 1922, the former Bishops' Palace began to house the world's largest collection of its famous local son's work, which re-opened in 2012 after a ten-year restoration.

Fifty miles northeast from the regional capital of Toulouse, Albi has, since medieval times, occupied a pole position on the trading routes between Le Puy, Bordeaux, Lyon, and farther on to Italy and Spain. All merchant roads led to the Pont Vieux, whose burnt sienna arches have traversed the Tarn since the year 1040 and still do today. But it is the Albi Cathedral, said to be the largest brick building in the world, which dazzles against the dusty sky. It is as majestic as it is forbidding, constructed as a monument to religious righteousness following the brutal twenty-year suppression of the Cathars who were considered heretics by the ruling Catholics. In 1282, the Bishop of Albi began construction of the cathedral as a defensive fortress as well as a commanding show of strength against all heresy that stated unequivocally: The Catholic Church was back and indisputably in charge. It took 200 years to complete. With its imposing 256-foot tower, the exterior is austere and militaristic and lumbers more like a prison than a place of worship over the city. Inside, though, it's a different story, the kaleidoscopic opposite of the severe Gothic façade.

If you believe in the interchangeability theory of the European cathedral—that they all blur into a single gray structure as you gaze blankly up at the flying buttresses—this one will disabuse you of that notion. Every inch of the vault is covered in vivid blue and gold frescoes painted in the early 1500s by Italian Renaissance artists. It is wildly elaborate, its richness digestible only in tiny slices. Even if you think you can't take another church, this one will prove you otherwise; it will lodge in your brain and give you lapis wishes and gilded dreams.

The atmosphere takes a sharp turn next door in Albi's other 13th-century rose-colored gem, the Palais de la Berbie and its formal gardens, designed by Versailles gardener André Le Nôtre. The palace was erected by the city's bishops, many of whom were inquisitors, to protect themselves against potential invaders (or retaliatory Cathars) while they plotted the demise of ever more heretics. These guys left nothing to chance, constructing the fortress with walls twenty-three feet thick.

Today, the Palais belongs to Toulouse-Lautrec's world and it's a surprisingly joyous one. He was born to an aristocratic mother and father who happened to be first cousins. Family inbreeding transmitted a tragic form of dwarfism not only to Lautrec, but several cousins. He stood 4'11" tall, and suffered from brittle bones and other congenital deformities that painfully crippled him and probably shortened his life. He died at thirty-six, of syphilis and advanced alcoholism, leaving an astonishing body of work that is iconic and utterly his own. Haven't we all, at one point, visited a hotel bar in Hartford or Tucson that was hung with posters of the dancers La Goulue and Jane Avril? His work is deeply lodged in our subconscious, one of our earliest, headiest pop culture references.

The collection, hung under the palace's vaults, takes you through Toulouse-Lautrec's life, self-portraits, drawings and paintings of his family and the horses and riders that enthralled him. It is, of course, the Montmartre paintings of prostitutes and dancers in brothels, cafés and the Moulin Rouge that exhibit a realism that actually transcends reality. Outsider, voyeur, bon vivant or just plain tortured soul, Toulouse-Lautrec's rendering of these women is neither detached nor fetishistic, but entirely as they are: tired, human, fully realized emotional and creative beings. They are people he knew well. "He never condemned prostitutes, because he had been condemned himself," says Julia Frey, author of the excellent biography, *Toulouse-Lautrec: A Life*. Frey points to his childhood in a houseful of women, with a very protective mother whom he adored, as the roots of his compassion. "Very early on, he was sensitive to the feelings of women," she says. "But like every human being, he needed to be loved."

He did not stand a chance with fashionable ladies of the time, however, so he found kindred spirits, even the love he craved, in the brothels. He was observer and participant, each of which aspects were reflected in his pitiless and tender gaze. In *Salon de la Rue des Moulins*, women are perched expectantly on red brothel cushions while others are slumped, looking exhausted. They are not sex objects but rather, non-idealized, ordinary people. In *Les Deux Amies*, two women sit together in an embrace, an image that evokes devotion and kindness. They are prostitutes, but he gives them dignity without sentimentality. "He showed their life as it was, and as only he could have painted it," says Frey.

Upstairs at the museum are the crowd pleasers, the posters and lithographs depicting the music halls and Can-can dancers that seem so familiar, still and always rendered with the understanding so unique to Toulouse-Lautrec. "Art was his way of consoling himself," says Frey. It was at the family stronghold nearby at Château du Bosc, where young Henri slipped off a chair and first broke his femur, an episode that ushered in his destiny as an artist and observer. From there, he went to study painting in Paris. If it's the opposites in life he sought as context for the emergence of his genius, he surely found it at night in Montmartre, a world away from his red city in the sun.

⁂

# 30 White Horses, Pink Flamingoes and the Black Madonna

## THE CAMARGUE, LANGUEDOC-ROUSSILLON

When you visit the Camargue you may want to stay forever, which is what Texas-born Lauren Laval did after spending a year there as an exchange student from the University of Colorado. "I married a typical French cowboy," she says in a drawl that is straight out of Lubbock. Today she works as a guide, a human encyclopedia of alpine mistrals, agricultural irrigation and the finer points of bull semen, who pilots visitors in a bare-bones 4x4 Range Rover through one of France's most exotic landscapes and some of Europe's most important wetlands.

In Arles, the Rhône forks into two branches that form a delta. This is the Camargue, 360 square miles of brackish meadowlands, freshwater marshes, salt ponds (*étangs*), and fields of round-grain Camargue rice, which cover 15 percent of the area's land mass. Whether you head east or west, in Lauren's capable hands, it's not a long drive—perhaps an hour—to the Mediterranean. But as you make your way south, the surroundings will repeatedly fake you out, switching from fertile meadows to desiccated grazing land to clusters of umbrella pines, and the sky from battleship gray to midsummer blue—even in October.

What will make you stop your safari vehicle, though, are the Camargue's hardy mascots, all of whom seem to run free: first, black, long-horned bulls that provide the "cow" in France's cowboy country. These are bred for the cruelty-free bullfights called *courses camarguaises* that take place in hundreds of arenas throughout southern France (including Arles and Nîmes), in which the bull is not killed but rather the matador known as a *raseteur* attempts to snip ribbons tied beneath the charging beast's horns. The second are the horses that turn pure white after four years, bred to help ranchers wrangle the bulls, great herds of which roam in pastures on either side of the road. Heads crowned with a blond surfer forelock that spills over limpid brown eyes, they seem to be the gentlest of creatures. Last are the flamingoes, which gather in force in the shallows of the Étang de Vaccarès. First you will notice a thick pink streak in the water and as you get closer, you can discern the individual birds in greater relief, each one with a rounded, cotton candy back. And those legs, which are a deeper, darker shade of almost tangerine orange.

If you can't do like Lauren and move to the Camargue, a voyage there should have three destinations. The first is a horseback ride, and you don't need to be Annie Oakley (trust me). They seem like kindly beasts, and they are. They are also small ("They are horses, not ponies," insists Lauren) and manageable for the nonequestrienne. But if you do know your way around a bit and a bridle and are familiar with the Portuguese trail-riding saddle fitted onto the horses, you will still be rewarded. Both main roads to the sea are studded with places for a *promenade à cheval*, and the owner of the riding club will determine your level, match you with a horse and accompany your ride. But what may be the most beautiful trail of all is to take a spin along the Étang de Vaccarès, toward the dike and over the sea wall past oleander, bulrushes (used for roofs on the local

dwellings), tamarix bushes and flamingoes by the thousand, wading in the shoals.

The second is the town of Les Saintes-Maries-de-la-Mer, a luminous fishing village and gateway to the thirty miles of unspoiled lighthouse-dotted beach that extends to the east and west. It is also a place of pilgrimage for seekers devoted to the sacred feminine. The town is named after Saint Marie-Jacobé (sister of the Virgin Mary) and Saint Marie Salomé (mother of apostles James and John) who are believed to have arrived here by boat after Jesus' crucifixion, along with Mary Magdalene and Martha, the latter two of whom departed for other parts of France. But Marie-Jacobé and Marie Salomé, along with their servant Sara, remained here. Sara became the patron saint of the gypsies and a carving of her, known as the Black Madonna, resides in the fortified Romanesque church Notre-Dame-de-la-Mer. A visit to this smoky, primal shrine is crucial to the gypsies, but anyone may light a candle inside the crypt. Every year on May 24th, gypsies from all over the world make their pilgrimage here and form a procession to carry the statuette to get blessed in the sea. And in late October, on the Sunday nearest the 22nd (Marie Salomé's saint's day) gypsies gather again in Sara's honor for another blessing of the sea.

Finally, Aigues-Mortes is an immaculate medieval fortress town and Louis IX's staging area for the Seventh and Eighth Crusades in the 13th century. The ramparts are worth exploring and nearly pristine, due to the fact that Aigues-Mortes was neglected once its military usefulness was over. Here, I walk the circumference of the walls; it doesn't take long, and the dreamy afternoon sun is balm on my shoulders. It is often compared to its grander crenellated companion to the west on the River Aude, something remarked upon by the American writer Henry James on his solo journey of 1882 documented in *A Little Tour in France*. "Next after Carcassone," he wrote, "...it is the most perfect thing of the kind in France."

But unlike that behemoth, Aigues-Mortes is almost untouched by crowds and commercialism.

What will further electrify in this otherwise sleepy town is the vision of Les Salins—the saltworks. Salt, including fleur de sel, the pretty mauve stuff we use on roasts, has been harvested in the Camargue since Roman times and is piled up in tidy white hills called *camelles*. Adjacent to them are vast salt ponds of iridescent bright pink (from algae) and tiny brine crustaceans, loaded with beta-carotene and staples of the flamingo diet, which is why the birds turn pink. These sultry rose, salmon, peach, and thulian pink waters are echoed at the Camargue's other saltworks in Salin-de-Giraud, thirty miles away, clear at the other end of the beach.

Carried away on a white horse to a fairy tale fortress, pink water, pink birds, and there's probably some chilled rosé nearby. Who wouldn't want to stay in the Camargue?

# 31 On the Street of Dreams

## LA CROISETTE, CANNES

When I was eighteen, I spent the summer in a flat on the Promenade des Anglais in Nice. One day my sister and I took the train up the coast to try the beach at Cannes. While she went to stake a spot on  one of the public beaches, I decided to wander La Croisette, the fabled avenue of movie-star struts. There was not much money in my crocheted purse, but I was sporting a deep Côte d'Azur tan and held myself high, as one must do to blend into the luxury. I had already learned that lesson in France: whatever you do, act like you belong there. Walk tall and whisper.

The world's flashiest film festival was already well-known to me, and it was palpable—the gowns, the gems, the parade of celebrities waving to adoring fans. The town had an atmosphere that, at that young and unseasoned stage of my life, was entirely new and bewitching. I was a college freshman from the staid suburbs of Boston, so naturally I made a beeline to Cartier just to peer in the window, Holly Golightly style, where all that separated me and a diamond solitaire ring was a pane of glass. And then I crossed back over to the seaside.

I spun around to take in La Croisette. *Belle époque* façades that shone bright white in the summer light, the pointy gray dome that crowned the Carlton Hotel. Ladies of a certain age who dangled leashes attached to miniature poodles. Men in mirrored sunglasses clinging to much younger and blonder women in white sundresses. The aura that melded Beverly Hills and Paris with a fairy tale limestone village and a sun-splashed beach town. With a little bit of excess thrown in. Or maybe, a lot.

That aura still is the allure of the Croisette. If you begin on the far eastern end of the city by the Old Port, you see men (and the occasional woman) playing pétanque, spinning and tossing silver balls in the air on a dirt course separated into six or so playing fields. On the weekend, you may wander into a *brocante*—a street flea market—for vintage Chanel mules, lace gloves or Art Deco cocktail shakers. Soon, the Palais des Festivals, where the Cannes Film Festival swirls every May, looms like an ocean liner. Take a second to imagine you are Marion Cotillard and pause at the bottom of the fabled stairway while a million cameras snap away at you. Cross the Croisette to begin window-shopping in earnest. The designer swag is not within reach of most mortals, but walking is free and the people-watching and luxury-lust is unmatched.

The strip is glamorous and unabashedly so, but it is also relaxed enough to stroll in comfortable beach clothes. *Nice*, comfortable beach clothes. Out of respect for the $1,000 bejeweled sandals on display as well as a certain French sense of decorum, leave the sweats and Dos Equis t-shirt at the bottom of your canvas tote for this walk. These days, you will hear a lot of people speaking Russian along the Croisette, and though many now come here on their private jets, this is nothing new for Cannes. Frozen Muscovites have long sought refuge in the balmy air of the Riviera. In 1894, Saint Michael the Archangel Orthodox Church opened its doors in Cannes so the growing community of Russians would no longer have to traipse to Nice to attend service.

Right across from the palais is Prada, where the boutique's floor is laid with a soft, inviting carpet. There are Chanel, Moncler, real estate agencies with listings posted only in Russian. There is Louis Vuitton, then Gucci whose vitrine is stacked with a collection of delicious handbags in earthy hues. Marvel at the luscious prints at Dolce & Gabbana. If you were thinking ahead or otherwise can get in, you can have a spectacular lunch in the yummy, modern Park 45 restaurant in the Grand Hotel. Or just skip to dessert: how does chestnut cream on brioche French toast sound?

If you're not up for a big to-do, there is a quieter option set back beyond a cluster of palm trees and rosebushes, where you'll find the gleaming white temples to Céline and Giorgio Armani, complete with a casual café out front. Admire a grape-colored Hervé Léger bandeau dress at the boutique 55 Croisette.

Because you never know, gaze lovingly upon the window displays at Cartier.

Don't forget to look up at the detailed façade of the Hotel Carlton, now an InterContinental, the undisputed heart of the Cannes Film Festival, and one of the first places Grace Kelly appeared publicly with her future husband, Prince Rainier of Monaco. It was also a key location for Hitchcock's classic *To Catch a Thief,* featuring Kelly and Cary Grant. If a potentate has not rented out the entire hotel for his daughter's wedding, as was the case the last time I was there, detour to the Carlton Bar for a Lady Carlton cocktail—champagne and coulis of fresh strawberries.

By now if you still require sustenance, stop just past the Carlton patio's yellow and white awnings at the always-packed Brasserie Le Voilier for a *café crème.* Admire through the window the unusual parquet floor at Yves St. Laurent and the black and white fixtures at Balenciaga. Picture yourself in a leather coat on display at Burberry, and trace the snake handles on the doors at Roberto Cavalli. Now, turn around and take in La Croisette. The Carlton's ornamented dome sits sentry on the right, and a row of palm trees does duty on the left. The sun flickers through the fronds. Across the street are the mysterious shapes of islands beyond the shoreline. If you have not bought anything by now—or if you have—end the walk at the Grand Hyatt Cannes Hotel Martinez.

Stroll past the Lamborghinis and Bentleys into the Bar l'Amiral, where you will be greeted by a U-shaped wooden bar and seemingly hundreds of orchids. Order a Martinez Cocktail, concocted from champagne, grenadine, and Passion liqueur. The glass will arrive adorned with pineapple, a sprig of red currants or something else tart and exotic. It may put you in the mood to splurge on something as you make your way back up. Act like you belong there. Diamond solitaire, anyone?

❧

# 32 *Walk the Walk*

## HIKES IN THE CALANQUES, THE MASSIF DE L'ESTÉREL, AND THE GORGES DU VERDON, PROVENCE

One thing is certain: the older I get, the harder I walk. Away or at home, I am convinced that a strenuous ramble is the key to all manner of well-being—sanity, limber joints, optimism, good posture, youth (broadly speaking). Walking and hiking get the introvert in me off the computer, force me to pass strangers on the trail, look them in the eye and wish them good morning. Sturdy trekking shoes must always be squeezed into the suitcase (in addition, of course, to less practical but more *comme il faut* options for Paris). When you hike a trail in the Calanques, the Estérel or the Gorges du Verdon, you are not merely burning off last night's *crème brûlée*, but participating in one of the most indigenous rituals in France, especially on the part of her women, some of whom were truly inspired wanderers.

George Sand crossed the Alps—alone and on foot!—in 1834. "I had always kept in the bottom of my trunk, should the need arise, a pair of linen pants, cap and blue shirt, in anticipation of a climb through the mountains," she writes in *Story of My Life* about her springtime trek from Italy, through Alpine crests and cool green valleys, ending up in Chamonix just ahead of a rainstorm. Sheesh, and I fret over having the proper Patagonia layers and changing up my SPF. Equally hardy was another solitary walker, Simone de Beauvoir, whose time in Marseille at age twenty-three was, she wrote, "charged with significance" for the budding intellectual, who went there to work as a teacher. For nine months, every Thursday and Sunday, from dawn past nightfall, she traversed a new stretch of Provence, aided with little more than a *Guide Bleu* and a Michelin map. "I would slip on an old dress and a pair of espadrilles, and take a few bananas and buns with me in a basket," she writes in her autobiography *The Prime of Life* about her day-long hikes. She seemed to relish the challenge of getting lost as she clambered up every peak, hilltop, ridge, and along the coasts, gullies, ravines and gorges—without a single PowerBar. The sense of accomplishment gave her great pleasure, and like all of us when we push ourselves, she congratulated herself at day's end. It's one of the best reasons to stretch our limits, no matter where they lie. In France, you do this by heading outdoors.

And there is a lot of outdoors in France. There are 7 national parks and 301 natural reserves. Seven mountain ranges, most of which contain mini-ranges within them—the Cévennes and the Chaîne des Puys, for example, are in the larger Massif Central. There are over 2,000 miles of coastline—rugged, rocky, sandy, forested—most of it lined with littoral trails with astonishing, sweeping vistas. There are some 368 ski areas in France, many of which turn to hikeable sloping ravines carpeted with wildflowers over the summer. In all, there are 74,500 miles of local trails, of which 37,000 are part of the vast network, marked with the telltale red and white paint, of the Grandes Randonnées or GR, the extensive web of long-distance walking routes that crisscross Europe.

If you love long, strenuous climbs and overnights in sleeping bags, there are hundreds of ways and places to design a trip that will satisfy that more urgent sense of adventure. What I personally crave, and what I outline here, is a challenging hike with stunning scenery. A good workout on my legs and lungs, lugging only plenty of Évian and a salty nibble, with a gorgeous payoff, preferably one flecked with gold reflections of streaming light on the water or canyon walls. And then, chilled cocktails and a hot bath on level terra firma at the end of the day. If this is your idea of the perfect hike, here are three spots that satisfy on all counts. All are in Provence, all are soaked in Mediterranean sunshine—and best to skip in the summer if they are even open. The forest fire risk during the hot months is great in wild maquis brush of Provence, and often the parks close, full stop. As is the case in much of the south of France, early June and late September are optimal, even winter when the water and air are equally bracing.

Calanques National Park extends for about 12 miles on the coast between Marseille and Cassis. The *calanques* are a series of steep-walled inlets that resemble fjords—long, narrow pools of electric blue-green sea that extend like fingers between bleached white cliffs. This combination creates a microclimate in the inlets, little sun traps that can be brutally hot and dry at times. The desert-like vegetation follows suit, and 900 species of plants sprout in tufts from the creviced stone, from Aleppo Pine to wild olive trees and fragrant rosemary to pluck, just a few spears, and inhale.

There are dozens of different hikes up, down and around these geological wonders. A map is essential—you can get one at the tourist office in Cassis or Marseille—and a car is a godsend. All of the *calanques* have names, and all of them have distinctive features and hikes. The walk down to Sormiou passes through a spectacular lookout point and ends on a luminous white sand beach with a flat, turquoise stretch of water. From Callelongue, you can walk 1½ miles to the pebble beach of Marseilleveyre. The path down the ravine to Sugiton is circuitous and steep, with a staggering view of a giant limestone pinnacle, blinding white against the iridescent water. Near Sugiton, the coastal path opens in two directions—toward Morgiou and l'Oeil de Verre *calanques*.

Even more efficient is to hike from Cassis, a pretty Provençal town set snugly among the limestone cliffs. The Port Miou and Port Pin *calanques* are fairly short hikes from the harbor, and the difficult but doable and vista-laden hike to En Vau takes about two hours each way; the end of the trail is a lovely little beach that sparkles like sugar crystals against the water.

Farther east on the coast, near Saint-Raphaël, are the copper-red cliffs of the Estérel Massif nature reserve, softly rounded headlands of Paleozoic volcanic rock.

Each twist and turn on the ridge and hillside paths brings a revelation of perspective, topography, and color—blue rippled sea, a range of greens from the brush, the russet outcrops, and swaths of wildflowers. There are four separate bite-sized hikes along wide forested paths infused with the aroma of eucalyptus, none more than 2½ hours round-trip (without distractions, and there are many), and a longer one to the Lac d'Écureuil. My favorite is to summit Le Pic de l'Ours, a 1,600-foot peak with an incredible view of everywhere—the fissured escarpments and on the way up, the Bay of Cannes. If not for the twinkling promise of the Riviera across the water, it would feel utterly remote.

North of here, between the towns of Moustiers and Castellane, is the Gorges du Verdon, whose plunging 2,300-foot canyon and clear, neon blue waters straddle the Luberon, Var and the Alpes-de-Haute-Provence. A day here on the trails is the antidote to too much rich food, champagne, and sybaritism in general, especially after a few days' debauch at the beach in Saint Tropez. Here, I can stretch my bones and clear my senses with healthy desert oxygen. My friend Sophie Sutton, who knows the canyon well, agrees. "It's the nondecadent countryside here and a great place to revitalize," she says. "The crisp, fresh air is like a rush of energy."

Like the Grand Canyon it is often compared to, there is a north rim and a south rim, a sixty-mile drive around. The tourist offices in Moustiers and Castellane sell easy animated flyers—*fiches*—with the hikes, including short ones, outlined in detail. The Sentier Martel—aka the Martel Trail—is the most famous and long, about four to six hours, depending on how much you rest—quite steep in parts, but not extreme for a fairly fit person. The trail leads through several tunnels, for which you need a flashlight or a really well-charged smartphone, and the home stretch near Port Sublime is the most arduous part of the trail. Anyone who has hiked in the American Southwest will find echoes of it in the steep, shady descent to the valley of the gorge and the fresh (swimmable) waters along the way. The soft scent, too, of sagebrush and sand, and lookouts of languorous slopes, indented gorges and placid sky.

When Simone de Beauvoir finished a walk, her state of elation made her wish to start all over again. She was twenty-three; I am not. But like her, I thrive on these outings, and find it pleasant to brush my legs against gorse, rock roses and juniper trees with the sun on my back and my shoes holding me steady; to feel the engine of my own body in a state of exertion as it carries me forth to something beautiful.

᪐

# 33 *Napoleon Slept Here*

## MALMAISON, RUEIL-MALMAISON

In June of 1961, President Kennedy opened his news conference in the French capital with this quip: "...I am the man who accompanied Jacqueline Kennedy to Paris, and I've enjoyed it." JFK did not, however, join Jackie on her visit to Malmaison, Napoleon and his wife Josephine's country home outside of Paris (which became her permanent residence after their divorce in 1810). Jackie's companion that day was France's Minister of Culture André Malraux, the brilliant author of *Man's Fate*, who despite losing both of his sons in a car accident the prior week, braved his grief to play host to the American First Lady. A Francophile who spoke the language beautifully, Jackie had surreptitiously hired a French decorator, Stéphane Boudin, to bring some Parisian sophistication to the White House after the dour Eisenhower years. Boudin had been the designer on the recent revamp of Malmaison, a 17th-century château Josephine had bought herself in 1799, which remains today a reflection of the captivating woman who lived there.

It's understandable how this grand but not excessive château would resonate with America's most stylish first lady. Every inch of it exhales taste and refinement that never pushes the boundary into gaudiness or overblown vanity. The château and its gardens were a respite from the dreary formality of their city residence at the Tuileries. Here in the fresh air, Napoleon and Josephine lived out many chapters in their legendary love affair that blossomed and faded during one of history's most turbulent times.

A visit to Malmaison, just a half hour from central Paris, is to be immersed in Josephine's story, from her dazzling wardrobe to  the roses she nurtured to the enduring shadow of her heartbreak. In this house, it's easy to feed my fascination with Josephine. I can't envy the woman who was discarded by her husband the Emperor, but it's inspiring to imagine her life as a divorcée managing valiantly to carry on without the man who had carried her to such heights.

After the French Revolution, Napoleon rose quickly to become emperor in 1804, leading his armies across Europe, Russia and the Nile in some of the bloodiest battles ever waged on earth. But after each victorious day on the front, a cold and weary Napoleon turned into a besotted lover, petulantly pining for his wife while giving her the news of the day about enemy casualties, troop crossings, and his slow but sure conquest of Europe. Napoleon's letters to Josephine show a lonely man seeking comfort in erotic musings, such as this one from the Italian campaign:

> I am going to bed with my heart full of your adorable image.... I cannot wait to give you proofs of my ardent love. How happy I would be if I could assist you at your undressing, the little firm white breasts, the adorable face.... You know that I will never forget the little visits, you know, the little black forest...I kiss it a thousand times and wait for the moment I will be in it. To live within Josephine is to live in the Elysian fields...

His letters are also a little bit scary, not because of the icy calculation (or even nonchalance) with which he sent his soldiers into slaughter, but because of the portrait they paint of obsessive love. Really obsessive love.

"I don't love you anymore; on the contrary, I detest you. You are a vile, mean, beastly slut. You don't write to me at all; you don't love your husband; you don't write him six lines of nonsense," he writes from Milan, waiting for word from her and suspicious she might be having an affair in his absence. "Soon, I hope, I will be holding you in my arms; then I will cover you with a million hot kisses, burning like the equator."

She was born Marie-Josèphe-Rose Tascher de la Pagerie in Martinique in 1763, the daughter of white Créole plantation owners. Shortly after moving to France with her father in 1779, she married her first husband, Alexandre de Beauharnais, who had been a general in the Revolution and guillotined in 1794. Josephine, too, was briefly imprisoned, and when the Reign of Terror was over, she became known as one of Paris's most beguiling and sexually alluring women. When she and Napoleon were introduced in 1795, she was 32 and the mistress of a powerful French statesman (one of several high-ranking lovers she had as a widow). Napoleon, short, six years her junior, graceless and not much of a looker by any standards, fell hard. They married in 1796, and though she had two children by her first marriage, Josephine was unable to give Napoleon an heir, one of the main reasons compelling their divorce over a decade later.

Malmaison was initially Josephine's passion, but Napoleon soon grew sufficiently attached to create a library and council room where he could summon his ministers, particularly in the years

before he became emperor. By 1802, he spent more time elsewhere, and Malmaison became her private sanctuary, supported
and maintained, of course, by her husband. She created a botanical garden, a park with rivers and cascades, and introduced exotic
plants from Australia and the Americas. She built her own zoo and
filled it with kangaroos, zebras, llamas, emus and other wildlife
from around the world.

She invested even more passion in amassing her stupendous
wardrobe and finery. It was said that Josephine had more jewels than Marie Antoinette, with diamonds, rubies and emeralds
bursting from her cabinet; but clothes were her real obsession,
and they were exquisite, low-cut creations that, in the fashion of
the day, bared her porcelain décolletage. In Napoleon's drawing
room, a portrait of her in a silver sheath, wrapped in sapphires,
hangs near one of the emperor in his coronation robes. One year
alone, Josephine ordered 985 pair of gloves, 520 pair of shoes and
136 gowns, many of which were made to match the décor in a given
room, and some of which are on display at Malmaison.

The sumptuousness at the château is not on the level of
Versailles, as royal excess was officially finished along with the
monarchs. It's intimate, not intimidating, and invites you to glide
rather than tiptoe through the rooms. There is the Empress's soft
pink-and-green boudoir, her gold-and-crimson tentlike formal
bedchamber and the sweet extra bedroom that holds the jewelry
chest, lit by sunshine that pours through the château windows. She
or her husband would repair here when one of them was ill. Or
maybe when Napoleon snored?

Josephine did not wither up when Napoleon left her and remar-
ried the eighteen-year-old Archduchess Marie-Louise of Austria.
She settled permanently at Malmaison, but she worried incessantly
about him as his fortunes began to turn. His once steamy letters
turned into missives of concern for her depression and health.

She continued to entertain lavishly, and it was Tsar Alexander I of Russia, a frequent visitor, who was most distressed when Josephine caught a cold as they walked together in her beloved rose gardens in May 1814. She died of pneumonia four days later, in her son's arms, at Malmaison.

In 1815, two days after Napoleon's triumphant arrival in Paris from exile in Elba, he returned to Malmaison, went upstairs alone and wept.

❧

# 34 The France of Our Desires

## THE LUBERON, PROVENCE

When we travel, at least for pleasure, we tend to seek what we are most lacking, the *chiaro* to our *scuro*. Life in the 21st century is cumbersome, and I don't know a person who is not overcome, overwhelmed, overburdened by responsibility—financial, familial, technological and otherwise. This is why Provence is spoken of with a mystical incantation. In our modern lexicon, the word has become synonymous with the place that will set you free.

To a French person, Provence refers to the administrative region (there are 22 in France) of Provence-Alpes-Côte d'Azur, which is a toothsome chunk of the southeastern part of the country. On the Mediterranean coast, Provence begins at Menton on the Italian border and extends west down the Riviera through the Var toward Aigues-Mortes. From there it continues north through the Vaucluse and westward into the mountains and the winter playgrounds of the Alpes-de-Haute-Provence and the Hautes-Alpes, which sound the same but are not. The paradise of our Pastis-drenched fever dreams tends, though, to be a narrower swath of the region, the Provence *profonde* of Marcel Pagnol's *Jean de Florette* and *Manon of the Spring*, of M.F.K. Fisher, and Paul Cézanne. The Provence of olive groves and fields of sunflowers, Savon de Marseille, baskets of figs and the world's sweetest melons from Cavaillon.

Here, we are fascinated by the still lifes in the landscape—the pale blanket of almond blossoms or the spear of a cypress tree posed beside blanket ochre wall—and we come to crave this spellbound state. We hear whispers about the mistral, the peculiar windy weather phenomenon unique to Provence, and wish to experience it with all five senses.

The most *profonde* of all, if one dares offer such superlatives, is the Vaucluse and within that, the Luberon. This elliptical-shaped region, studded with hills hoisting ancient, amber-colored villages, begins about 30 miles east of Avignon and is a valley framed by the Grand  and Petit Luberon mountains to the south and the Vaucluse Plain to the north. This is the Provence of Peter Mayle and of Russell Crowe and Marion Cotillard in *A Good Year* (based on another Mayle book), which is one of the great cinematic blues busters of all time, and as good a kick as any to chuck the rat race, find a fixer upper château and start living again. If going to Provence has become a bit cliche, it's because it is foolproof, geographically gifted with a near perfect mix of light, shadow, scent and color—all of which can be distilled in a single visit to the Saturday market—that gently triggers the pleasure centers in the brain. No one is immune to its charms and anyone who visits has moments of exaltation.

My friend Betsy Ennis is a public relations advisor in the art world and a superb traveler—a person I seek for travel advice. Usually, she is drawn to Italy or other corners of France, but recently she celebrated her twentieth anniversary in Provence in the sharp sunlight of mid October when the crowds had dwindled to a sprinkling. "Finally, I get it," she wrote me from Les Baux. "I can

see why people come here and never leave." Les Baux—the entrancing clifftop village high in the Alpilles Mountains where the ruins
of the citadel and castle look down on the Val d'Enfer—the Valley
of Hell. These fantastically-shaped remains of white limestone and
bauxite (named for Les Baux) are especially entrancing in the evening, sluiced in starlight. I love Simone de Beauvoir's memory of
arriving there, as told in her autobiography: "When I reached Les
Baux, at night, again for the first time, the wind was blowing; fires
twinkled down in the plain, and a fire was crackling in the grate at
the Reine Jeanne, where we were the only guests." The moment
exudes warmth and quiet satisfaction.

You must have a car to properly explore Provence, and a good
old-fashioned map is helpful as well, since sometimes the GPS
signal vanishes, as if by design, in the medieval streets. One of the
most iconic towns in the Luberon is L'Isle-sur-la-Sorgue, fifteen
miles from Avignon. This recalls a little Venice or a mini-Bruges,
an island village with canals, bridges, and waterwheels, as well as
hundreds of antique stores. Even in this region of already exceptional markets, the one that materializes here each week is distinguished for its purity and perfection, where you can stock up on
sausage, olives, linen dish towels, and herbes de Provence at stalls
that wind around the narrow streets. There is also one of France's
most storied *brocantes*, for old Ricard pitchers, chrome lampshades
or silver demitasse spoons. For lunch, my friend Betsy tried the pig
knuckles over garlicky lentils—"Really, they're good!" she insisted
over my arched eyebrow—at Café de France, which is full of hip
locals as well as sturdy older matrons.

Make haste for the Petit Luberon and Oppède le Vieux, a town
literally carved into the side of a cliff and abandoned for centuries,
but which artists have been slowly reviving, Brooklyn style. In other
words, craft breweries might soon be popping up, if they haven't
already. Above the Romanesque church and the castle ruins is a

sprawling view of the crests and ravines of the Luberon, and trees permanently bent from the mistral winds.

In the perched village of Ménerbes, which soars above the cherry orchards and vineyards of the Côtes du Luberon, Pablo Picasso installed his mistress Dora Maar in a house that is now a retreat for artists and writers. Betsy recommends Maison de la Truffe et du Vin du Luberon, a place for an al fresco lunch of scrambled eggs with truffles, a glass of rosé on a beautiful terrace overlooking the tiled roofs and green hills. In Provence, I'd rather sit for hours at a table in the sun than do much of anything else, close my eyes and feel the breeze push up from the valley.

Little remains of the Château de Lacoste, which was gutted during the Revolution, but you can clamber up to its vestiges. Its erotic history clings tantalizingly to the castle's crumbled bones, as this is where the Marquis de Sade began his scandalous career as a literary bad boy and chronicler of the principle that would one day bear his name.

The town of Lourmarin is a cross between Capri and St. Barts, trendy and stylish—and often crowded. I wouldn't pass it up since it is indeed beautiful and packed end to end with cafés (which somehow don't detract from its charm). One of the most enchanting places in the Luberon is the medieval village of Cucuron, where several scenes from *A Good Year* were filmed. In the center of town is a large reflecting pool filled with fish and surrounded by ancient plane trees, their forked white trunks graced with pale green foliage that shuffles slightly. In the corner of the square, in a pretty house with steel-blue shutters, is the restaurant La Petite Maison de Curcuron, where the chef gives group cooking lessons here every weekend. Enough said. No wonder Russell Crowe didn't return to London.

Strangely, my seminal Provençal moment was not in the sun-steeped Luberon in July, but Christmastime farther north in the Vaucluse, at the foot of Mont Ventoux. My husband and I were in the village of Crillon-le-Brave in the hotel of the same name, which had everything and nothing and absolutely all we needed. We had spent much of the prior summer in nearby Vaison-La-Romaine, with its fountains and Roman ruins, and in the intervening months had married, honeymooned and collapsed from celebration fatigue. The sun that had burned our shoulders in July hid behind an opaque sky. We could see the Luberon from our window and Mont Ventoux under the first snow of winter. We went outside and ambled along the stone paths, whipped by the legendary mistral that lifted my hat and sent it aloft. Inside the hotel we had a warm fire, a bowl of dried apricots, and each other. There were bottles of Châteauneuf-du-Pape and Gigondas wines, grown from nearby grapes that grow sugary in summer. It proved to us that Provence was always Provence, even in the dead of winter. It is always hard to leave, but in three months we would be back, just as the almond trees were beginning to blossom.

❦

# 35

## *A Country of Green*

### SOME OF FRANCE'S MOST SPECTACULAR GARDENS

Some choices are harder than others. I could no sooner name France's most excursion-worthy gardens than I could pick the best seaside promontories for sunsets, or choose whether I prefer to be outdoors among the burnished oranges of autumn or the spring's profusions of pastels. What I can do is encourage you to make time not just to visit, but to inhale deep and long in some of the thousands of green spaces that flourish all over the country.

Whether this simplifies your task or makes it more difficult, in 2003, the French Ministry of Culture upped the stakes when it created a new designation: Remarkable Gardens of France. Today there are 396 of them, and that's not counting other spectacular private or public enclosures that aren't even officially classified. They are everything—royal enclaves or urban preserves, Renaissance or romantic, wild or austere, with flowering camellia bushes, orderly rectangles of chestnut trees, or rows of kitchen herbs and vegetables. France's gardens  are as diverse as they are abundant. They reflect varying climates, local histories and the preferences of their architects and owners— or long-deceased former owners—because many of them are centuries-old preserves of personal proclivities and testaments to the tastes and landscape fashion of the times.

Many tour outfits specialize in visits to parks and gardens. Some will focus on regal enclosures such as the Parc de Chantilly, designed by André Le Nôtre, the genius behind the gardens at Vaux le Vicomte and Versailles (when you see Le Nôtre's name, it's like a text alert that says, "Go!") or the tree-shaded lawns of Château de Cheverny—a visit that features a daily dinner call for the seventy resident hunting hounds. Others will lead you to secret places through Normandy up to the granite Channel coast, while others will reveal the sun-kissed courtyards and citrus groves of the Alpes-Maritimes. But if exploring on your own is more your style, you will never regret carving out time to visit the marvels that bloom and blossom in every corner of France. Here, to start you off, are six of my favorites.

Russian billionaires are snapping up homes for hundreds of millions these days, but the *ne plus ultra* of real estate in St-Jean-Cap-Ferrat, the gilded promontory between Nice and Monaco on the Côte d'Azur, belongs to the Ephrussi de Rothschild Villa and Gardens. This is my kind of place—tame but sexy, with rangy palm trees and lookouts over pristine views of the sea. The *belle époque*-style Venetian palazzo was built between 1905 and 1912 by Baroness Béatrice Ephrussi de Rothschild to house her art collection and ménagerie of wild animals. There are nine separate gardens behind the pink villa, each with a different theme ranging from Japanese to Spanish, but the overall effect is of symmetry between formal and exotic. The various gardens, all designed by leading landscape artists of the day, include waterfalls, musical fountains, hidden grottoes and tangles of roses—100 varieties of them, one of which is named after the Baroness.

Architect Barbara Griffin Cole, based in Princeton, New Jersey, loves the International Garden Festival at Château de

Chaumont-sur-Loire, Catherine de' Medici and Diane de Poitiers's old haunt, and finds inspiration in the innovative installations woven together by meandering paths and ribbons of meadows. "Each exhibit stretches the boundaries of garden and landscape design," she says, "and is a wonderful respite from the crowd-packed grand châteux." Every year since 1992, up to thirty artists, landscape gardeners and designers are chosen from all over the world to create a unique garden based around an annual theme such as Water, Memory, Color and in 2014, the Deadly Sins. Set within separate plots of 240 square meters each, the installations range from highly conceptual, featuring mirrors, stoneworks or canvas, to the purest of rambling, overgrown environments. Many invite passage of man through material by being completely immersive, with places to climb, lounge, inhabit, touch, meander and even disappear.

A charming steam train stops in La Bambouseraie de Prafrance on the route from St-Jean-du-Gard to Anduze, right in the heart of the Cévennes mountains, not far from Nîmes. Not all gardens are ideal for contemplation, but this drenchy-green and airy one decidedly is. Merry Mullings, a textile entrepreneur in Paris, says it's one of her favorite idylls in all of France. "You can spend all day here," she says. "It's utterly transporting." Here, over 84 acres ribboned with trails, around 300 species of bamboo flourish. Some are wispy and silver, others are so tall they make tunnels over the allées, which ripple with sunlight. The collection was established in 1856 as the passion project of Eugène Mazel, a wealthy spice trader and amateur botanist, who brought exotic trees and plants home from his frequent travels to China and Japan. He also planted a pair of giant sequoias, now 130 feet tall. They may keep sentry over the gardens, but it is the bamboo that reigns in this dense, green kingdom.

Every Thursday evening in July and August, when the air cools down and softens, you may explore the dreamscape at Château de Marqueyssac in Vézac by candlelight (it's open in the daytime, too). The terraced gardens soar above the Dordogne River, and if you are early enough, you can still see the land stretched before you and behold the eye candy that is Beynac, one of the locations for that sweetest of cinematic bon bons, Lasse Hallström's *Chocolat*. The gardens are set in a 16th-century château, and though the view is thrilling, it is the walk among the boxwoods that made me sigh in satisfaction. The bright-green shrubs—150,000 of them—are sculpted (by clearly overworked gardeners) into dynamic whirls and puffs that seem to drift like bubbles, resulting in a landscape that is both playful and polished.

The vision of the three-tiered garden at Château de Villandry in the Loire Valley provokes a singular rapturous awe, the kind that arises when drifting through pure but indescribable beauty. It presents as a veritable sea of boxwood and parterres, but on closer inspection could be the world's most elegant *potager*, or kitchen garden, planted with a rotation of over forty vegetables as well as flowers, in dazzling color-coordinated parcels. There is an herb garden, too, soft leafy arrangements of medicinal and cooking plants, as well as tranquil fountains and lawns. Villandry's most irresistible draw is the ornamental Gardens of Love, the most fanciful swath of green in France, a Renaissance narrative on the agony and ecstasy of romance. Here, the clipped boxwoods are carved into allegories in four separate beds: hearts and flirty pink flowers representing Tender Love, fractured hearts that form a maze and represent the mad whirl of Passionate Love, the yellow blooms of betrayal, horns and conceptual *billets-doux* symbolizing Fickle Love, and sharp blades and blood-red flowers meaning heartbreak or rivalry in Tragic Love. It is impossible to remain unemotional here. The garden seems to transmit encoded messages, and moves us to reflect upon our own romantic histories.

Lastly, there are many places to pay homage to the rose, the emblem of Picardie, but one of the most enchanting is the roseraie of the fortified Château de Rambures in the Somme. The castle is a paragon of feudal architecture, an almost perfect specimen fashioned from brick and capped with black stone turrets. This fairy tale fortress makes the ideal counterpoint to the vast 25-acre garden where nearly 500 varieties of roses bloom from June to September. Bow your head and smell the sweet perfume.

❧

# 36 In the Shadow of Rome (plus two romantic hotels)

## NÎMES AND ARLES

When visiting France, it's easy to gorge on a diet of Gothic cathedrals, Romanesque abbeys, and Renaissance châteaux. It can be difficult to consider another historical landscape to behold, know and love. Ignore the Roman twins of Arles and Nîmes at your peril, however. Your long days will be complete with a bit of cosseting at a duo of singular hotels—counterpoints to the yellow-lit relics of raw, imperial power.

Many people have traveled these paths before me, and I will encounter their memory along the way. In Arles, I land at l'Hôtel Particulier on a leafy side street. My friend Thérèse Verrat, a high fashion photo stylist in Paris, recommends it highly. "It's so chic but not overdone, and the courtyard smells magnificent," she says. It was also way beyond my budget, but when a taxi from the train station stopped on the rue de la Monnaie, the *coup de foudre* caused me to take leave of my senses. Thérèse was right. Even at the reception desk, I could smell *fleurs d'oranger*. The courtyard was so serene, the white sheets so pressed, and the tucked-away bar with the wine menu scrawled on a chalkboard so inviting, I did not consider cancelling my reservation for more modest accommodations. As travelers, we have to weigh these options. Blow the bank on spectacular lodgings, and it's bread and cheese for lunch and second-class passage on the train. So what's wrong with that?

In Arles, the Rhône River ends its journey before splitting into branches and reaching the Mediterranean, so the hotel, appropriately, serves me a bracing glass of Côtes du Rhône on a silver tray with a clipping of jasmine. As darkness begins to lower, I exit and make a few quick turns on back streets, which lead to the Place du Forum, the onetime center of what was once called Arelete. The Romans arrived in the 2nd century B.C. and during the Gallic Wars, Julius Caesar took the land from Massalia (Marseille) and gave it to his victorious Roman soldiers. Arles became a sort-of second capital for the empire. Just two blocks away are the Thermal Baths of Constantin, which were excavated in the late 19th century. It is after hours, but a walk around the exterior reveals the splendid decay of antiquity. Just as I had hoped, the crumbling stone structures appear more sensual with age.

Vincent van Gogh moved to Arles in 1888 and painted many of his masterpieces when he shared a house there with Paul Gauguin, but it is not the gold of *Café Terrace at Night* that intrigues on this fall evening, but that of the Roman amphitheater lights. The recently-refurbished limestone edifice known locally as "les Arènes" was built in A.D. 90 to seat 20,000 people and it still has many uses today, among them concerts (including the Arles-born Gypsy Kings). The amphitheater's vastness seems magnified by the glow of the floodlights. It is a powerful emblem of the Empire's staggering reach and might. At night, there is only stillness, and the sky in outline through the double row of arches.

Aided by a good map and the incandescence of streetlamps, my steps lead to the Roman theater. It's an easy and safe walk back along the Rue de la République to l'Hôtel Particulier and a supper of *saucisson sec* and a glass of La Clotte Fontaine Louise, a Languedoc rosé. Before climbing the marble staircase to that perfect room, I fish out the card the cab driver had handed me for the next day's ride to the train station and dial his number. "Just a quick trip," I assure him. *Places every woman should go.* He drives a short distance, and I clamber onto a stone walk that overlooks a riverbank.

Among the travel books in my bag this time is Henry James's *A Little Tour in France.* When he chronicled a voyage from Tours to Burgundy, the poor guy had a rare, miserable disappointment in Arles. "Nothing could be more provincial than the situation of Arles at ten o'clock at night," he wrote as he descended perhaps this same stone path to the Rhône, looking for something under a moonless sky, and finding nothing. That was 1882. At ten o'clock this night, the stars are out, but not shining as brightly as they were when Van Gogh painted *Starry Night over the Rhône* from this very spot in 1888.

Nîmes is about twenty miles away crossing into Languedoc-Rousillon, and it is a quick walk from the train station to Jardins Secrets, my hotel on the rue Gaston Maruéjols. It is a dreamlike, enchanted place, whose courtyard is iridescent just after a rain and holds the damp scent of lavender and rosemary. There are five downstairs living rooms adorned with lush Napoleon III detail, where every corner of every space is a beautifully crafted still life. A farm table is strewn with wooden bowls of pomegranates, striped melons and fresh autumn apples that are so perfect I have to ask. "Are they real?" The owner nods sweetly, and holds forth a basket of girolle mushrooms just picked in the nearby Cévennes Mountains. My room has a spacious bathtub, and I walk around the hotel's many outdoor spaces to see the array of views, terracotta roofs under scrims of foliage and vines.

Nîmes is more manicured than Arles and seems less of a relic to Roman splendor than a great city that grew up around antiquity when it joined France in the 13th century. Even with the ballast of its ancient ruins, Nîmes has a lightness of spirit. Here, I feel welcomed and well, and it seems as if the sidewalks are propelling me forth, urging me along so the city can reveal its glories. There is the central canal that is the picture of an urban oasis, gurgling green and fresh under a curved canopy of plane trees; and the formal 18th-century Jardins de La Fontaine, where black swans paddle around inky water. Even this owes its existence to the Romans, as it was built around a stone sanctuary worshipping the god Nemausus (after whom the town was named), which Louis XV wished to preserve. It is a noble sprawl of green and white, thick with the smell of marjoram and pine, the intermittent rustle of running water, palm trees, balustrades, terraces, reflecting pools and stone nymphs. One spring, when she was on tour with a theater troupe, the writer Colette danced around these fountains and the soft stones of the Temple of Diana. Here, she exulted in the aroma of cedar and jonquils. "One wants to stop, lie down with a sigh, sleep here and never wake up," she wrote.

This early-evening stroll is about night vision and the tug of history. Nîmes joined the empire in 121 B.C. and reached prosperity under Emperor Augustus, becoming one of the wealthiest towns in conquered Gaul. The Roman amphitheatre dates from about A.D. 70, just ten years after the Colosseum in Rome, and it lords over the town with the swagger of the ages. Its two-story row of arches forms an ellipse, which was built to seat 24,000 senators, magistrates and commoners who gathered to watch young men meet their demise at the hands of a lion, tiger, bear or wolf.

The modern world begins to get swallowed by the darkness. A straight shot down the Boulevard Victor Hugo leads to the Maison Carrée, built in the 1st-century B.C. from limestone quarried in the nearby Rhône and one of the few Augustan temples still standing. The white stone glows burnt orange. The building is intact, and I circle around it as if to seek out a flaw. There are none. Its architecture—Corinthian columns, wide stairs and a classical pediment—is both familiar and unfamiliar. I don't recognize the building, but the image is deep in my memory. Across the square, it is reflected in—and mimicked by—the 20th-century glass walls of British architect Sir Norman Foster's Museum of Contemporary Art.

I think of another traveler who was similarly transfixed by the structural perfection of the ancient, unsullied temple—Thomas Jefferson, in 1787. "This is the second time I have been in love since I left Paris," he wrote in a letter to Mme. La Comtesse de Tessé, the aunt of the Marquis de Lafayette. "I am gazing whole hours at the Maison quarrée like a lover at his mistress." Thus inspired, he based the design of the Virginia State Capital on what he saw in the Roman genius at Nîmes.

In the morning, after breakfast at Jardins Secrets, where I slathered five different homemade jams on my bread just to taste them all, I stroll past my reflection in the courtyard pool and then over to town. My feet lead me back to the museum and up to the third-floor restaurant, Le Ciel de Nîmes. The temple looks even more perfect from above, pure white in the daylight. Even when my coffee and then my lemon meringue tart arrive, I can't seem to avert my eyes.

꙰

# 37 The Turquoise Waters of the Haute-Savoie

## LAKE ANNECY

You have to prize a man whose final words pay ardent tribute to the first woman he ever loved, the person who fifty years earlier taught him the great lessons of the human heart. In the last paragraphs of his last work, *Reveries of the Solitary Walker*, Romantic philosopher Jean-Jacques Rousseau writes of his years on Lake Annecy, where he arrived at sixteen from his native Switzerland and over four years shared a house with the twenty-nine-year-old formerly-married Françoise-Louise de Warens, "a charming woman, of extreme wit and beauty," he writes. "There is not a day I do not recall with melting joy this only and short time of my life where I was wholly myself...," he continues, "and where I can truly say, I lived."

Annecy rests in the snow-topped alpine breast of the Haute-Savoie, an hour west of Chamonix and thirty minutes south of Geneva. It's easy to see why Rousseau found his singular happiness there. It sits on a turquoise lake of the same name that presents with a hue more Caribbean than Savoyard. The town itself dates to the 10th century and is a network of pristine canals that flow past narrow streets of low-slung weathered stone buildings blessed with the charm (and archways and huddled doorways) that Epcot and Ye Olde American diners try so valiantly to ape. It is because of this latticework of rivulets and footbridges that Annecy is known as the French Venice.

For Jean Davis, who travels the world for her job in international trade, it is one of her most treasured spots in France. "I love to wander through the Vieux Quartier," she says, where the market, known for the region's excellent cheeses—especially Tomme de Savoie—is held three days a week. "This town puts it all together—the view of the mountains and this incredibly beautiful and clean lake. It's really restorative."

And then there is the food. Annecy is the place to lose yourself to a steaming fondue, or the local Savoyard specialty, *tartiflette*—an addicting concoction of potatoes, cream, and chunks of bacon baked under a chewy crust of Reblochon cheese—that is one of Christendom's most wicked comfort foods. If you are like me, you will be content to while away the hours over lunch or wander around the Old Town and the Palais de L'Isle, a medieval prison that sits in the main Canal du Thiou. Flowers are everywhere, in tidy window boxes and studiously messy thickets along the canals and footbridges.

But you may also feel the pull of the water and a craving for the sweet mountain air, even if it is not ski season. Isabelle Mathez, the

creator of the Malle W. Trousseau, a case full of everything wonderful for the house of a new bride, has had a home near Annecy for twenty-five years. She loves to hike around the hills, when jonquils, violets, star gentians, campanula, edelweiss, veronica flowers and wild raspberries burst from the earth when the snow melts and cows are brought up to pasture. "This is why the milk is so good, and why the air has such an incredible perfume," she says.

And then there is the aquamarine lake, with bike paths along the shores, which are walkable as well, and lots of places to rent *pédalos*—pedal boats—on a sunny day. Just over halfway down, across the ten-mile lake, is Talloires, a little far to pedal even on the fairest day. But you can take the forty-five-minute ferry ride, a water taxi or an old-fashioned wooden motorboat from Annecy and get delirious from the mountain scenery and crystalline air. Talloires's beauty has long drawn creative genius, and its storied abbey that was painted by Paul Cézanne is now a luxury hotel. It is here that Mark Twain, who visited in 1891, also fell in love: with Lake Annecy's radiant waters. "It is a miracle," he wrote in *Europe and Elsewhere*. "It affects you just as all other things that you instantly recognize as perfect affect you—perfect music, perfect eloquence, perfect art, perfect joy, perfect grief."

Or, in the case of Jean-Jacques Rousseau, that one, first, perfect love.

※

# 38 Eileen Gray's Masterpiece (and Le Corbusier's Little Gem)

## E-1027 AND LE CABANON, ROQUEBRUNE-CAP-MARTIN

In 2009, a chocolate-leather Dragon armchair by the Irish furniture designer Eileen Gray sold at Christie's in Paris for $28.3 million, shattering the record for 20th-century decorative art. Those in the know were always aware of her massive but somewhat unrecognized talent, but the auction officially—and finally—crowned Gray as one of the immortals of modern design. She moved to Paris in 1902 and distinguished herself as a pioneer in the use of the lacquer so paramount to the Art Deco movement. In the 1920s she incorporated chrome, steel and glass in her designs concurrently with her peers Marcel Breuer and Mies van der Rohe. But it is the peers Le Corbusier, her contemporary and onetime friend, with whom Gray's history on the Côte d'Azur is most intertwined.

If you don't have a boat, you reach Le Cabanon and E-1027 in Roquebrune-Cap-Martin via the narrow path that loops around the drowsy but glittering coast between Monaco and Menton. Gray and her lover, Romanian critic Jean Badovici, were looking to build a beachside love nest on the Côte d'Azur, and here Gray found the perfect secluded site. From 1926-1929—without any clue that she was creating a masterpiece years ahead of its time—Gray oversaw every detail of construction of the house, including wrangling the mules that hauled materials up and down the hills to the site. She named it E-1027, a numeric code: E for Eileen, 10 for J as in Jean, 2 for B as in Badovici, and 7 for G as in Gray, devised as a tribute to their entwined lives.

Set on a gentle slope saturated in Mediterranean sunshine and thick with pines, the house was the pinnacle of modernism: tiered with squared-off planes of white, floor to ceiling windows, sliding doors and open spaces making full use of the sea and sky. Gray furnished it with her own designs, adding ingenious touches such as a black tiled swimming pool that she filled with sand and where she repaired for cocktail hour. "I really admire her sense of modernity and daring, and her absolute iron will in getting this house done," says Lanie Goodman, a journalist based on the Côte d'Azur and an expert on Gray, E-1027 and the villa's turbulent history. "And remember she wasn't even an architect."

Enter Le Corbusier, who visited Badovici and Gray often at their seaside idyll. Whether he was or was not threatened by her talent, most scholars agree that Le Corbusier was obsessed with Gray and her triumphant E-1027. So much so that in 1938, after the bisexual Gray split with Badovici and returned to loving women, Le Corbusier took it upon himself to paint—some say defile—the interior walls with eight garish murals depicting charged lesbian imagery. To add to the insult, he took photos of himself doing so, wearing nothing but his trademark glasses. When she heard about this brazen act of disrespect, Gray was horrified and vowed never to return. But Le Corbu continued to visit the area.

In 1951, Le Corbusier arranged with the owners of the café L'Étoile de Mer in the lot adjacent to E-1027 to construct a beach hut connected to their restaurant. The concept, ingenious to be sure, was to live in a house attached to the place where he could eat all his meals. Soon, he added a hyperefficient guesthouse next door to the property.

At E-1027, the drama turned to tragedy. Nazi soldiers looted the house and used it for target practice during World War II; in 1996, its morphine-addicted owner was murdered there. The house was abandoned and left for dead, battered from disrepair, appropriated by squatters, junkies and drifters. Finally, in 2000, a group of concerned conservationists and the local landmarks commission stepped in to rescue one of the country's most distinct architectural treasures from the wrecking ball. As of this writing, the renovation is approaching completion, and though those concerned are hopeful for a speedy opening, the project remains mired in setbacks—bureaucratic, structural and otherwise.

You can get a good glimpse of its exterior from the steps near Le Cabanon, and it is a marvel of elegance and simplicity, with right-angled roofs and walls fashioned from white concrete, the kind of house that by now we may have seen before, but which no one but Gray could have dreamed of in 1929. It is a sheer drop past olive trees and rosemary bushes to the cliffs below.

Whatever your theory of Le Corbusier's role in Eileen Gray's disappearing into decades of obscurity, his little Cabanon is ingenious, a masterstroke of high style and low maintenance, nestled among the citrus as if house and trees were joined at the roots. Corbu believed that a house should be a machine for living in, and this one is a feat of efficiency, where the bedroom, dining table, chairs that double as storage boxes, bathroom, and cabinets either have their dedicated corner or disappear into the walls of this tiny, wooden space. Everywhere are Cubist-looking bright blue, electric green and yellow murals that Corbu loved to render, the architect most at home in another medium. The miniature restaurant connected to the house by a door is a chic set piece, and every corner of the room, from the rounded bar lined with vintage carafes and painted with fish, to the tiny table in the corner, has the patina of wear and style.

Le Corbusier spent many peaceful holidays at Le Cabanon, and each time he walked down the steps to jump in the waves or back up to resume his painting, he passed by E-1027, a couple of arm's lengths away. One wonders what his memories were of the place, or of Eileen Gray, or if he even chose to access them. Le Corbusier was said to truly admire his former neighbor's work, but it's hard to imagine what possessed him to appropriate the walls of a villa that did not belong to him. Some have said that later, Corbu may have taken credit for some of Gray's design. Lanie Goodman doesn't sugar coat it. "Corbu's murals are an unquestionable act of sabotage, whether he was conscious of what he was doing or not," she says. "As Gray's former friend and mentor, he was certainly not very invested in her success."

Certainly he owed her some gratitude for drawing him to this lush corner of the Riviera in the first place, at least while he lived. In August 1965, he drowned while swimming in the water at the foot of the hill, on the beach just below Le Cabanon and E-1027.

❧

# 39 *From Market to Table*

## COOKING CLASSES IN NORMANDY, NICE, LYON AND BOULIAC

In 1948, a young American diplomat and his 6'2" wife from Pasadena disembarked ship at the port of Le Havre and drove their imported Buick to Rouen where they dined on *sole meunière*, wine and oysters. A year after what she called "the most exciting meal of my life," Julia Child would enroll in cooking classes at Le Cordon Bleu in Paris. Within three years, she would join forces with Simone Beck and Louisette Bertholle to open L'École des Trois Gourmandes, an informal cooking school in Julia's kitchen, which developed a great following among Americans living in Paris. *Mastering the Art of French Cooking (1961)* was borne from this collaboration, and in its wake, our ongoing love affair with French gastronomy.

Cuisine française: to revere it, to devour it, and even better, to prepare it ourselves. That is the enduring legacy of Julia Child: to find joy in the kitchen. There are hundreds of cooking schools all over France, and several of them take cues from the Trois Gourmandes and teach the fundamentals in their well-equipped kitchens. I am listing here the best I have found, run by women who are actually chef-scholars, not just gifted cooks and instructors, but passionate emissaries for French culinary culture and history.

Rosa Jackson is a journalist and food writer who gives daylong workshops on the cuisine of Nice, her home of the last ten years, along with lots of local lore, gastronomic and otherwise. "It's really about being Niçoise for a day," she says—and that is not necessarily French, since Nice belonged to Italy until 1860. Unlike much of France, whose food is based on buckets of butter and cream, cuisine Niçoise is based on olive oil, and features lots of produce grown in the southern sun. She and her students begin the day at the market and return to Jackson's kitchen to prepare *pistou*, the French version of pesto made without pine nuts, or perhaps *pissaladière*—caramelized onion tart—or *chicken bouillabaisse* and a mixed berry gratin.

Lucy Vanel is an American expat originally from upstate New York, who has lived in Lyon for fifteen years. She offers one-day pastry workshops and market classes (where students create meals based on what is freshest at the outdoor *marchés*) from her Plum Lyon kitchen in an old boulangerie in the heart of the city. Yes, she has earned her certification as a pastry chef—*un pâtissier*—via a very difficult test to pass in France. But she is also a food historian, with

a wealth of knowledge about women's major role in making Lyon the gastronomic capital of France, which her students learn while exploring the markets for ingredients for their menu—fish or ripe young cheeses or mushrooms picked that morning.

In her pastry classes of up to six people, Vanel helps students create wonders from simple *pâte à choux*—the stuff of cream puffs and profiteroles. There is Paris-Brest, a ring filled with caramel, almond and hazelnut pastry cream; the *religieuse*, draped in coffee fondant that resembles a little nun; or savory versions of the éclair—what Vanel calls "the cupcake of France—they're really popular now." All of them boggle the mind. "When you see the dizzying array in the pastry case, it's hard to imagine everything is basically made from butter, eggs, flour, water and salt," she says. "It's really humbling."

Susan Herrmann Loomis is the author of eleven cookbooks, including a gorgeous, recipe-filled memoir of her food-rich life in Normandy, *On Rue Tatin: Living and Cooking in a French Town.* She offers three- and five-day classes at her home in a lovingly-restored convent in the heart of Louviers. Students stay in nearby guesthouses and spend mornings scouring the local markets and the region around the Eure River for the area's famous shellfish, cream, apples, poultry and in springtime, red fruits. "Ninety percent of what we cook and eat comes from within five kilometers of the house," says the long-expatriated Seattle native. "I want the participants to make things they've never made before," she says, "and to eat food they've never tried." Wine, too. Loomis pairs their creations with small production, handcrafted wines impossible to find elsewhere.

Beyond Julia's tradition of kitchen-based cooking classes are the many high-end hotels that are also beginning to offer hands-on facetime with their equally high-end restaurant chefs. Le Saint-James in Bouliac, a hotel high in the vineyards just north of Bordeaux, actually has a cooking school on the Jean Nouvel-designed premises. Celia Girard, the young and amiable sous chef to the Michelin-starred chef Nicolas Magie, taught my session in a spectacular white-on-white Poggenpohl kitchen classroom fully-loaded with All-Clad everything. Each day the class has a theme, and in my case it was scallops—*les coquilles St. Jacques.* We incorporated the first clementines of the season, tiny onions, lots of olive oil and espelette, the heated red pepper from the Basque country, for a citrusy tartare, and then, cauliflower purée and scallops seared to perfection—by us.

As I jumped in my taxi for the ride back to Bordeaux I was woozy with delight, armed with new knowledge and a resolve to replace all my knives at home with shiny new ones. I recalled a passage in M.F.K. Fisher's memoir of her first years in France, *Long Ago in France: The Years in Dijon,* and how she returned to California to find she could not once succeed at the cauliflower casserole she prepared almost every day in Dijon. "How different it was, the manner of doing it, the flavor, everything," she writes. "The vegetable was watery, there was no cream thick enough...the cheese was dry and oily...and then, where was the crisp bread, the honest wine?"

Yes, things taste better when you cook them yourself, but everything tastes better in France.

※

# $40$ *Sweeter than Wine*

## THE CANELÉ, BORDEAUX

There are thousands of delicious reasons to visit Bordeaux, and you can drink nearly all of them. There is only one excursion-worthy pastry, however: the *canelé*. It's not clear to me if it is a breakfast

food or a dessert, and that ambiguity allows you to punctuate the day with them. Of all the regional pastries in France, and there are many hundreds to love—the cream-filled *tarte Tropézienne* from Provence, or the flaky, apple *pastis gascon* of the Midi-Pyrénées—it is the *canelé* that has me most in its thrall. My ardor for it verges on evangelical. It is a small (I prefer the bite-sized ones), dark cylindrical cake with fluted sides, a crunchy, caramelized exterior and a moist, custardy interior.

A day in Bordeaux begins and ends with this most mythical of French confections. First, a jaunt around the corner from my hotel to look for the bike rental spot by Cathédrale Saint-André. Here in 1137, the Archbishop performed the marriage of a hugely wealthy fifteen-year-old duchess, the most eligible heiress in Europe, to Prince Louis VII. Five months later, Eleanor of Aquitaine was crowned Queen of France. The sun glazes the limestone towers and façade in a wash of apricot and gold, and the massive rose window gives no hint of the colors streaming through it inside the nave. A flying buttress here, a gargoyled belfry there, France's historic temples of devotion to crown and to God provide a layer of texture to Bordeaux's singular beauty.

I've found the bicycles. I'm not a citizen of Bordeaux (yet...), so I'm not able to abscond with one of the new yellow-tired bike-scooter hybrids designed together by Philippe Starck and Peugeot to help rid this burnished city of traffic. But I can rent one, and I do, in search of sweet perfection.

It's around the corner at Baillardran, which is warm with the scent of vanilla and browned sugar. The cakes must be ice-cold before they are baked, then are freshly sprung from their special copper molds. I buy six for the road, and stop at my bike to eat one. The story of the *canelé* is bolstered by legend, but it probably owes something to the truth. I learn that the precursor to the *canelé* was first made in the 16th century by sisters in the Convent of the Annunciation in Bordeaux, who formed the cakes around a stick of sugar cane and fried them. They made the batter from egg yolks discarded by local winemakers who used only the whites in their production. Later, the local bakers known as *canauliers*, who specialized in making bread to be blessed in church (and were not yet allowed to use sugar and milk—only the pastry chefs had that right), probably created a version of what we know today out of flour reaped from the holds of ships that sailed on the Garonne into Bordeaux, as well as vanilla and rum that arrived into port during the slave-trading years.

The recipe vanished during the Revolution and slowly reappeared by the 1920s. By the mid 1980s, the *canelé* was officially revived and designated the official pastry of Bordeaux, with its own cadre of dedicated *pâtissiers* who maintain the secret recipe. Like the graceful buildings and grand public spaces on which Baron

Haussmann, once a prefect of Bordeaux, based the rebuilding of Paris, the *canelé's* loveliness is a point of civic pride.

My bag is bursting as I proceed along the cobblestone paths, past the achingly radiant neoclassical Grand Théâtre, which was restored to its original splendor in the 1990s. High above the façade's Corinthian columns, twelve women watch over the Place de la Comédie, the Nine Muses and Roman goddesses Juno, Venus and Minerva. In the evening, they are illuminated and somehow appear more formidable glowing out of the darkness. By day, it is the sun that defines their gestures and drapery. Calliope, the muse of epic poetry and eloquence, wears a crown and carries a stack of books; Juno, the queen of goddesses, stands with her shoulders back and a peacock by her side.

The city is wide open, it exhales vast gulps of clean air. I pedal to the Place de La Bourse and behind the 18th-century skyline along the quai where the biannual Fête du Vin takes place in June, and around the Esplanade des Quinconces, one of Europe's largest squares. I cross the Garonne on the vertical-lift bridge and true engineering marvel, the Pont Jacques Chaban-Delmas. I ride south along the opposing quai, past the botanical gardens and back via the Pont de Pierre, a majestic structure with seventeen stone arches and rows of wrought iron street lamps. It's been a flat ride, not too exhausting, but I stop anyway for water and a snack of *canelé* by the Basilica Saint-Michel, whose 400-foot belfry spire dominates the Bordeaux skyline like a Gothic space needle. I find a place to return my bike (it has cost me one euro on my credit card) and eat lunch: foie gras and a glass of white Pessac-Léognan that is just dry enough. I grab another bike, just because.

After coffee and my own dessert, I circle back along the esplanades, past the Hôtel de Ville. I have passed literally hundreds of people on bicycles, and I will again later that night, long past dark. By the cathedral, I replace my bike and climb Pey-Berland, the free-standing bell tower. All 231 steps. The view makes it clear why Bordeaux is always in the throes of a golden age.

The afternoon passes quickly without much consequence, as they often do in great European cities. An hour at a café in Bordeaux qualifies as busy, and I'm content. For dinner, I slip into a tiny spot called the Bar à Vin near the Place des Grands Hommes. I order a plate of cheese—Tomme, St. Nectaire, some *saucisson* and *jambon noir*, with a thick glass of Château Martinat red. The whole thing costs me eight euros and dessert, which I pop into my mouth, is free.

Going home, I try to connect the pieces of this day. Open expanses, medieval spires, a bike ride through time and green space, a river flowing through all of it. Beauty and glory and wine, accented with a jewel of a pastry that seems to embody the essence of this city. Rich, gold, balanced, a soft, sensual core cloaked with a strong but delicate shell. Bordeaux.

✥

# 41 The Simplest Fantasy

## ABBAYE DE LÉRINS, ÎLE SAINT-HONORAT

There are two major islands in the Lérins archipelago, and both are a breezy fifteen-minute jaunt from Cannes. The Île Sainte-Marguerite is a eucalyptus-scented idyll laced with wild coastal paths and views of Cap d'Antibes. There, you may ponder one of France's strangest and most enduring unsolved mysteries by visiting the fortress prison where the Man in the Iron Mask was held a few years before he died in Paris's Bastille prison. People have puzzled over his identity for centuries, and in the last book of the *Three Musketeers* trilogy, Alexandre Dumas speculates that the prisoner was the identical twin brother of King Louis XIV. Both men—the prisoner and the monarch—were portrayed by a fresh-faced, flaxen-haired Leonardo DiCaprio in the 1998 film *The Man in the Iron Mask*. The film also boasts a truly formidable cast of our coolest actors juicily hamming it up: Jeremy Irons, John Malkovich, Gérard Depardieu and Gabriel Byrne as D'Artagnan.

The other island, Île Saint-Honorat, is a place to ponder weightier mysteries, or simply pose your own questions and find the silence in which to resolve them in the dry heat among 17th-century olive trees and gatherings of palm, parasol pines and cypress. This is where to come for a spiritual retreat (you don't need to be Catholic—you just need to crave some solitude) and to live from two to six days as the monks do: simply, closely connected to the land they carefully tend. You may also make a day visit from Cannes.

When I disembark at the island's tiny harbor, I head past lavender bushes along a densely packed red soil path that leaves a claylike residue on the soles of my shoes. I ask my friend what smells so sublime. Eucalyptus, pine, dry wood, tea olive blossoms and vine, perhaps something sweet that blows in over the waves. The island is blanketed by the pastel shadows of the Mediterranean sun and supported by a foundation of secluded coves, chalky cliffs and rugged beaches, which frame the vineyards and wild vegetation that cover the parts of Saint-Honorat that the remains of medieval chapels do not.

For seventeen centuries, the island has been inhabited by monks, and it has suffered its share of maritime indignities at the hands of pirates, Saracens, and Spaniards, all of whom inspired what Alexandre Dumas called the "square tower of the Benedictines,"

an 11th-century fortified monastery on the southern spit of the island. It juts out confidently into the sea, a specimen of perfectly squared-off pale stone, crowned with crenellated ramparts so symmetrical it could be a child's toy castle. You will explore this on your retreat and climb to the top on the central staircase with seventy-two steps for the seventy-two orders of Benedictines, because at the top is an unobstructed view of what I assume to be heaven—as well as Saint Tropez, Monaco and on a very clear day, the Alps.

Today the twenty-five monks who live, pray and work in silence at the Abbaye de Lérins are Cistercians, the order that arrived from Provence in 1869 and replaced the Benedictines who had resided there since the 7th century. Their labor mostly takes place among the vines, where they grow six different varieties of grapes over about twenty acres of vineyards, whose tidy rows occupy the central part (and a good chunk) of the island. The wines—a Pinot Noir, a Mourvèdre and a Chardonnay—are rather swell and very expensive, and though you can buy them in the abbey's gift shop, they will not be included in the modest price of your stay, which includes all three meals. They also produce liqueurs from herbs and berries they raise and forage on the island, as well as from lemons and mandarins grown nearby on the Côte d'Azur.

The retreat area consists of thirty-five (five of them for couples) 8' x 9' rooms they call "cells" containing just a bed, furnished with your own sheets. You are expected to perform simple chores—wash your dishes, keep your room neat, but with no Internet, there is ample time to tidy up. Your phone service will follow you to the island, but you'll have to hide if you want to chatter away on your mobile. The experience is meant to be contemplative for all, and even one person braying on a one-way conversation shatters the peace; meals, too, are passed in strict silence. It is a spiritual retreat, and the point, though difficult for some, is to disengage. It may be the reason you need to step aside in the first place: to quell the buzz of electronics and activity that seems to be burning a hole in our 21st-century brains. In fact, these little respites should be required of all of us in this day and age, what must be the noisiest epoch in human history. A little quiet time in a monastery on a Mediterranean island, with church bells the sole, glorious ring tone.

❧

# 42 Stories the River Tells

## THE DORDOGNE AND
## JOSEPHINE BAKER'S CHÂTEAU

When you drive through the Dordogne, the area of Aquitaine between the Loire Valley and the Pyrénées, the names will fall from your tongue like drops of truffle honey sold in the local markets alongside Cabécou goat cheese and *magret de canard*. Sarlat, Castelnaud, Souillac, Issigeac—with each passing *commune*, the seduction grows more poetic and somehow, more persuasive. People succumb to the Dordogne's allure with a sense of destiny, lasting love from *coup de foudre*, and I know plenty of people for whom France is not Paris or Provence but rather this untrammeled southwestern slice of valleys, rivers, farms and vineyards. Such understatedness may be why passion for this area is unusually potent and the attraction so enduring.

Author Kimberley Lovato remembers when she fell, a moment that could only be called a conversion. "When I first saw Château de Beynac, I drove off the road," she says about the medieval fortress that roosts dramatically on a cliff face high above the Dordogne River. "I called my husband and said, 'You wouldn't believe what I'm looking at.'" Inspired, she began to delve into the stories behind the cuisine of the region the French still call Périgord—the raspberry growers, the purveyors of foie gras, the creator of the sublime lavender crème caramel. The result is *Walnut Wine & Truffle Groves: Culinary Adventures in the Dordogne*, her cookbook, memoir, and tribute to the food, markets and people of the area. "Everything you love about France is here, but better," she says. "Lifestyle. Physical beauty. Uncrowded markets and restaurants, where dinner is usually cooked by the owner. And life exists around the table."

In the Dordogne, cuisine is king, but so is the history of royals who resided there and the architectural reminders of the many battles fought on its soil. The *bastides* of Monpazier and Beaumont-du-Périgord, fortress towns from the Middle Ages built around an arcade-lined central square, remain largely intact. The Dordogne also lays claim to some 1,001 châteaux, many of which came under attack during the Hundred Years' War between France and England, and they rise from the vineyards and undulating green meadows in various degrees of splendor. They are at their most sublime when seen from the river itself, either in a hired *gabare* or better yet in your own rented canoe or kayak. If you depart from La Roque-Gageac, where the village's honey-colored houses descend to the riverbank, you will paddle past several of the castles built high upon the craggy cliffs. At journey's end your car awaits you, and you may explore the medieval villages, including Beynac and Castelnaud and the castles that loom above them, which clutch centuries worth of stories. Among the most fascinating tales is one of the most recent, and it is told at Château de Milandes, the former home of one the 20th century's most intriguing women and a genuine French war hero, Josephine Baker.

As an eight-year-old foraging for food in the slums of Saint Louis, Baker worked as a maid until she found her way to New York, where she danced at the Plantation Club cabaret in Harlem. In 1925, at age nineteen, her beauty caught the eye of an impresario looking for performers to play *La Revue Nègre* at the Théâtre des Champs-Élysées in Paris. Topless, her hair slicked into a helmet, clad in oversized gold earrings and a pink flamingo feather between her limbs, Baker was a *succès fou.* Janet Flanner, the *New Yorker*'s legendary Paris correspondent known as Genêt, wrote a belated tribute to Baker's opening night at *La Revue Nègre*, which, she writes, "remains to me now like a still-fresh vision, sensual, exciting and isolated in my memory today, almost fifty years later." Within a half hour of the curtain fall, Baker had catapulted

into the stratosphere. "The two specific elements had been established and were unforgettable—her magnificent dark body, a new model that to the French proved for the first time that black was beautiful, and the acute response of the white masculine public in the capital of hedonism of all Europe—Paris." Soon, the woman known as Bronze Venus or the Black Pearl, with an entourage that included a pet cheetah named Chiquita, had her own show at the Folies Bergère and was the richest entertainer on the continent, and a movie star too.

In 1937, Baker saw and fell in love with the Château de Milandes, a Renaissance castle complete with gargoyles and massive stone staircases. During the war, she hid Jewish refugees there while she spied for De Gaulle's Free French Forces, for which she was awarded the Rosette of the Résistance in 1946 and in 1961, the Légion d'Honneur and Croix de Guerre. As a crusader for civil rights in America as well, Baker was the sole woman to speak at the March on Washington with Dr. Martin Luther King, Jr. in 1963.

By then she had bought the château and adopted twelve children from eight countries to raise there. Her great wealth allowed her to transform what she called her "Sleeping Beauty Castle" into a theme park dedicated to her life, complete with an African village, theater, dance hall called the Sans Souci, and a J-shaped swimming pool. Her extravagance came at a high cost, and she was forced to sell Milandes for a fraction of its value and abandon it in 1968.

It was rescued by a local family, and today, a modest museum there honors her memory and role in French history with film clips, photographs and of course, the famous banana skirt from the time when she was the toast of all Paris. The pièce de résistance is a regal bathroom befitting the glamorous entertainer-turned-châtelaine decorated in the gilded black palette of her signature perfume, Lanvin's Arpège. It's a long way from Paris and even farther from St. Louis, but in the Dordogne, Josephine Baker takes her rightful place among the great women of France. The region, famous for its food, memorialized by its villages, but sustained by the people who loved it and still do, is the richer for it, and so are we.

❧

# 43 *Oysters and Sand*

## THE DUNE DU PILAT AND THE
## BASSIN D'ARCACHON, AQUITAINE

One of my French girlfriends, Sophie, was elated when on one jaunt to the U.S. she finally got to visit "9-2-K," which is how the word "Nantucket" emerges when spoken with a dainty Gallic lilt. I was similarly enlightened when I made my way, at long last, to the Bassin—or Bay—d'Arcachon. Just as Nantucket may seem to a European like some sort of windswept vacation promised land frequented by those in the know, the Bay also seemed that way—distant, exclusive, elusive.

It's none of that, of course. It's simply one of those secrets that insiders don't care much to divulge. "I first went for fun and was so struck by the charm and importance as a destination for French people (despite being almost unknown to Americans)," says *Travel + Leisure*'s Paris correspondent Alexandra Marshall, who returned there on assignment and loves the area's beaches, oyster shacks and accessibility from Paris. "And on the TGV to Bordeaux, it's incredibly easy."

After about an hour's drive or a short train ride from Bordeaux, you arrive in the town of Arcachon, the main hub of the area. The town is also a staging area to the beaches and dunes due south or, via speedboat or a wooden *pinasse*, across the bay to Cap Ferret (no relation to the oligarchs' playground Cap Ferrat on the Côte d'Azur) and to the oyster beds and nature preserves that flourish there. There is also the beautiful neighborhood of Ville d'Hiver— Winter Town—a stretch of turreted and gabled *belle époque* villas built as private homes for wealthy consumptives, as the air around Arcachon—a salutary combination of Atlantic winds and mountain breezes from the Landes—was thought to be a tonic for the lungs.

Unlike the island of Nantucket, the Bay of Arcachon is an inland sea, shaped roughly like a horse's head, with a narrow channel on the western side (its "neck" as it were) where the Bay opens to the Atlantic. The delta of the Leyre River is on the eastern part of the Bay, so fresh water flows in and blends with Atlantic seawater. On the western (ocean) side of the Bay, there is a long narrow peninsula, a ribbon of sandy beaches with a hardcore surf scene that stretches from the village of Cap Ferret north to the lighthouses that mark the entrance of the vast Gironde estuary, for which this department is named.

The area has long been a popular refuge for luminaries seeking a low-key break from the limelight or prying camera lenses. In 1914, at the outbreak of World War I, the actress Sandra Bernhardt— dubbed in her time as "the most famous actress the world has ever known"—came here to disappear into the folds of the French countryside after learning she was on the Kaiser's list of hostages he hoped to haul to Berlin when Paris was defeated. Hollywood-sur-Seine still comes here (as do assorted French tycoons and their families) to decompress and dress down, and though you may catch a glimpse of Audrey Tautou, Marion Cotillard, Philippe Starck or Jean-Paul Belmondo at a café in Cap Ferret, be assured that the only flashy thing about the Bay of Arcachon is the water itself, calm and sparkling on the bay side, angry and agitated, like frothy milk, on the other, with waves that unload surfers while crashing under harsh Atlantic sunlight.

There are three things to cross off your list when you visit the Bay. First, rent a bike and ride it (Locabeach has branches in the train station, Cap Ferret, and elsewhere). Everyone else does. There is only one main road that winds around the bay, but over 125 miles of bike paths. You can cycle for a short stretch or all the way around—50 miles from Arcachon to Cap Ferret—past salt marshes and under forest shade in the shelter of the bay. The bay's beaches expand into a giant sand basin during low tide, when the water dips from 60 to 15.5 square miles in area, and people walk to and from their grounded boats to visit friends. Much of the path is through a substantial pine forest, and on the cape you may cross to the Atlantic side where the surf roars and the heat dissipates when you approach the water's edge.

Whether you rent your bike in Arcachon or Cap Ferret, you will come across dozens of oyster farms and traditional villages with wooden houses, where a farmer steeped in the tradition of *ostréiculture* (Arcachon is the country's most important oyster breeding center) will demo some serious know-how including how to open one of those bad boys and serve it with a spray of lemon. What would  cost me five minutes and possibly a flesh wound, the sea-farmer does in seconds. L'Herbe, Piraillon, Le Canon, Arès and Grand Piquey are low slung, rambling settlements on the bay and ideal for an afternoon plateful on ice. "Probably the best part of the journey is sitting on the bayside after a long day at the beach and having a half-dozen oysters and very cold Chablis for an aperitif," says Alexandra Marshall.

The last must-see is the great Dune du Pilat, which in the summer you access by boat from Cap Ferret. At 2 miles long, 550 yards wide, and 360 feet high, it is the largest sand dune in Europe, a natural triumph of shifting sand and westerly winds off the Atlantic. It's a steep but short climb to the top, which gives you one of the most remarkable views, it seems to me, in all of France. Deep forest on one side pans to the bluest water studded by sand-bars, streaming with cottony whitecaps at precisely the point where the ocean rushes in and out of the bay. The day is so clear I swear I can see all the way to Boston or at least, to Nantucket.

# 44 *Millions of Flowers*

## MAKE YOUR OWN PERFUME, GRASSE

Grasse is a quiet hilltop town in Provence, fifteen miles and a world away from the dazzling beaches of Cannes. There is a sweet languor here on an early morning, eating breakfast at a table in the sun, wearing sandals, with a breeze riffling in from the valley. The village is up high, surrounded by red-tile rooftops and the blue-green vistas of olive trees and the maquis, and swirls with the scent of cypress and pine that grow on the hillside. This slight detachment, just far enough from the sea, is what allows the town to wear its singular history well.

With its nearly perfect combination of water, climate and soil, Grasse is a geographic fluke that enabled fields of hyacinth, tuberose, mimosa, lemon groves and jasmine to flourish in the surrounding countryside. Once it was the center of France's tanning industry, but the leather smelled so putrid that during the Renaissance a local perfumer named Galimard had the idea to infuse a pair of gloves with local floral scent, giving birth to the era of *gantiers-parfumeurs* (glovemaker-perfumers). According to legend, he presented a pair of these fragrant gloves to Catherine de' Medici, wife of King Henry II and mother of three more eventual monarchs, which helped usher in Grasse's golden age as the perfume capital of the world. Although Catherine was more infamous, and probably inaccurately so, for her alleged expertise in the poisonous properties of plants, she undoubtedly brought the passion for perfume to France with her entourage from her native Italy. When the fashion for scented gloves eventually died out (largely due to high taxes on leather goods), the *gantiers-parfumeurs* moved away from leather-making and focused on perfume instead.

By the mid 17th century the development of cold enfleurage allowed the extraction of essences from the most delicate blossoms, and by the late 19th century, Grasse harvested 600 tons of flowers annually. The early 1900s saw the rise of synthetic essences that were often more powerful than real ones, and Coco Chanel, who subscribed to poet Paul Valéry's dictum that "a woman who doesn't wear perfume has no future," collaborated with renowned Russian perfumer, Ernest Beaux, to create the world's first "modern scent." When No. 5 was launched in 1921, it was the first fragrance to be dominated by synthetic scents. (According to one legend, its name came from the laboratory sample she selected, based more on her belief that "5" was her lucky number rather than the formula in the vial.)

Today, the annual flower harvest is reduced to about thirty tons but Chanel still owns vast fields of jasmine and May rose, the flowers that are the heart of their fragrances, as do Dior, Hermès and other industry leaders. The world's greatest noses are rigorously trained and often based in Grasse. As I stroll past a 12th-century palace and the Notre-Dame-du-Puy Cathedral, I recall Patrick Süskind's novel *Perfume: The Story of a Murderer*, when the whole of Grasse erupts into a massive carnal revelry induced by the intoxicating scent of twenty-four virgins, with which Grenouille, France's unparalleled nose, has doused himself for his execution.

Here in town, it is the traditional houses, rather than the corporate behemoths that billow beyond the city, that maintain the legacy of Grasse, one that is documented with great style in the charming

Musée International de la Parfumerie. Fragonard, named for the locally-born Rococo painter, and Molinard, another family operation from the mid 1800s, both offer tours and perfume making. But I head a few miles out to Galimard—once famous for its perfumed gloves—to create my own scent.

My private instructor (and nose) is the white-jacketed Siliang Guo, an amiable chemist. "A perfumery is just like a pharmacy," he says, leading me to a perfumer's organ, which consists of three levels of bottled essences, and on the table, a ready array of beakers, funnels and pipettes. First, we choose the base notes (or fond notes). They are, he says, "like the foundation of a house," the longest lasting element that will leave my fragrance's ultimate impression. They can be woody—sandalwood or vetiver, animal—musky, or sweet, like vanilla. Next we select the middle (or heart) notes, which influence the depth of the base notes. They can be floral—rose, violet, jasmine, peony, magnolia or honeysuckle—or reminiscent of foods, like pomegranate, spicy licorice or cinnamon. The last step is to pick the very volatile top or peak notes, the light ones that last only fifteen minutes but which define the first, crucial impression of a perfume. Often they are fruity—grapefruit, lavender or orange.

I indicate my preferences: I want light, light, light, or citrus, citrus, citrus or floral, floral, floral—rose preferably, lavender's okay, orange flower, too, is cool and fresh. Please, no vanilla. No cedar. No ambergris or praline. Please God, no narcissus or honeysuckle or gardenia.

One step at a time, I inhale, concoct, wave the vapors towards my nose, compose. I drip precise quantities into a beaker and when I add an extra milliliter of something I love (lily of the valley), I'm gently chastised. This is science after all, and as a writer I'm decades removed from my last chemistry lab. After about seventy-five minutes, I have chosen tuberose and lilac, floral musk, jasmine, peony, green tea, grapefruit, lemon and lavender, among others. Three base notes, six heart notes and five peak notes—the last being the clean ones I like best of all, the ones that, sadly, will not endure on my wrist or behind my ear.

Guo asks me to name my perfume, and after making sure it isn't the name of some tropical disease I'm not aware of, I call my blend Avarée, a hybrid of both my children's names, sort of. We mix it one last time, and he disappears into the lab. He emerges with a gorgeous bottle of what he calls a "fresh, clean, elegant and very springy scent"—everything I asked for. Galimard will keep the formula locked up tight in Grasse for when I need to stock up. But it takes two weeks for the molecules to become balanced in the solvent—a process known as maceration—and the perfume to be ready.

Precisely fourteen days later, during a thunderstorm at home in Connecticut, I smell Avarée for the first time. It is light, delicate and thankfully without a hint of sweet or spice, the qualities I feared the most. I'd like to think I'm going to wear it but it hardly matters. It is France, and I have her flowers in a bottle, a potion created by combining centuries of science with an eternity of art and my one very particular nose. It is also uniquely and forever mine.

*

# 45

## The End and the Beginning of the World

CARNAC, BRITTANY

When you enter a Gothic cathedral, whether it's Notre-Dame in Paris or Notre-Dame in Reims, you expect to be overwhelmed by heroic arches, 200-foot ceilings and imposing decorative structural icons—crosses, altars, naves, statuary. The experience is always one of gazing skyward, of air and glass and windows letting in heavenly light. We are supposed to be dwarfed by a church's verticality and openness and aware of our own small selves, contained inside the house of the divinity. This is entirely different from the experience—equally humbling—at Carnac, the largest of the megalithic sites bunched throughout the Morbihan region of southeast Brittany, and one of the most important fields of prehistoric standing stones in the world. Here, the majesty is on a human scale rather than a divine one. We move and dwell among the ruins, and as we do so, partake in a primal ritual, one that gives the brain a workout by asking questions rather than offering solutions. We wonder how, and by whom, these unfathomably dense and heavy granite stones were quarried, moved and installed. And unlike in a church, we will never know for what purpose.

When I learned I would be writing a book on 100 places for women to experience in France, Carnac was the first item on my list. It's not simply because I live with a stone sculptor, who has taught me (or will die trying, anyway) to see life and movement in rock, even in abandoned quarries. Nor is it because the chic beaches in coastal Carnac and nearby Quiberon are some of the sugar-sandiest in all of France, and the port town of La Trinité-sur-Mer has an afternoon light not unlike my native New England (not to mention plenty of crêperies serving up the star of Breton cuisine). It is Carnac's scope and sense of permanence that has haunted me since I first set eyes on the fields there. It is both more accessible than a cathedral and infinitely more enigmatic. I love the chance to ponder the unanswerable, especially in a sweetly swaying meadow of tall grass and wildflowers.

There are at least 3,000 stones at Carnac configured into various alignments over seven fields that stretch for about two miles. Its overall resemblance to an army striding across the landscape is perhaps what gave rise to the most enduring legend about the megaliths: that Saint Cornelius, the patron saint of cattle, was pursued by Roman soldiers across Brittany. Cornered, he froze them into stone. The earliest monuments date back to the Neolithic period around 4500 B.C. and carbon dating suggests that they were erected over a period of 2,000 years.

Bear with me on the basics and try to imagine a hypnotic and endless landscape of granite forms, which really do resemble figures, sentries keeping watch over millennia. Carnac's upright standing stones, called menhirs, are arranged into avenues comprising several distinct alignments, some of which fan outward from circular rock formations called cromlechs. There are dolmens—little covered stone chambers made up of clusters of menhirs, and tumuli—manmade mounds of earth, which are burial sites, the most famous of which is the Tumulus de Saint Michel. At the Kermario alignment, 10 rows of approximately 1,000 menhirs, some reaching 10 feet tall, extend outward with obvious symmetry. In the Ménec system, as in Kermario and Kerlescan, which consists of 13 rows, the stones at the western end are taller than those at the east. At Ménec, 1,100 menhirs extend in 11 converging rows for about 1,200 meters, roughly 7/10 of a mile.

It's little wonder that new agers and seekers of all stripes have come to channel the energy of the stones, treating Carnac as a sacred site for whatever purpose they desire. The Cruz-Moquen dolmen and the Grand Menhir in nearby Locmariaquer—the largest in the world now broken into four smooth stones—were both long considered touchstones to help with a woman's fertility.

And why not? Scholars have been baffled by the stones of Carnac for centuries. It may have been a giant calendar, for farmers to know the arrival of winter and summer solstices, or observatories to predict solar or lunar eclipses. They could be burial grounds, or the remains of a Roman camp, or fairy grottos or places of worship. In his 1904 book, *Over Strand and Field: A Record of Travel Through Brittany*, Gustave Flaubert debunks the antiquarians and archbishops, ecclesiastics, Egyptologists and scholars of Druids and Celts, who by their "vanity" have tried to dignify Carnac with a history. "This is my opinion," he writes. "The stones of Carnac are simply large stones!"

Well, so they are, but ones with raw power, which when you walk among the ruins, you both give and receive. And unlike in a cathedral, where the wonder lies in how man carved detailed decorations into massive stone blocks, here it is how he arranged them. We still feel their natural beauty. And strangely, the forms at Carnac are so close to human statuary that you can actually convince yourself that they were once Roman soldiers. Except I like to think that they are female forms—all curves and cleaves, softness and natural contours—that like women, get more beautiful and more formidable over time.

❧

# 46 *La Vie en Lavande*

## THE LAVENDER ROUTE, PROVENCE

There are a few feats of nature so particular to their place and time they manage to leap across the merely picturesque into full-blown icons. Japan has cherry blossoms in springtime, Vermont has its autumn leaves, and the south of France has lavender in the summer. Long before its scent infuses our Trader Joe's dryer sheets or its oil is extracted to give my salt scrub its headiness, billions of these tiny purple-blue flowers grow in great swaths from Mont Ventoux to the Drôme Provençale, through the Luberon and the towns of Sault, Apt, Simiane-la-Rotonde, and Gordes and finally, across to Forcalquier, Valensole and Digne, whose Bishop Myriel forgives Jean Valjean for making off with his silver, the spark that sets *Les Misérables* in motion.

Unbutton something and give it up to the summertime. You can always visit this corner of the Côte d'Azur and Provence again when the crowds go home, but the lavender blossoms come only in June, July and August. This is when you must make your pilgrimage, not once before you die, but when you are as vital as you ever will be, all senses poised. Rub the flowers between your fingers, and inhale their pungent beauty. There will be festivals celebrating the season and markets to distract you that brim with on-theme wares that, even when it seems like overkill, you will never regret bringing home. Bunches of dried blossoms, sachets in linen pouches, essential oils, extracts, soaps in waxy wrappers and potions that will do what lavender has been known to do since Roman times: smell glorious, first of all. Fight infection, clean you, cure you, and elevate your spirit. But have a gander at the raw stuff in the early quiet of morning, and it will move something else in you.

*Lavender*

If lavender is the soul of this part of France, gazing upon fragrant fields of it somehow triggers the essence of us, too. Unlike roses that are womanly and sensual, or sunflowers that manifest a statuesque glory, or girlish fields of daisies laced with pixie dust, lavender as it grows here has a purity of purpose. Chances are, you won't just feel intoxicated by the vision and the aroma of buds that expand into softly rolling columns, but rather—even you, the deepest, darkest cynic—will feel cleansed. I'm not sure how to convey this without too much dramatic emphasis except to compare it to other head-clearing vistas that have served me well: the Sonoran desert has this quality, as do certain Adirondack peaks and every isolated beach I've known from Maine to Paracas, Peru. In these places, I breathe in the stillness, whether balmy or crisp, and the effect is exhilarating.

One early morning, I walked by myself the easy 2.5 miles down from the medieval village of Gordes to the Abbaye de Sénanque. In high summer, framed by that eternal blue sky, the simple Cistercian structure was luminous white. Set dramatically behind the lavender fields, the abbey is photo opportunity No. 1 in Provence, if not in all of France. I had seen the image a hundred times before, radiant, arresting but all too familiar and was prepared to head straight into a high-kitsch painting. Instead, I heard the drone of honeybees, a rustle of butterflies. I was confronted with something I had expected, and yet the effect was thoroughly unexpected. Convex mounds of lavender were aligned in rows perfectly perpendicular to the Romanesque abbey that was so pale, it almost faded into the glare. The Provençal sun was just starting to penetrate the passing cool of dawn.

Travel writer Constance Hale also visited the lavender fields at Abbaye de Sénanque one July in time for the 5 P.M. mass. Just as she entered, a thunderclap shook the monastery, and the sky unleashed a driving rain that poured right through the opening of the roof over the stone chamber. "This is one of my strongest memories ever of France," she says. "The afternoon I was no longer in a postcard of these beautiful lavender fields, but also in the presence of grace."

There was no storm the morning of my visit. But as I stood there alone under a still-gentle sun, immersed in all the smells of Provence and adrift in those great purple waves, I'm sure I was too.

᷂

# 47

## A Sisterhood of Wine

### WOMEN WINEGROWERS OF BURGUNDY

On a Saturday morning, a black SUV makes its way along the narrow thoroughfare through Chassagne-Montrachet in Burgundy's Côte de Beaune, just off the Route des Grands Crus, unleashing sprays of mud from the previous night's rain in its wake. When the car stops in front of the Abbaye de Morgeot, its Scottish-born proprietress, Amélie de Mac Mahon, the Duchess of Magenta, bellows, "Welcome!" She is youngish, with a bob of honey-colored hair and appears distinctly unroyal this morning, clad in earthy cords and scuffed boots, despite the fact that her home is the Château de Sully (whose Renaissance courtyard is considered one of the most magnificent in France), which she has inhabited since marrying Philippe, the 4th Duke of Magenta in 1990. The Duchess is meeting me that morning for a tour of her twenty-two-acre domaine—the vineyards planted by Cistercian monks in the 1100s, which surround the abbey. It is she who runs the estate and all the operations for producing eight different wines and, in that capacity, belongs to Femmes et Vins de Bourgogne—the Women Winegrowers of Burgundy—now thirty-six members strong, aged twenty-one to sixty, all of whom you may visit with an appointment.

The group formed in 2000, not simply in recognition of their mutual womanhood, but as like-minded professionals who shared the desire to run successful businesses and make the best wines possible. From Roman times to the clergymen who settled in Burgundy and delineated the various *climats* based on geography and sunlight, through the Dukes of Burgundy, up until today, wine production has been dominated by men, and for the minority of women in charge, this camararderie and support is a godsend. "When my husband died, all of a sudden I had this huge responsibility and a ton of questions," says Amélie, who took the reins in 2002 and points to the unique perspective she shares with her colleagues. "As women, I suppose we feel as though we need to look after our grapes and our wines as if they're our children."

Unlike in Bordeaux, where vineyards surround a single château, winegrowers in Burgundy often have several parcels of land scattered around the area. Given that the whites are almost exclusively made from Chardonnay grapes and the reds from Pinot Noir, the versatility of these wines is enormous—as is the expertise required to run a successful operation.

The wine women of Burgundy are a fairly diversified lot, extending as they do through the five main regions—Chablis and Grand Auxerrois in the North, through the Côte de Nuits, de Beaune and de Chalonnaise, and finally down to the Mâconnais. Many, like the group's dynamic leader, Virginie Taupenot-Daniel, are from wine-growing families. She is a seventh-generation vigneron who studied business in Paris and returned home to run Domaine Taupenot-Merme in Morey-St-Denis on the Côte de Nuits, which produces gorgeous wines—sixteen reds and three whites. These include the eponymous Premier Cru, a Grand Cru Gevrey-Chambertin, and the delicate Charmes-Chambertin, smooth and tasting of red berries and cherry. Virginie has the relaxed demeanor of a working mother but also that polished refinement that befits a French chief executive. "We are feminine but not feminists," she says about the group. "I like to think we formed in homage to our mothers, who tended not to be involved in the business in the past."

Part of her role as head is to organize field trips—to study the fabrication of barrels for example or hire a speaker who can discuss the cork versus the screw top. Gathering knowledge can pose a lot of questions, and within the group—one of whose aims is to learn from one another—someone will usually know the answer. "None of us ever has the same question so we really help each other a lot," she says.

Five minutes south is Domaine Anne Gros, who creates some of Burgundy's finest Premier Crus in the geographically blessed, southeastern-facing slopes of Vosne-Romanée. Anne, the only child of a sixth-generation winemaker, studied viniculture in Beaune and took over the estate in 1988. She led me on a tour of her cellar, and I tasted some of her 2013 baby wines that would remain in the barrel for another year, including a Grand Cru Echézeaux, which will eventually sell for about $175 a bottle. "We are all the heads of our enterprises, and we share the same problems," says Anne about the women's group. "It's also a chance to have fun, and a really good meal together."

I stayed at her maison d'hôtes called La Colombière, a tony but unpretentious (and wildly comfortable) guesthouse right on the property, outside of which her mother tends to the flowers and her daughter, now working for the domaine, will happen by. Anne custom-designs packages with a tasting, all of which include breakfast with sublime jams made by Maman, but I liked the fridge in my kitchen, stocked with her friend Virginie Taupenot-Daniel's wines and those of other women winegrowers. I opened a bottle of Anne's own Hautes-Côtes de Nuits Blanc Cuvée Marine, a crisp white Burgundy and a bargain at fifteen euros.

Over in Auxey-Duresses, Estelle Prunier, from Domaine Michel Prunier et Fille, is a fifth-generation winegrower who shares responsibility with her father for thirty acres of vines, which produce 39,000 bottles a year of red, white, and sparkling wines. She walks me through the cellar and, like her colleagues, speaks fluently about terroir, maceration, soil quality and sun exposure. These women run businesses but they are farmers and scientists as well, de facto experts in everything from microbiology to the weather. We taste seven of her selections, and finally I grasp how to *"grumer"*—sip and suck air through the liquid to create bubbles, which oxygenate the wine and send a message to the brain. I loved the dry, white Auxey-Duresses 2011, with an aroma of lemon and exotic fruits and the Volnay Premier Cru, with its spiciness and persistence.

I finally get to Chablis where I meet Clotilde Davenne, who bought and built Les Temps Perdus in Préhy eight years ago after two decades in the business, and now oversees an astonishing thirty-five acres of vineyards. It is late Sunday morning, and the house is warm with the scent of a roast in the oven, but she is all passion and focus about the oyster fossils in the soil and climate, which makes Chablis unique. In her tasting room we first explore an Aligoté made with seventy-five-year-old vines, which, she says goes wonderfully with snails. I love the fresh, perfumed Saint-Bris, a rare Sauvignon for Burgundy, which is leafy with the presence of white flowers. Most unusual is a red called Irancy, made partially with the César grape, a big fruit that gives the wine a remarkable taste of cherry pits. But it's Sunday lunchtime, and it's time for me to leave Burgundy.

I think about all the words used to define the many wines I tasted in the last days—good balance, complex, delicate, elegant, subtle, strong but not overpowering, profound. All the same words I would use to describe the women winegrowers of Burgundy.

# 48

## You Are Never Too Old

### FRENCH LANGUAGE IMMERSION COURSES

When I taught high school French, I found that some of my best speakers were the school thespians. Even when grammar was iffy or vocabulary fleeting, if she were willing to vamp it up, imitate a French person and *pretend* she was fluent, she was halfway there. *That* was a kid who would do fine on her own at the Gare du Nord in Paris; not so the student who aced every chapter test but could barely utter a word. I used to encourage the kids to exaggerate, feel the words in the throat, pucker the lips—really, really pucker them because a mouth is meant to do that when speaking real French. I showed them how to shrug the shoulders when saying, *"Je ne sais pas,"* which no French person actually even says. A French person says, *"Sais pas."* With no disrespect to grammar, which is necessary, and vocabulary, whose many uses are obvious, what you really need to speak French is to try to speak French.

The rest will follow. Go to France, immerse all your senses in the words and music of this beautiful language. Eat it, dream it, get lost on a bicycle in it and drink it without ice. If you love France, if you wish you could speak French, if you're actually tired of winging it with three cards in your deck (*merci, s'il vous plaît,* and *très bien*), you owe it to yourself, at long last, to make this effort. And go alone. "If you travel with a friend, you will inevitably speak English, and that

really defeats the purpose," says Anna Kate Hipp of Greenville,
South Carolina. Years ago, while in Paris on one of her frequent
voyages to France, she couldn't tell her cab driver right—"*droite*"—
or left—"*gauche*," because she could no longer recall from her high
school lessons which was which. That experience propelled her to
an immersion program the following summer, and now she has
been to six, earning her rare bona fides on the subject.

Over the years, Anna Kate has studied in an intimate château
and twice with Centre Linguistique pour Étrangers (CLÉ) in
Tours, which has nice small classes. In Vichy, at the CAVILAM
program, she rented an apartment off-campus with her two daughters, who were also studying. When she attended CAREL in Royan,
she shared housing with other international students. Most reward-
ing and effective for learning, she recalls, was when she landed in
homes with a series of French hostesses. "That stress and adventure
were a large part of each experience for me," she says of chatting
through dinner—some memorable, some lousy—with her hostesses,
even after five hours of classes each day. "It forces you to learn."

We are fortunate. When Abigail Adams moved to Paris to join
her husband John, a Congressional Envoy at the time, she did not
have the luxury of any of the terrific intensive courses we have now
in many of our big cities, at say, L'Alliance Française, which would
have beautifully prepared her right at home in Boston (AF, by the
way, also has several affiliated language schools in France). Instead,
once she resolved to learn French, she devised her own immersion
program, which consisted of reading plays by Racine, Voltaire, and
Corneille, and with the help of her *dictionnaire*, translated one a day.
"I must read French or nothing," she wrote her niece, in 1784.

That would take more discipline than most of us can muster
(let alone sustain), and luckily immersion programs are not exclusively for diplomats anymore. I encourage everyone to plunge into
those waters.

Sometimes I wonder if there is a reason, besides geography and our English-language solipsism, why Americans in general (not all Americans, of course) struggle with foreign languages. I wonder if culturally, we are so self-conscious that we fear sounding pretentious, or foolish, or like an actor hamming it up—which, as I saw with my students, is kind of the point. Take a cue from that rascal Mark Twain. Even he gave it a college try in *The Innocents Abroad*. "*Madame, avez-vous du vin—du fromage—pain*—pickled pigs' feet—*beurre—des œufs—du bœuf*—horseradish, sauerkraut, hog and hominy..." he asks the waitress moments after setting foot on French soil in Marseille, before she cuts him off and answers in English. Twain played at being humiliated, but the dear boy gave it a shot and had fun with it. You should too.

Finally, for the plane ride to your immersion class, download some songs by Carla Bruni—yes, the model and former first lady of France. Her voice is surprisingly lovely and the lyrics are crystal clear. After a few weeks in France, your efforts boosted by a little necessary theatricality, I believe you will be able to understand every word. Meanwhile, speak up, loud enough so they can hear you.

ॐ

# 49 Tender Was the Night

## PLAGE DE LA GAROUPE, CAP D'ANTIBES AND HÔTEL BELLES RIVES, JUAN-LES-PINS

If you have ever loved any book that was set in France, it can become somewhat obsessive to transpose yourself into that fictional world when seeking out a landmark that you know from reading about it. The effect is similar to that of being in the presence of a much-adored celebrity, except in a setting where you can freely gawk and openly idolize the object of your infatuation. The second aspect of literature and place is that it can be pointless to try to separate what transpired in the fictional setting from its other, actual history. For example, despite its prominence as an imposing masterpiece of Gothic architecture, it's impossible for a *Madame Bovary* fan to enter the Rouen Cathedral and not think of it as the location of Emma's first liaison with her young lover Léon and recall the tone-deaf verger who leads them on an unsolicited tour of the church.

The last and most alluring phenomenon of books and travel is when the life of the writer conflates with the setting of a novel. Nowhere is this more palpable than at the spot where *Tender Is the Night* begins (although for the sake of fiction, it is somewhat shuffled geographically): Plage de la Garoupe in Antibes. Here, you can imagine the ghosts of F. Scott Fitzgerald, his wife Zelda and their daughter Scottie leaping into the waves or having a languorous lie-in on the sand. Along the coast in Juan-les-Pins is the former Villa

Saint-Louis, now the Hôtel Belles Rives, where the Fitzgeralds lived in the summer and fall of 1926 and where he worked on the manuscript whose working title was, at one point, *Our Type*. There is dense fictional meaning here, but there is also a separate atmosphere of timelessness, of a weathered ideal of heat, light and the sea.

*Tender Is the Night*'s is not Fitzgerald's most perfect book, but it is my favorite, for reasons I won't bore you with here. The first pages root the story in the glory days of the French Riviera, which to many of us is poetically alluring. "In the early morning the distant image of Cannes, the pink and cream of old fortifications, the purple Alp that bounded Italy, were cast across the water...." I swoon for  Fitzgerald's portrayal of the hard sunshine of a Mediterranean morning, the little town waking up, of cocktails on the beach, striped umbrellas and a suntanned beauty on the sand draped in a string of pearls. Today La Garoupe is jammed every summer day, but if you go in the morning before the crowds arrive, you can walk along the curving expanse of sand, brown your shoulders and dream.

In the 1920s, the Fitzgeralds expatriated to France to write and await publication of *The Great Gatsby*. In Paris, they were introduced to Gerald and Sara Murphy, the American couple who later inspired the term "Living well is the best revenge" after a *New Yorker* profile by Calvin Tompkins. The Murphys had befriended many artists and writers who toiled in the ateliers and cafés of Jazz Age Paris, among them Hemingway and Picasso. Because of their American vigor and charm, they became popular hosts with a devoted following, and in 1922, they rented the ground floor of the Hôtel du Cap d'Antibes, which was shuttered for the summer. Hosting one memorable fête after the next, the glamorous Murphys created the concept of "the season" on the Riviera as we know it today. Until then, it was a winter holiday getaway for the wealthy, who boarded up their villas when the air got steamy and relocated to the cooler breezes of Deauville.

The Murphy's company was so coveted and their hospitality such a draw that the brilliant and the celebrated flocked to join their circle in Antibes. They built a villa there and led their friends in a jolly, relaxed social life that took place between the rose-colored hotel (now the Hôtel du Cap-Eden-Roc), amusing dinners at their house and elaborate picnics on La Garoupe.

In *Tender Is the Night*, Fitzgerald drew heavily on those heady summers, conveying what he treasured most about the Murphys into the better parts of Dick and Nicole Divers's characters, especially their easy social grace. By the summer of 1926, Fitzgerald's alcoholism was worsening, and Zelda was beginning to show signs of the mental illness that would ultimately incapacitate her. But today, here at the Belles Rives, you can immerse yourself in the man, his work, his era and the idea of better times. You just can't help it.

Some of his original furniture—Art Deco tables and chairs left undestroyed by German soldiers during the war—remains, as does the building, renovated to five-star sheen and polish. The dining room that was his office looks out to the terrace and the Bay of Juan-les-Pins. The deep-green islands split the vista of sea and sky in half. Fitzgerald sat at his desk in this room and could see the clouds sweeping across the water. He spent long hours drinking with Hemingway in the sexy little bar now decorated with moody scarlet lampshades and an antique map of Cap d'Antibes.

The terrace restaurant, La Passagère, stretches grandly towards the sea and is enclosed by olive trees, bougainvillea and bunches of other heady blossoms. You can imagine the great Fitzgerald standing outside here, cocktail in hand. Slowly turning the view and the life he led from this vantage point into words. This is where the writer ends and the story begins. Or perhaps, it's the other way around.

❧

# 50 *Beautiful in Any Language*

## VILLAGES OF THE PAYS BASQUE

The Pyrénées divide France from Spain, and early morning on the highway from the city of Pau through the Béarn to the Atlantic coast, the strip of mountains are a veritable distraction. On my left, due south, they extend in curves of violets, blues and grays, and it contributes to the sense of a border that in these parts is otherwise quite fluid. Signs on the highway begin to appear in both French and Basque and when I arrive in Saint-Jean-de-Luz, one of the seaside jewels of the Western Pyrénées, Saint Sebastián, Spain is a ten-minute walk along the beach trail, no passport required. But this adventure is about going back inland, eating *pur brebis* sheep's cheese and buttery cake in the towns of the Pays Basque, in this most unusual, pitch perfect southwestern corner of Aquitaine.

Here, it's almost impossible to hit a false note. There is an exquisite and palpable balance between where to go and feeling good when you get there. Mountains meet the waves in glamorous port towns via green hills grazed by milking sheep called *manech*—with colored faces and legs. Sturdy villages erupt from bends in the road, and they don't have to try hard to entice you with comfort. What the Pays Basque has, like the Pays d'Auge in Normandy, is a sharply delineated identity, customs found nowhere else in France and pride to match.

"We celebrate everything here," says my guide Nathalie, and she is not exaggerating. The press dossier on festivals in the Pays Basque and the Béarn (very connected spiritually, though slightly inland) takes fourteen single-spaced pages. On any given day, all year long, somewhere there is a party. They celebrate salt, shepherds, corn, hake fish, tuna fish, ham, pigs, pepper, Irouléguy wines, the grape harvest, dance, the river Nive, night surfing, and yes, the beret and everything else Basque. Espadrilles. Peaches. Cheese. The big sports of the region—rugby and pelote (like jai alai)—played in *frontons* in the center of every town, or in *trinquets* that resemble wooden squash courts.

Saint-Jean-de-Luz is a perfect place to begin. It's also a nearly perfect village, the kind of place where a woman feels not just safe and undisturbed, but good. Really good. It's a walking town attached to a broad beach with crystalline water, a creamy surf, and a boardwalk with barely a glimmer of bling—if you want, you can find that in Biarritz about thirty minutes up the coast, but even there you'll have to look hard.

After coffee in the Place Louis XIV, across from the house where the Sun King lived when he married the King of Spain's daughter Maria-Theresa here in May 1660, I peruse the shopping district. First stop: Sandales Concha on rue Gambetta, for espadrilles. Everyone genuinely wears them, as they must have been designed for long strolls up and down the beach promenade. I buy mine in black, with a little wedge heel, and a flat pair with stripes that I slide on at once. I discover a dreamy shop called Artiga Maison, which carries the most beautiful quality thick Basque cotton fabric and towels, pillowcases, and canvas bags.

From Saint-Jean-de-Luz, I go to my hotel, the Arguibel, on a quiet road in the uplands behind the mythic beaches of Guéthary, less than ten minutes from Saint-Jean-de-Luz. It is an ideal midpoint to branch out in all directions. The next day, drinking my

French press coffee on the terrace as I observe the coming morning, I inhale the quiet isolation and scent of grass. Sheep come up to pasture from the farm below, their neck-bells clanging in a joyful racket.

In barely twenty minutes, I am in line at the Petit Train de la Rhune to begin my thirty-five-minute ascent up the highest mountain in the area. The train is ninety years old, and it is made of smooth varnished wood, with red and white striped curtains. We cross into Spain and climb to the summit, almost 3,000 feet. Along the way are vistas of wild ponies called *pottok*, fields of buttercups and scattered outcroppings of granite. The panorama on top is endless—the Pyrénées, Spain and long stretches of coastline and pale ribbons of beach. I stop for hot chocolate, thick as ganache.

After the train, I drive about twenty-five minutes to Espelette, where the famous red pepper of the same name seems to hold sway over all else in town. Basque architecture dominates the landscape and villages and consists of red asymmetrical roofs and colorful shutters on half-timbered houses. It looks almost alpine, but it is distinctive and always patriotic. The red, white and green Basque flag flies freely here and elsewhere. I procure a jar of black cherry jam seasoned with espelette, and a jar of pepper, ground. From there, I drive to Ainhoa, a quiet village. Nothing can distract me from a deep sense of languor and contentment here, which only increases at my simple lunch at Hotel Ithurria. Sliced *jambon de Bayonne*, chewy chunks of bread, local Ossau-Iraty sheep's cheese, and spoonfuls of fig confit.

Next stop: Sare, another almost comically well-appointed enclave with a handsome stone *fronton* in the town square and buildings with alternating red and Basque green shutters. Wisely, I stumble into Hotel Arraya, a stately timbered beauty with an Armagnac bar on the ground floor. Outside, a stand sells their famous *gâteau Basque*, dense, yellow butter cake filled with cream or cherries. I choose the latter and do like an American and gobble it up on the way to my car. After all, I am about to walk to Spain.

Fifteen minutes away, just above the Grottes de Sare caves— I join up with an easy footpath, well-indicated by blue horse icons. The trail is almost flat, passing under blooming dogwoods, Lawson cypress, oaks and goat willows. I snap pictures of purple wild orchids, Alpine narcissus and snowbells and cross over bridges and rushing streams. Forty-five minutes later, I arrive in Zugarramurdi, just over the Spanish border, with its own set of mysterious caves and history of Salem-like witch trials in the 17th century. I get hydrated in the town square near the church that has no similarity to the French Basque architecture I've left behind, and return the way I came. Next time I will continue another forty-five minutes to Urdax, but I am alone and getting tired.

I pass through Ascain and over the Nivelle River on a bridge that is decorated—for no special reason—with garlands of spring flowers. I stop at the 1910 Lartigue factory, where they weave cotton thread into bolts of chic, beachy fabric out of which they make household linens and espadrilles. I want to take ten of everything and ten meters of cabana striped canvas as well, but I show restraint and buy a few dishtowels, striped gray, blue and earthy brown. I arrive back at the Arguibel and pour myself a tumbler of Jurançon wine and sit back outside, craving the good cheer of those adorable sheep. All is beautifully still, and at that moment I find the pace of modern life completely overrated. I wonder if one day, they might throw a party for this—life in the balance, Basque style.

❧

# 51

## Eat— You Are in France

### AN UNFORGETTABLE MEAL, ANYWHERE

Some of the best meals I've ever had in France have been haphazard affairs, slapped together with a quick trip to the Marché d'Aligre near the Bastille—ripe Rocamadour cheese and *saucisson aux noix*, bread, and a salad of *mâche* trucked in that morning from the Loire Valley. It's important to dine like this in France, to spread out your samplings from the market before you (even in your hotel room) while uncorking a decent Beaujolais from the corner store. You don't need to eat expensively to eat well. But chances are that if you do eat expensively, you will eat unforgettably. So I make the case that you should save up and surrender yourself, just once in this short life, to a master French chef.

In late February or early March, the folks at Michelin announce their annual benedictions and death sentences to the *chefs de cuisine* of France and the restaurants they oversee. Careers are made or lost, wrists are threatened with sharpened blades, culinary celestials are anointed into or plucked from the galaxy. In 2014, 504 restaurants in France received 1 star, 79 were awarded 2 stars and 27 earned that third most-coveted golden star. The tradition gets knocked by both the French public and press, and some critics believe it has an autocratic sway over gastronomic destinies (and that includes focusing too much on up-and-coming chefs and not enough

on the unassailable established stars), while others lambaste the
mandarins at Michelin for ignoring the new "bistronomy" movement—affordable haute cuisine—that is democratizing fine dining
in France.

Fair enough. But let's buy into this system, however flawed, for
the sake of pleasure. There is artistry, even genius, behind these
single, 2 or 3 stars. In this rarified universe, these chefs have made
the cut. So seek one out. Put on your best dress. Go ahead and eat.

Use the salad fork. Order the good wine, and
drink it all. Unless you suffer from celiac disease
or your food allergy is truly life-threatening, try
to forget that you can't tolerate gluten or dairy.
You may also have to swallow some foie gras,
which most French chefs have no moral qualms
about preparing in seventeen different ways.

If food is memory and memory is destiny, then you could
make the case that food is destiny, and nowhere more so than in
France. This meal may be what lingers most enduringly in the hidden reaches of your mind. A table littered with wine glasses, the
remnants of dessert and you, utterly satiated. You may not recall
what you ordered or what the chef delivered, but the scene will glow
more brilliantly over time and take on new meaning in retrospect.
Here's one such memory from writer Abigail Pogrebin about her
long-ago visit with friends to Les Prés d'Eugénie, Michel Guérard's
three-star idyll in Landes:

There are few lunches that stay with you because of the light
as much as the meal. But that's what comes back to me: the
kind of sunlight that made the crystal twinkle and dance on
the table, that swept the immaculate gardens outside the
restaurant's window. I don't remember what we ate but I
remember moaning—literally making some involuntary,

grateful sounds—after almost every bite. We kept pinching ourselves. Who were we to get to have this? We weren't rich, we were like kids playing dress up. And then I was in the pool. In my long summer dress. I'd leapt in on a dare, because I was so giddy with it all.

And here's another. Nancy Evans, my former boss, relates the following:

Seymour and I had just gotten married and were driving up from Perpignan to Paris when we stopped at Oustau de Baumanière in Les Baux. The restaurant is in the bottom of a valley, surrounded by mountains. We ate outside on the terrace. When I leaned back on my chair, I saw nothing but stars, like I was inside a planetarium. Waiters came and went. Foie gras. Escargots. Something *en croute*. I ate it all. Crème brulée, I ate that too. Cheese tray, ah, yes. With a sigh of satisfaction I leaned again towards the stars. I discreetly undid the button of my pants, and as I breathed again, I thought this was the perfect dinner with my perfect husband (thirty years later, he still is), and this was the most magical place I ever had been.

And here's my most recent experience, the memory of which intensifies as I recall it:

I was traveling alone for work, as I often do. By some stoke of luck, I landed at Le Mas Candille, a fancy hotel in Mougins, in the hills behind Cannes. Lonely, desperately missing my husband and children, and expecting to dine and sulk in my room, I was surprised by a generous invitation. The owner had apparently taken pity on me and arranged for a chef's table—some really fine hotels will do this—whereby I sat at a simple stainless steel station in the corner of the kitchen to savor a gourmet meal. Serge Gouloumès, the one-Michelin-star chef de cuisine, bustled alongside his staff while I wrote it all down.

He fed me foie gras with apple and Armagnac. He handed me a slab of potimarron squash to nibble on, and a few shavings of white truffle that were just in from Alba. He oversaw the staff—"*Oui, mon chef,*" they repeated again and again. He adjusted this, added garnish to that, spooned caviar onto dishes and onto a round of—more—foie gras. He spun around, chatted with me. He squeezed a splash of lemon-infused olive oil onto my hand. He fed me bread, baked into a brick color from beet juice. He fed me rare beef, scallops and more truffles. He fed me Fourme d'Ambert and goat cheese from the Auvergne. He poured a simple Le Saint André rosé, and poured some more. He fed me wheels of chocolate with drops of chestnut purée and eglantine jam. Finally I wrote, "THIS DINNER IS TOTALLY INSANE."

I recall my loneliness dissipating as I sat snug inside his kitchen, wishing I weren't alone of course, but grateful, overwhelmed and so deeply satisfied. Long live France and power to the system—imperfect as it is—and the artist chefs who strive only to amaze us and turn us delirious with pleasure. Serge works for every point on his Michelin star, but I think he deserves at least two.

※

# 52 *Yards of Luxury*

## THE HISTORY OF SILK, LYON

Lyon exudes greatness. It is a sweeping Gallic kind of greatness rivaled only by Paris, with which it is connected by what was, until recently, the world's fastest train. But although I never would advise anyone to overlook the capital, nor would a sane person want to, Paris is busy being Paris, the center of culture, government, international politics, media, and entertainment. That leaves Lyon to be the most French city in France.

How fitting, then, that couture, or at least the luxury fabric that was used to create luxury fashion, originated here. The heritage of Lyon is encapsulated in the story of the rise, fall and preservation of the silk industry that defined it for centuries. It is told in various places throughout the city. At the Maison des Canuts, you can see how and where the industry thrived, and at the Musée des Tissus, some of the most magnificent dresses, capes and tapestries are on display. The city is loaded with mansions built by the bankers and businessmen of the silk industry. And lastly, the story permeates the hills, rivers and *traboules*—those hidden passageways unique to Lyon, through which the city's silk weavers—the *canuts*—carried their bolts of fabric down to market in the center. In 1831, the workers gathered clandestinely in these *traboules* to prepare for an open revolt against silk manufacturers for low wages and poor working conditions. It was the first recorded uprising of the Industrial Revolution, and a landmark in the history of organized labor.

In Europe, a city's prominence is in direct proportion to its geography, and in this regard, both internally and externally, Lyon is unusually blessed. Two hills dominate the city. To the west is Fourvière, site of Lyon's excavated Roman ruins and a gleaming basilica that overlooks the Saône, which flows from northeast France, and the Rhône, which comes from the Alps. Both rivers would prove indispensable to the silk trade. The confluence of the two rivers forms the tip of the Presqu'île, the central peninsula whose northern point is the Croix-Rousse. This is the city's second hill, the heart of Lyon and the neighborhood where the silk industry flourished, faltered, and repeated that cycle until Asian competition, synthetic fibers and industrial advances all but killed off Lyon's raison d'être.

The city is sufficiently south and east to be a crossroads of Europe and major trading center since the reign of Louis XI (1461-1483), who set up a silk manufacture in Lyon in 1466 after deciding to build a French luxury textile industry. By the mid 1500s, King Francis I had broken the Italian hold on silk weaving, and in 1536, the first fabric was produced in Lyon. In 1599, agriculturalist Olivier de Serres convinced King Henry IV that sericulture could succeed in France, so the king planted mulberry trees (whose leaves are the silkworms' only food source) at the Tuileries in Paris and throughout France. By 1620 there were 10,000 looms in Lyon. By 1786, as the demand for luxury fabric exploded in the court of Louis XVI, there were 15,000.

The Revolution almost fatally wounded the industry. All that changed under Napoleon Bonaparte, whose wife Josephine had a voracious appetite for extravagant dresses. The Emperor also commissioned the redecoration of all the imperial residences and finally, required the courts of his conquered lands to buy Lyonnais silk. These were the boom years, which lasted through most of the 19th century; at its peak, nearly three-quarters of all industry in Lyon was related to silk production, with 400 companies and around 105,000 weavers.

The Maison des Canuts is in the heart of the old silk quarter, the Croix-Rousse, where high-ceilinged houses, now luxury lofts, were built to accommodate the massive Jacquard looms, invented in 1801. These allowed the weaving of increasingly complex patterns like brocade and damask through a punch card that resembles a computer printout, into which the design is programmed. The loom here has a system of 1,344 needles, each connected with a vertical hook, integrating a total of 7,040 fine strands of silk. The director, Philibert Varenne, demonstrates the painstaking work as he weaves, thread by thread, sumptuous brocaded silk, sliding the shuttle back and forth at—literally—warp speed (in weaving, the weft goes across, and the warp is longitudinal). In the next room, a *canuse* creates fabric for a wealthy client at a cost of 2,000-3,000 euros per meter. Consider this. When Versailles was renovated, it took 17 years to complete the upholstery silks that were woven at the rate of 1 inch a day. All of it by hand.

Today, France's modern textile factories are scattered on the outskirts of Lyon, where centuries of expertise has been updated for the 21st century. And alas, there are no public tours, but there is great symbolism in the fact that the planet's most iconic silk extravagance, the Hermès scarf, has been produced in a facility on the edge of town since the 1930s. Silk and luxury are forever woven together, as tightly as the finest brocade. The city of Lyon wears its history well.

※

# 53 Nowhere in the World More Lavish

## MARIE ANTOINETTE AND
## THE PALACE OF VERSAILLES, VERSAILLES

On the morning of October 5, 1789, three months after the storming of the Bastille Prison, a crowd of women from the marketplaces of Paris, angry over the shortage and high price of bread, took to the streets. The crowd swelled to over 6,000 and continued to gather steam. The angry women grabbed makeshift weapons—pitchforks, pikes, crowbars and kitchen knives—and began their defiant, rain-soaked advance 13 miles to Château de Versailles. When they arrived at the palace at 1:30 A.M. on October 6th, they stormed the gates and demanded bread, killing two guards and forcing their way into Marie Antoinette's bedchamber, from which she had escaped moments before through a secret door in the wall. The Women's March on Versailles marked the true beginning of the end of the *ancien régime*. For over a century the palace had been the seat and symbol of the absolute monarchy in France. That afternoon, King Louis XVI, his wife Marie Antoinette and their two surviving children passed through the gates of Versailles and left for Paris. They would never return.

It is a strange bit of history that the queen who grew from child bride to party girl to devoted mother to determined (if misguided) monarch was brought down by a throng of women, whose desperation and plight she could not deign to understand. Marie Antoinette had tried but failed to portray herself in public as a loving mother to her own children and by extension, to all of France. By the time the monarchy expired, she was too reviled and her image too far gone for burnishing. In the end they wanted her blood and in the end, they got it.

Marie Antoinette will forever be an object of fascination. Despite, the fact that she was only one of many queens and mistresses to inhabit Versailles, it is she we inevitably seek when we visit Louis XIII's old hunting lodge, transformed into the grandest royal residence in Europe by Louis XIV, for whom André Le Nôtre designed what are still, arguably, the most magnificent gardens in France. We immerse ourselves in her contradictions, try to weigh her outrageous wild-child excess and indolence against her later  years as a devoted mother against the brutality of her tragic end. We walk around her private estate where she sought refuge—the bucolic hamlet of thatched cottages where she played at being a peasant shepherdess and frolicked with farmyard animals. We walk to the Petit Trianon, built for Louis XV's first mistress Madame de Pompadour, who died before it was complete. Louis XVI gave it to Marie Antoinette, and she loved to look out at the English gardens and Temple of Love from her room.

We gaze at her portraits by Madame Vigée-Lebrun. One that hangs upstairs in the antechamber at the Petit Trianon, painted in 1773, shows a dressed-down Marie Antoinette holding a pink rose. She looks serene in her muslin dress and straw hat, shedding all royal artifice for freshness and simplicity. The mountainous wigs with ribbons and birds had been hung up for good. In another from 1787, displayed in the antechamber of the Grand Couvert, she is posed with her three children; the eldest, seven-year-old Louis Joseph, points to an empty cradle in memory of Princess Sophie who died before her first birthday (while the portrait was a work in progress). The dauphin himself would die of tuberculosis two years later. Soon after this tragic loss, Marie Antoinette's world would shatter.

One can't help but conclude that she was the wrong person for France, married to the wrong guy who became the wrong king for the times. But she earned emotional maturity over the years, firming her sense of entitlement on behalf of her children and the crown they were born to inherit. These stubborn political instincts strove to maintain an absolute monarchy at a time in France's history when the populace had no patience left. But it is important to remember that from the outset, she chose none of it—neither her birth nor her husband nor her destiny as the last queen of France.

It is difficult not to sympathize with the girl, herself no stranger to grandeur, who was thrust onto center stage at Versailles, where she arrived at fourteen for her wedding to the king's grandson and heir to the throne. Louis XVI would ascend as king four years later, but meanwhile, she had to make her way in and around this palace where Madame du Barry, Louis XV's latest mistress, reigned supreme. This was now her home, and eventually, in the eyes of the revolutionaries who tried and executed her in 1793, the scene of her crimes, the only indisputable one of which was simply being Marie Antoinette.

The extravagance of Versailles makes the jaw grow slack. In fact, the first time I visited, I fainted in the Hall of Mirrors from what was probably the crush of the crowd, but I prefer to think was a case of Stendhal Syndrome. This is an attack of dizziness and panic, by all accounts psychosomatic, which occurs when looking at a work of sublime artistic beauty. Many years later, my daughter, who was seven at the time, collapsed in fatigue on the grounds outside the

Grand Trianon. The estate is massive, and the palace's dimensions beyond comprehension: 700 rooms, 67 staircases, and 2,153 windows for the Austrian archduchess to stare out of after arriving from Vienna. The park and gardens cover almost 2,050 acres, where 50 fountains, a grand canal and 200,000 trees fill in the landscape.

You too will be overwhelmed. In fact, it is part of the experience at Versailles to get a bit dazed while under the spell of the opulence and scale. And the throngs. There is no way to soften this blow. The simple fact is that the doors in Versailles were not built to have 20,000 people like us pass through daily. I propose two ways to keep your wits about you on a visit to Versailles. Three, if you include good walking shoes, because you will wear out some leather on the avenues, groves, colonnades and parquet even if you see the bare minimum.

If you are going on your own, I highly recommend *Secrets of Versailles: A Visitors' Survival Guide,* an e-book by Heather Stimmler-Hall. It is an essential sixteen pages of information that clears up a lot of questions, from the different classes of tickets and how to get them to precise walking directions to the Trianons and when best to visit.

There is another brilliant way to visit Versailles: from mid March to mid November, see it on a bike. This takes almost all the preordained chaos, confusion and obligatory exhaustion out of a trip there. Bike About Tours has it all figured out, and they hold your hand from the moment you board the RER train from Paris. In the town of Versailles, you are given your made-in-France 3-gear bicycle with a basket. You buy your own picnic lunch at the town's outdoor market, and ride straight up to the gardens, the Trianons, the hamlet, and around the lakes and fountains. The day finishes with a tour of the château and then, you catch the late afternoon train back to Paris. By the end of the day, you've gotten a little exercise and experienced the grounds as a true, living out-door space.

What is ideal about this approach is that when you avoid, for the most part, the other thousands of people who are there at the same time, it leaves time, space and sanity for contemplation. Here, we consider a girl who was an outsider, who became a woman, mother, queen, prisoner and legend. Whatever we feel for her, whether compassion or contempt, we never feel envy. We get to hop on our bike at the end of the day. She had a lot of shoes and a lot of dia-monds, but Marie Antoinette was never, ever free.

❧

# 54 *Celebrate*

## THE CHRISTMAS MARKET, STRASBOURG

The holiday season was always my favorite time of year when I lived in Paris. It is cozy rather than raucous, and the outdoor markets smell of clementines and pine needles. People head there all bundled up with a keen sense of purpose, as if they are preparing for a month of great feasts. As in the rest of France, Christmastime arrives almost imperceptibly, not as it does in the States, with our cacaphony of sleighbells and *Féliz Navidad* on continuous loop from the moment the Thanksgiving turkey gets trussed, if not sooner. Even though France is a traditionally Catholic country, the holidays are very much tied into the early darkness of wintertime, a time for home and family and turning inward, a season of candles, illumination and most of all, food. Take some time to gaze into pâtisserie windows, where garlands and ribbons swoop over red and gold macarons and *bûches de Noël* with snowy layers of fondant and stumpy meringue mushrooms.

Although France does the holidays almost pitch-perfectly, this does not mean it's understated. Paris shimmers under galaxies of tiny white lights strung in the butcher's window and around the topiaries on Avenue Montaigne. In one of the country's most festive displays, Lyon goes DayGlo when the Fête des Lumières kicks off the holidays with a technicolor bang for four days in early

December. The staid façade of the Saint-Jean-Baptiste Cathedral becomes a resplendent lime green, hot pink and electric blue as does the Basilica of Notre-Dame de Fourvièvre way up on the hill. All along the banks of the Rhône and the Saône rivers, the rest of the city follows suit with installations created by visual artists lighting up the Presque'île and beyond.

From Lille to Perpignan, festivals take over the urban avenues and village squares, with the tree set up in the middle of town and stalls to help you with your shopping and fill your baskets with seasonal, edible treats. But the undisputed king of all holiday bashes around France is the Christmas Festival in Strausbourg, a fantastically lush fairy tale wonderland since 1570.

There is no such thing as a brief history of Alsace, the long narrow strip of land hugged by the mighty Rhine, that jogged between French, German and Prussian rule and back again to where it is now, suspended on the easternmost reaches of France. Sometimes, the countries have been fatefully joined. In 1770, Austria offered fourteen-year-old Marie Antoinette to France on a small German island near Kehl so she could marry the dauphin who would become Louis XVI. Today, Kehl and Strasbourg are connected with a modern footbridge, the Passerelle. Because of its past, Strasbourg has more than a tincture of Teutonic flavor in the rows of half-timbered buildings with flower boxes festooned with Christmas lights during the season, that together resemble a backdrop for a Grimm's fairy tale before sugar was added—much as I adore Disney's *Sleeping Beauty*.

Strasbourg is Alsace's capital and as the seat of the European Parliament, one of the most important cities on the continent. At Christmastime, there is no inkling of any bureaucratic drudgery. Come late November, the moment you step off the train, you are enveloped in the spirit of the season, the chilly wind, the smell of baking gingerbread and mulled wine, called *glühwein*, another holdover from Germany. A small market has been set up at the exit of the station, with stalls of roasted chestnuts, ornaments and baubles, cookies and information points for visitors. You can easily find a copy of one of the very readable maps of the ten different markets, which though separate, are clustered in the historic city centre.

The walk takes you along twisting cobbled streets, past the river Ill that drifts through town and Christmas tree displays. It all portends the approach of something unforgettable. Aromas waft with you along the banks: nougat candy, *glühwein* and *choucroute*—Alsace's signature dish, served with heaps of sausage, all year round.

Strasbourg Cathedral is one of Europe's most remarkable Gothic churches, whose tower can be seen on a clear day from the Black Forest in Germany right across the border.  During Christmastime, there is a notable crèche and lots of evening music at the church—organ and chorale concerts and caroling events—an argument for spending the night and seeing the festival as it is meant to be seen: twinkling in the winter darkness. The Marché de Noël surrounds the entire cathedral, and it's a bit otherworldly to do your shopping right beneath the 12th-century stained glass windows that were removed and stored in a salt mine during World War II.

Mostly, you browse and eat your way around all day; though all the markets have a different theme, they merge into one dazzlingly cinematic set-piece. Place Broglie is the oldest Christmas market in Strasbourg. You cannot escape *glühwein*; it runs thick and warm on every corner and in every market and comes dressed up for the holidays—red or white wine flavored with liqueur, berries, lemon, vanilla, or the traditional way with cider, cinnamon, orange and cloves.

The Alsatian small-producers food market is on Place des Meuniers and is stuffed with local honey, jam, cheese, *pain d'épices au gingembre*—a ginger cake—and French *lait de poule*—eggnog. Place d'Austerlitz, as well, has Christmas specialties from Alsatian tradespeople: wine from the Couronne d'Or, ornaments and other handiwork, foie gras, *choucroute*, traditional pretzels, Bredele Christmas biscuits, beer, and waffles. And endless, fragrant mounds of gingerbread men, cinnamon stars, chocolate-covered marshmallow cookies, chocolate-covered everything else, and Stollen cake.

Somewhere during the day or better yet at night, you will see the statuesque tree on the Place Kléber, Strasbourg's central square. Even if you don't believe in—or celebrate—Christmas, you may be inspired to believe in something when you sit, gripped by the vision of this skyscraper of an evergreen draped in blue and white lights. To me, it seems the very embodiment of the divine.

❧

# 55 The First Liberated Woman

## GEORGE SAND'S HOUSE, NOHANT

Novelist Edith Wharton's travel memoir, *A Motor-Flight Through France,* is as formidable as its author. The book, reissued in 2014, is a compendium of essays she wrote for the *Atlantic Monthly* on three automobile voyages taken in 1906 and 1907. Her observations integrate a scholar's breadth of knowledge with the elegant, incisive prose that is her trademark, as she and her traveling companions traverse blue hills and soft flowing rivers, noting the moods of light and landscape as they stop to admire, for the most part, the great cathedrals in France. The exception to this fascinating, often architecture-focused narrative occurs on two identical occasions: when she and her companions (which, on the second trip, included the writer Henry James) wind through the Loire Valley and the area known as Berry to Nohant, the home of George Sand.

On both pilgrimages, the encounter is emotional for her and gripping for the reader: to see the incomparable Edith Wharton humbled in the presence of greatness—female greatness no less, in the countryside home of the writer she admired and strove to understand. "Does a sight of Nohant deepen the mystery, or elucidate it?" writes Wharton. "—one can only answer, in the cautious speech of the New England casuist: *Both.*"

If you are in awe of either of these women, the image is overpowering. The author of *House of Mirth* peers behind the hedges and inside
the parlors of the author of *Mauprat, Valentine, Indiana* and *Lélia*—novels
of manners with a soothing style that reveals her acute understanding

of human character. Like any visitor, Wharton
is mystified at how the rural housewife Aurore
Dudevant became the great George Sand.
And as I did upon entering the pale brown
manor house shaded by trees, Wharton
attempted to conjure the rare air breathed on
the premises, from when Flaubert, Dumas,
Delacroix, Balzac, Liszt, Turgenev, and
Chopin—Sand's lover for nine years—escaped
here from Paris to relax and work in this idealized mini-château.

Today, the table is set in the dining room, complete with the
amber and pale blue stemware given to Sand by Chopin. In the
salon is his piano, and one imagines the after-dinner discourses
over brandy around the cherry table, carved from a fallen tree in
the yard. This is what Eugène Delacroix had to say about the summer of 1842, where he painted among the streams, thickets and
orchards in the place Sand christened the Black Valley:

> When not assembled together with the rest for dinner,
> breakfast, a game of billiards or a walk, you are in your room
> reading, or lounging on your sofa. Every moment there
> come in through the window open on the garden, gusts of
> music from Chopin, working away on one side, which min-
> gle with the song of nightingales and the scent of the roses.

That atmosphere, and certainly the scenery, does not appear to
have much changed at Nohant in the 138 years since Sand's death,
and the museum is an exceptionally well-maintained tribute to the

woman born Amantine-Lucile-Aurore Dupin. She spent much of her girlhood here, had her children, and often repaired to its comfort from the chaos of Paris, which she once said, "strains our nerves or kills us in the long run," and at seventy-one, died here. Until old age, she explored the countryside around her as she had as a child, taking daily eight-hour botanical walks and delighting in the scenery, mitigating the inconveniences of her aging self.

Sand's ascent to the literary pantheon is exceptional not only because of her prodigious output (including at least sixty novels, twenty-five works of nonfiction and seven plays), but because of the immense life she led, much of it right here in Nohant. None of Sand's books, besides her autobiography *Story of My Life,* are much read these days, so we remember her, unfairly, more for her legendary life—she dressed like a man, smoked cigars, had an open marriage and numerous love affairs, including, say some, with women, and of course, those friendships with the prodigious artists and minds of the day. She also had huge domestic cares, battled lifelong cycles of manic depression, and during the political upheavals of 1848 and 1871, tirelessly campaigned against corruption and for better conditions for the working classes. But as a writer, there is no greater inspiration.

Sand had aristocratic blood through her father, a great-great-grandson of King Augustus II of Poland. Her mother was the impoverished daughter of a bird merchant in Paris. She was born in 1804, the year Napoleon crowned himself Emperor, and after her father was killed in a riding accident, she was raised by her grandmother in Nohant, also spending time at a convent school in Paris. At seventeen, Sand inherited the house with its significant lands and the next year, married a provincial baron, Casimir Dudevant, with whom she had a son Maurice and daughter Solange.

But soon she began to feel the stirrings of restlessness and frustration, and stronger bouts of depression. This longing for something else would resonate throughout the body of her work, as she continually explored a woman's hunger for emotional expression and equality—sexual, financial and otherwise—and against what she explicitly named as a form of enslavement. "I was in the servitude of a given situation, from which it was not up to him to free me," she wrote about her husband and the need to pick up her pen, which thereafter, she never set down. "And then, in spite of myself, I felt that I was an artist, without ever having dreamed I could be one."

She moved to Paris, changed her name to George Sand, and embarked on her career at a moment that also saw the rise of other great Romantics—Victor Hugo, Dumas *fils* and Honoré de Balzac. In writing, and through the lens of her own desires, she found her voice and her freedom. "This emotion, which had slowly accumulated during the course of a lifetime of reflection, overflowed as soon as the vessel of a given situation opened to receive it," she wrote in *Story of My Life*.

Throughout her career, whose output astonished even other prolific writers ("How the devil did George manage?" wrote Colette. "I am completely staggered when I think of it."), she returned to her pastoral roots, both in her books and in her life. She found consolation tending her expansive garden here and was placated under pergolas and along the property's sunny lanes. "Mine is a practical life," she wrote. "I live in the trees, upon the heath, on the sand,—I lie in Nature's activity and in her repose." Sand's grave, set amidst those of her family in Nohant's little churchyard, rests in the shade of a giant, fragrant cedar.

❧

# 56

## Step into a Painting

### MONET'S GARDENS, GIVERNY

The conundrum of many of France's most beautiful places is that they reach the pinnacle of their glory during the summer tourist season. There are too many of us *voyageurs de passages*—short-term travelers—and too few days to spare for everything we wish to see. So the cleverest among us devise ways to block out the swarms of people and circumvent the shadow of tour buses. Such sleight-of-hand is surprisingly simple at Claude Monet's house and gardens at Giverny, which consists of two parts, the Flower Garden ("Clos Normand") and the Water Garden across the road, and it works any day during the seven months a year the garden is open.

Forego the big, organized tour and approach these gardens as a pilgrim would: on your own. It is about an hour's drive from Paris, or a short skip in a taxi from the train station at nearby Vernon. Arrive early in the morning, find an empty bench, sit silently, close your eyes, drink it in. This is how you submerge in Giverny's irresistible beauty and feel the presence of Monet's hand, from the walkways packed end to end with a dense profusion of flowers to the Japanese footbridge where water lilies—the Nymphéas—float and fade as they did in the artist's time and in his estimated 250 paintings of them.

"Spend a day, not an hour," says professional gardener, writer and photographer Elizabeth Murray, whose adherence to these principles of patience has brought her a rare familiarity with Giverny, which she illustrates in her book *Monet's Passion*. "You need to give yourself time to slow down and connect with the spirit of place here." There are few people more qualified than Murray to

dispense advice on a visit to this blooming haven of color, texture and light. When she first saw Giverny thirty years ago, she was so struck by the glory of the place that she found a way to drop everything, including her gardening position in Carmel, California, and relocate to Normandy to volunteer her horticulture skills. Though she has long since returned stateside, Murray will never really leave Giverny. She travels there each year in late spring or early fall to photograph Monet's gardens for annual publications, and greets familiar blossoms as old friends. "I love autumn at Giverny," she says about late September and early October when the eye travels upwards to gold sunflowers and crimson vines, while dahlia, aster, marigold and nasturtium flourish where summer blooms have vanished. "The shifts of color and scale that happen every season is how Monet planned it, which is absolutely remarkable."

Impressionism was the art movement that pulled imagery out of focus to let the eyes absorb the interaction of light and color, and Monet was its lord and master. In 1883, he and his family (including eight kids) settled in a farmhouse at Giverny, and for the next forty-three years, he proved himself as adept and prolific a gardener as he was a painter, creating a rotating palette of color and texture as other artists would assemble still lifes. The overall design in the Clos Normand was unified by a formal geometric structure anchored by the wide hoops of the central Grande Allée, topped by climbing roses.

Monet was a collector of Japanese prints, which was the inspiration behind the Water Garden. The pond was dug for the painter, and he commissioned the large bridge and the many smaller ones to provide a range of views over the water. He strolled each morning past the willow, bamboo and wisteria to paint the water lilies that bloomed all summer long. Monet created an elaborate orchestration of color, some monochromatic, some shot through with the scarlet of poppies, the neutralizing white of clematis, or the strong yellow of black-eyed Susans. The waves of purple in spring's irises and lupine give way to the pinks and mauves of peonies and above all, roses, hundreds and hundreds of which are shaped and draped throughout Giverny.

The quality of light was ever-changing, so Monet factored in Normandy's turbulent rains, mist and skies that quickly rotated from thick cloud cover to sharp sunlight and back again. As he did elsewhere, Monet snatched images and layered one on top of another in the final oil paintings. Like the haystacks or cathedrals, the water lilies and flower beds he painted during his years at Giverny are not mere renderings, but complex amalgams of memory and sensation—in other words, impressions rather than simple portraits.

It's good to keep that in mind when visiting Giverny, a place that deserves to be sipped, not gulped. Elizabeth Murray suggests an overnight in one of the many B&Bs in town and dinner at the rustically charming Hôtel Baudy. Her wisest advice on savoring Giverny is a good tip for whenever you want to absorb the spirit of a place. First, you have to put down your camera. "Find something that moves you and make a little drawing," she says. Whether it's a bench, a spray of climbing roses, or a leaf clinging to an arbor, you will find something to sketch at Giverny. Even if it's just an impression.

# 57 *Rock of Ages*

## LE MONT-SAINT-MICHEL, NORMANDY

 Mont-Saint-Michel inhabits its bay like a monarch occupies its throne. It is arrogant, aloof, arrestingly dignified. All a person can do is supplicate before it. When it comes into view floating in the sun or rising from a great sea of vapor, you can't help but see it in the context of the interplay between our own human strengths and weaknesses, an effect that sometimes occurs when confronted by works of sublime genius. Strength from the faith and gall to think man could—and did—build an abbey atop a sharp granite outcrop in an angry sea whipped by some of the strongest tides on earth, corralling all the knowledge in Christendom of stonemasonry, mathematics and engineering. As for frailty, where do I start? The briefness of even the most extraordinary lives, and how temporal we are compared to this stone edifice and the rock it stands on, the ocean it rises from, and the God it was built for.

The abbey might be just a lovely relic if not for the milky expanse of the bay in which it sits. Each can only be understood in relation to the other—the ocean's perilous strength against the architectural beauty and vice versa. For centuries, the faithful and the curious had to take caution and wait for low tide to venture across the sand to the Mont. The natural causeway was built in 1879, but even then, people continued to get swallowed by quicksand and swept away in the tides that change, in Victor Hugo's words, "at the speed of a galloping horse." Today, there are still dire warnings posted and the occasional rescue of someone with too little fear of the currents.

Mont-Saint-Michel is a two-pronged experience—from a distance as a vision and up close as a sojourn and climb up through the village to the abbey itself. In both cases, we are struck dumb in the presence of one of the wonders of the world. Seeing it is easy, to circle the periphery of the bay and watch the constant shift of light and shadow. The abbey can look opalescent and pink or swarthy and glowering, and its countenance can alter in minutes. Between Avranches and Granville is la Route des Champeaux; at the turn of the 20th century, someone called it "the most beautiful kilometer in France," and the moniker stuck. From this vantage point, the Mont looks confident in its realm, a fairy castle that rules the waves.

Inside the Mont, however, it is a different story. The village (and the road to the abbey) is tiny and close on the inside, and suffers from its own popularity. It took me two tries to get it right. The first was forgettable, even regrettable—a July day as hot as an oven. I went barefoot over the sand as the outline of the abbey came arrestingly into focus. I had been looking at it for hours beforehand, a mirage that shimmered in its watery perch. I saw the glint from Archangel Michael's wings atop the spire; it was in his honor that the bishop first constructed a sanctuary on the mount in A.D. 708. Pilgrims flocked here, and in the 10th century, Benedictine monks settled into the new abbey, whose foundation was laid, miraculously, on the apex of the rock.

It must have been a powerful sight back when it was an island. When I arrived and brushed the sand off my feet, there was no room for contemplation. There was no room for me; it was claustrophobically crowded on the narrow streets. There was little enlightenment to be found, only commemorative mugs. I made my way through clogs of people like me, making the 900-step trek to the top of the abbey. I felt faint from the heat, and restless. I couldn't wait to return to the mainland, to admire Mont-Saint-Michel's power again from afar.

That's how I loved it for twenty more years, when I passed through Normandy and happened by: a marvel in the sea, built by man, inspired by the divine—and best admired from a distance. Until I returned one winter evening.

A large construction project is underway (nearing completion) to relieve the silt buildup that was trashing the bay and obliterating the maritime setting that defined Mont-Saint-Michel for centuries. The pedestrian bridge to the foot of the Mont was not quite complete, and the weather was abysmal anyway, so a bus ferried me from a remote parking lot on the mainland during an icy, February rain. By the time I reached the hotel in the village, I was soaked through and shivering. My room was warm as toast, and I ran a steaming bath. The storm slammed against the lead windows and the sea below was charcoal gray. I loved it. I wanted to stay cozy but instead, I hiked to the church. Just the occasional phantom joined me on the trek uphill. There was no one there.

It was raw inside the cavernous halls and crypts, in the newer Gothic part, down below to the Romanesque foundation and through the Merveille, the three-story complex of chambers, crowned by the graceful cloister. The nave of the church has airy strength, and is a haunting sea green—from oxidation, perhaps. I loved the monk's refectory with its thin, tall windows, and the massive fireplaces in the Guests' Hall. I had not remembered the enormous 19th-century wheel, designed from the original that hoisted cores of granite in the Middle Ages.

I stopped at the West Terrace, where I looked down and saw the angry sea and clouds like waves of steel wool, Brittany to the west, Normandy to the east. I gazed up at the spire. There was Archangel Michael, brandishing his sword skyward, hip thrust to one side, looking dull in the mist. I walked in near solitude around the colonnades of the cloister, whose boxwood hedges seemed impossibly green. I strolled back down to town on the outside steps and turned back to see the Merveille. Two hundred thirty-five feet of sheer verticality and simple lines, walls thrown up in some fit of ancient genius. I ate dinner at La Mère Poulard, whose pricy omelet was nevertheless perfection. I had made my reservation that day. July undoubtedly was already booked up.

The rain had ended, the remaining clouds lapped the full moon. I descended the hill to see the abbey from sea level, blazing like a fireball. The delicate spire looked blue, and Michael was gold again. I walked back up to the church to take in those walls that seemed to spring straight up from the rock I stood on.

I was completely alone. The sound of my boots on the stone path resounded in the night. There was no crowd, the Breton biscuit stands and T-shirt shops, locked up. The air was frosty. "One looks back on it all as a picture; a symbol of unity; an assertion of God and Man, in a bolder, stronger, closer union than ever was expressed," wrote the American writer Henry Adams in 1905 about Mont-Saint-Michel. More than any other cathedral or abbey in France, I get a sense here of what fragile, earthly creatures we are, but also how optimistic, and how unstoppable. If ever I need reminding of the latter, I will make my way there again some rainy winter night.

⁂

# 58

## The Most Powerful Woman, Ever

### THE TRAIL OF ELEANOR OF AQUITAINE

Eight centuries before *Game of Thrones*, there was the life of Eleanor of Aquitaine, a gripping, eighty-two-year epic of love, power and loyalty whose likes had never been seen before and have not been duplicated since. She was queen of France, queen of England, the mother of two other kings, and had political instincts equal to or greater than those of the shrewd and ambitious men in her family. Driven in equal parts by love of her children and love of her country, she was a paradox: the ultimate proto-feminist and the ultimate super Mom. She traveled to Jerusalem on the Crusades, across the Pyrénées, through Italy, the Alps, and nearly every other corner of Europe on horseback, arranging marriages for her children, overseeing her armies, fortifying loyalties and alliances throughout her heroic life. Her legacy is truly vivid in France, where her footprints are scattered from the Louvre to Saint-Denis to Falaise, Poitiers and the abbey at Fontevraud. Whether you savor one small bite or devour the whole Eleanor buffet, these are sojourns to make and—if we have them—take our daughters. And why not bring the men too? It's time to give the lady her due.

"She was the most extraordinary woman in the most extraordinary times," says Sue Morris of Pittsburgh, whose background as psychotherapist and history-lover created a special affinity for

Eleanor's complex story. Morris first visited Fontevraud twenty-seven years ago, became further intrigued by her life through the historical novels of Sharon Kay Penman, and joined the author on a 2011 cultural pilgrimage retracing Eleanor's trail in France. "What I find most fascinating is her resilience and humanity," she says.

Until the last century, Eleanor was a vague figure of legend, a great medieval queen who had two husbands, was imprisoned by one of them, and ended her days in a convent. But history has also subjected her to the speculative rumor mill that sadly is the fate of many formidable women. If she was mentioned at all in the textbooks, it tended to be in either negative terms short on substantiation—a woman of loose morals, as a bare-breasted Amazon on horseback  at Vézelay when she recruited for the Second Crusade, the black force behind the death of her husband Henry II's mistress—or in frivolous ones—the patroness of troubadours who softened the masculine edges of the royal circle by introducing poetry, romance and the concept of courtly love. Katharine Hepburn won an Oscar playing Eleanor in the 1968 film *The Lion in Winter* and chewed up a lot of scenery with Peter O'Toole and Anthony Hopkins. But even in this case, the nearly sixty-year-old queen was portrayed as both schemer and scorned and the Plantagenet family as irredeemably dysfunctional. What did come through in the movie was Eleanor's maternal force and her vulnerability. She was a queen, but she was also a human being.

Further scholarship is doing away with some of these notions, but the facts alone are remarkable. She was the beautiful and well-educated Duchess of Aquitaine, a hugely wealthy feudal land, which made her one of the most desirable heiresses in Europe. When she married Prince Louis of France in 1137 in the Cathedral of Saint-André in Bordeaux, she gave him a rock crystal vase that today is at the Louvre, having arrived there via the Basilica Saint-Denis. The mere fact of it is nearly miraculous—it is the only artifact that we can assume was touched by Eleanor's hands. She was fifteen, he was seventeen, and a week after they were married, he became King Louis VII of France and she, his queen. He was said to be more of a monk than a monarch, so one can imagine Eleanor craved a bit of adventure when she accompanied her husband on the Second Crusade, following her ride to Vézelay to rally forces to ride with her to the Holy Land.

The king's close connections with the abbot at Saint-Denis, the basilica near Paris, rendered it a logical ceremonial point of departure when, in 1147, they took the cross and set forth for Jerusalem. However, while on the unsuccessful crusade, the couple reached an impasse, which led to the dissolution of their marriage, despite their two daughters. Though Louis was clever, he was dull, and the lively young woman from Aquitaine met her match in Henry Plantagenet, whom she married in 1153.

A year later, the couple was crowned King Henry II and Queen Eleanor of England at Westminster Abbey. Eleanor bore Henry five sons and three daughters, and during the first two decades, she split time between England and her court at Poitiers, which at the time was the seat of Aquitaine (it is now Bordeaux). You can visit the great Palace of Justice and see Eleanor's immense ballroom, where she presided over lavish banquets in what must have been the height of style. The Saint-Pierre Cathedral in Poitiers, built by Henry and Eleanor, contains one of only two confirmed likenesses from her lifetime, a stained glass portrait that was commissioned by Eleanor and Henry of the couple and on either side, four of their children. They celebrated Christmas Court (the high social season) together in 1159 at Falaise in Normandy, a magnificent fortress stronghold built on the site of the birthplace of William the Conqueror, and today the palace pays tribute to her.

In 1173, Eleanor led a rebellion with her three surviving sons against the king. Perhaps she was fed up with Henry's infidelity; more likely it was an expression of her own political will, particularly her wish to share rule with her third son Richard (The Lionhearted) in Aquitaine, rather than with her husband. Henry quelled the revolt, arrested his fifty-year-old wife, and she remained imprisoned in England for fifteen years, though it more resembled a house arrest, where she was transported to different castles from time to time, but still only free when the king said so.

And then, upon Henry's death and Richard's ascension to the English throne, she rose again. The dowager queen defended the kingdom while he was away on the Third Crusade (and imprisoned by the Holy Roman Emperor), even against her machinating youngest son John, who had been Henry's favorite. "We can learn a lot about perseverance and hope from Eleanor," says Sue Morris. "She started a full second life after seventeen years in prison." And she rode until the end of her days, even in her early eighties, seeking wise political matches for her children and grandchildren.

By then, she was already installed at the convent at Fontevraud. It is believed she had a hand in designing her *gisant*—the tomb effigy that bears her likeness—and here is where the story of Eleanor ends with a breathtaking statement. Usually the tomb of a queen shows her in sweet repose, the bible laid peacefully upon her chest. Eleanor, however, is actively reading her prayer book. Alive, for eternity.

᚛

# 59 Who Was Madame de Sévigné?

## CHÂTEAU DE GRIGNAN, DRÔME

The sun-washed town of Grignan has changed little for centuries. But its name is starting to surface on the lips of two types of people: those for whom summer traffic in Provence holds diminishing charms, or those who tend to be ahead of the curve when it comes to unheralded havens of sweet French enchantment. Grignan, an hour north of Avignon, springs out of the olive groves and truffle oaks of the Drôme Provençale. Like a gorgeous woman who is unaffected by—or as yet unaware of—her beauty, it has many secret admirers. "I'm obsessed with Grignan," says Katherine Johnstone, the Attaché de Presse of the New York-based French Tourist Office who, incidentally, is a woman of exemplary style and taste. "It has become one of my favorite small towns to escape to in France."

The village is not so much unique as it is a perfect allegory for something we know only because we think we do. It is southern France, distilled. Slender streets lined with jumbles of ivy, clematis, climbing roses. Honeyed summer air by night at a café at the Place de La Fontaine, with floodlights that flicker softly on the foliage of plane trees. Grignan has effortless purity that refuses to call attention to itself. You know to expect lavender fields, and when you do, it is still revelatory and unforeseen. But something else makes Grignan soar above countless other achingly luminous places. This looker has substance, too, and her name is Madame de Sévigné.

She spent several years here, on and off, with her beloved daughter who married into the local aristocracy. The celebrated writings of Madame de Sévigné are forever entwined with Château de Grignan, whose lacy, blinding-white countenance dominates all from atop a high, steep hill overlooking town and, it seems, the whole European continent.

You could say that the crag itself is the pedestal that exalts Madame de Sévigné to the lofty position she deserves. One is hard-pressed to exaggerate her importance both to the country's literary heritage and its history. Madame de Sévigné was a prolific writer of letters. That's France—where the extraordinary rises from the ordinary, and out of that flowers genius. She and her 1,372 known letters—which when edited into an anthology make a total page-turner—continue to fascinate because of the near effortlessness with which she observes, documents and chronicles without parsing. She is like the most skilled reporter—invested but divested, free of judgment but wise to human folly, especially her own. She gets her material everywhere, from the corridors of imperial power to her son's bedroom, and uses all the tools of the natural born storyteller to force us to listen. In an adulatory essay, Virginia Woolf called her "one of the great mistresses in the art of speech."

Marie de' Rabutin-Chantal was born in Paris in 1626 on what is now the Place des Vosges. Superbly educated and sufficiently wealthy, she married a Breton nobleman, Marquis Henri de Sévigné. Six years later he was killed in a duel over another woman, leaving his twenty-five-year-old wife with two children, Françoise-Marguerite and Charles. She chose not to marry again, but was courted, fêted and admired for her intelligence and depth of knowledge, which distinguished her among society women.

Because of her birth, education and beauty, Madame de Sévigné was entrenched in aristocratic circles and the court of Louis XIV. She was a star of Paris's first-ever literary salon, held at the mansion of Madame de Rambouillet, where the city's greatest intellects and scholars mingled with the glittering social élite and where she legitimately straddled both worlds. She was a frequent guest at Versailles and was close friends with the woman who became Madame de Maintenon, the Sun King's second wife and queen.

With few newspapers at the time, her breezy but insightful letters addressed to some of the leading *personages* of the day, also her close friends, were passed around and made public. Centuries before blogging popularized off-the-cuff commentary, she wrote in one draft, knowing her gossip, news and opinions would be widely distributed, discussed, even debated. Taken together, they are a crucial historical document of 17th-century France. Her meticulously reported letters during the trial of the king's finance minister, her friend Nicholas Fouquet (see chapter 74), to one of her contemporaries reads like high courtroom drama. She took the further daring step of showing sympathy to the accused man in his legal battle against the crown.

In 1669, her daughter—known as "the most beautiful girl in France"—married the Comte de Grignan, a two-time widower. In 1671, she moved with her husband back to his home in the Drôme, and the separation was a crushing blow to her mother, though it proved to be the catalyst for Madame to start writing in earnest. For the next twenty-five years, she wrote impassioned letters as easily as she breathed, from wherever she was—her home in the Marais (now the Musée Carnavalet), or the Château des Rochers in Brittany, the Sévigné ancestral home.

Her letters to her daughter, published in part twenty-nine years after Madame de Sévigné's death, reveal more than just facility with language, but a tortured and irrational maternal love. "I am obsessed by your absence and can't get it out of my mind," she writes in every conceivable iteration. Virginia Woolf called it "a passion that was twisted and morbid," and when her daughter recoils, we see the disappointment of a mother who cannot give love in any measured dose, and requires that degree of love in return. As always, Sévigné pulls back from self-pity and returns, chastened by her own emotion, to society gossip or dispensing grandmotherly advice—all with chatty self-deprecation and incisiveness.

"Meanwhile, jollifications go on at Versailles," she writes, from personal knowledge.

"Everybody thinks that the King is no longer in love," she states.

"His little gee-gee stopped short at Lerida," she relates with howling amusement of her son's performance mishap in the sack with one of his mistresses. "In vain I assure him that the empire of love is full of tragic stories."

It is hard to know how Madame Sévigné spent her three long stays at Grignan, as there are marked gaps in her life story coinciding with these visits, each of which lasted between fourteen months and two years (she died and was buried there in 1696). One can only imagine how difficult it was to leave the sophistication of Paris she loved for the provinces, not to mention the six-hundred mile cross-country voyage over barely passable roads. But no reason to pity her. Yes, it was the 17th century, but when you come upon the town in early August, as she first did, and see the château aloft between the lavender and the outline of Mont Ventoux, it is a heavenly sight. And my kingdom for a night at Hôtel le Clair de la Plume, or a plate of foie gras with figs in Katherine Johnstone's favorite restaurant, Le Poème de Grignan. And the next morning, I would climb the hill to the château, look through bleached sunshine over the Drôme, sit down and write someone a letter. The kind with pen and paper.

❧

# 60 *Forty-Four Children*

## MEMORIAL MUSEUM OF THE
## CHILDREN OF IZIEU, IZIEU

Izieu is barely an hour from the center of Lyon but there is no train there, no bus or organized tour. So I hired a taxi. The driver followed the course of the Rhône due east to where it meets up with the Ain River, not far from the Alps. The countryside grew more idyllic as we drove further from Lyon, and when we veered off the highway, it was full-blown explosion of spring. It was early April, and white puffs of apple blossoms dotted the fresh, green hills on which farmhouses perched and cows grazed. When I arrived at the Maison d'Izieu, there was a clear view of the Chartreuse Mountains. A person can feel very safe here, buttressed against the uncertainties of the world.

It was a perfect day like this, full of springtime promise and the scent of new grass, when two German officers and a gang of Wehrmacht soldiers drove this same route from Nazi headquarters in Lyon on April 6, 1944. The regional Gestapo head, Klaus Barbie, had learned of forty-four Jewish children aged four to seventeen sheltered in plain sight by nine adults in Izieu east of Lyon, and ordered their seizure and arrest. As they sat down to morning hot chocolate, two trucks and a car drew up in front of the house. The Gestapo burst into the home and forcibly removed all forty-four children and seven adults, throwing them onto the trucks "like sacks of potatoes," said a witness. Within minutes, they were on their way to Lyon's fortress Montluc Prison. And within days, all but three were en route to the transit site at Drancy outside of Paris and shortly, sent to their immediate deaths at Auschwitz. Two older boys and a supervisor were sent to a labor camp in Estonia, where they were executed by firing squad. One of the teachers, Léa Feldblum, had impeccably forged papers that identified her as Marie-Louise Decoste. Once at Drancy, she revealed her true identity as a Jew and insisted on being deported with the children to Auschwitz, though the Gestapo offered her freedom. She would not abandon them.

The crime perpetrated against the Children of Izieu is one of the most inconceivable tragedies in an era defined by inconceivable tragedy. Today, it stands as a symbol of senseless and ruthless Nazi brutality. It has been said that old buildings are only worth keeping for the testimonies they carry. Here in Izieu, the stone farmhouse has the great responsibility to bear solemn witness to violence against innocence as well as to preserve the memories of those who lived here. This is what is so devastating and unusual about the museum and the farmhouse in its bucolic, unchanged setting. The spirits of the children and those who cared for them are alive and soaring at Maison d'Izieu.

The children had arrived in Izieu under the protection of Sabine and Miron Zlatin, two Jewish refugees who had fled Poland at the outbreak of the war. Sabine was a Red Cross nurse living in the southern city of Montpellier, and when she lost her job under anti-Semitic laws, she became involved in the Oeuvre de Secours aux Enfants (OSE), a humanitarian group dedicated to child welfare. The OSE promoted the rescue of Jewish children, assisting those interned with their families in domestic camps or setting up homes for those whom Zlatin helped escape or whose release she helped secure. When the situation became increasingly dire in early 1943, she went to the Italian zone east of Lyon towards the Alps where Jews were not hunted down. The deputy prefect of the town of Belley, in full support of her mission, found her a roomy 19th-century farmhouse in nearby Izieu where she set up the home for refugee children. She initially had 15 children with her, and over the next year, 105 (mostly Jewish) children were to be sheltered at the home. Some were brought directly by their parents, others came from clandestine children's homes, while still others, left alone when their parents were deported (until July 1942, children were spared the death camps), were brought to Izieu by hidden networks.

The children led idyllic lives, eating delicious meals, swimming in the Rhône, collecting drinking water from the huge fountain out front. Some of the older children even earned a little money working on neighboring farms. Classrooms were set up for lessons. Here you can see their artwork, as normal as can be—drawings of pirates, cowboys and Indians, Puss in Boots, and a cartoon strip depicting high drama on the Tartar steppes.

Photographs illustrating their carefree life provide particularly profound anguish, as do the letters on display. "Dear Maman," writes Georgy Halpern, seven. "I'm having fun here and I'm well. The war will be soon over and I will come back to you and we will go to Vienna and we will be together again." They write of walks in the fine weather, that they need more pants and socks, that they are eating well—soup, fromage blanc, pain au chocolat, bread and jam. You can feel their heartbeats, hear their voices, feel their hope and anxiety. A series of photographs taken by a neighbor days before the round-up show a group of kids laughing against a glorious mountain backdrop. The pastoral setting allowed them to live what turned out to be their last days in safety, beauty and peace.

That security was destroyed in the raid of April 6, 1944, when they were rounded up, imprisoned and sent to death. Sabine Zlatin was away in Montpellier, gaining support for her efforts, when she heard the news. One adult, Léon Reifman, escaped from a second-story window. Léa Feldblum, who had refused to leave the children, was released from Auschwitz when it was liberated in 1945. All of them lived to testify against Klaus Barbie, the "Butcher of Lyon," at his 1987 trial for crimes against humanity. "I loved them very much. The tiniest ones cried," said Feldblum, who was sixty-five when Barbie was finally extradited to France (through the efforts of Serge and Beate Klarsfeld) after hiding out in Bolivia for many years, and finally brought to justice in a Lyon courtroom. "The others sang.... They burned all of them."

Here in Izieu it's difficult not to imagine the violence on the morning their lives were about to be taken. But you can also picture the children running through a field of spring flowers, past grazing cows, on a morning as sleepy and pristine as this one.

❧

# 61

## The Most Beautiful Lines

### STATUE OF THE POET LOUISE LABÉ, LYON

On the Place Louis Pradel—right by the Hôtel de Ville and Opéra de Lyon, blown by the unrelenting winds off the Rhône—you can celebrate two great French cultural heroes in the statue of Louise Labé by Jean-Robert Ipoustéguy. The protagonist, the feminist Renaissance poet Labé, is honored by her city in a highly expressive sculpture that is figurative in most ways, with a touch of the surreal. But even before you go to Lyon, before you sort out your restaurant itinerary or reserve your boat ride on the Saône or the Rhône, order Labé's book of poetry and prose—there are several translations available. Savor them or devour them, but for a woman and a visitor to Lyon, it is essential, emboldening reading, both for her timeless insight into male/female conventions and exquisite grasp of the agony of love.

She has remained largely obscure, but is the kind of poet that poets themselves admire, a figure from the distant past who is startlingly contemporary. "Though sorely underrecognized, Louise Labé's poems contain some of the most trenchant explorations of Eros ever written by a woman," says my friend, the poet Kirstin Hotelling Zona, associate professor of English at Illinois State University and editor of the *Spoon River Poetry Review*. "Like Sappho before her and Emily Dickinson after, Labé was fundamentally a disciple of desire, drawn inexorably to the thrum of the almost-there, the delicious torment of anticipation. Labé's poetry, especially the Sonnets, are as relevant today as they were 500 years ago, affirming as they do the vitality of vulnerability and a brave capaciousness of heart."

One can imagine the courage it required to negotiate the landscape between the sexes in 16th-century Lyon. The dedication of her book, *Oeuvres*, published in 1555, is a letter to a fellow Lyonnaise noblewoman Clémence de Bourges, and is nothing short of a manifesto exhorting women to seek the equality with men that is their due, to set aside their weaving and to start writing.

Labé was a well-educated daughter of a wealthy rope maker, and eventually the wife of one as well, which is why she is also known as La Belle Cordière—the Beautiful Rope Maker.  Lyon was at the cultural nexus between France and Italy in the 1500s, and she became a dominant figure in the humanistic circles at the time. But like many famous women in history who aren't around to defend their posthumous reputations, lots of ink has been spilled on who this 16th-century poet may have been. She was a cross dresser, an Amazon jouster. She was a courtesan. In 2006, a scholar at the Sorbonne offered the shattering thesis that Labé didn't even exist and that her poems were written by a bunch of Renaissance pranksters. Men, of course.

I prefer to tune out the noise and trust that Louise Labé was Louise Labé, a woman of—and ahead of—her time. How fitting that Ipoustéguy's sculpture is poetic as well as humanistic, much like his subject, and like her work, filled with notions that went against the grain. His use of imagery and the figure defied the trends of abstraction and minimalism of his day.

Often compared to Giacometti, Ipoustéguy was considered France's premier sculptor during the '60s and the heir to Rodin. Backed up by winning a prize at the Venice Biennial in 1964, he was prolific in gallery and museum exhibitions but also one of few artists making large-scale figurative public sculpture in marble and bronze, which had gone out of vogue. He even proclaimed, in very melodramatic French style, that he would "crack Brancusi's egg"— meaning that he would stem the Modernist tide and bring texture to the surface, drama to the form and narrative to the sculpture. He had a unique interpretation of sculpture and shunned the overintellectualized notions of his time, always sticking to the basics that drove great art: passion and universality.

By the time Ipoustéguy was commissioned for his tribute to Labé, he was in his early '60s, a sculptor's prime. But he had been slowed by time, momentum and personal tragedy. Once a regular in art history surveys, he would be all but invisible save for a few public pieces, such as his 1985 tribute to the poet Arthur Rimbaud in Paris's Bastille. He had undergone a stylistic transition, moving to a more planar way of forming figures, using layers and sheets of bronze.

The artist defies the hearsay and presents Labé as unquestionably a woman, and a heroic one at that, left foot suspended while the right is placed squarely on the ground. His sculpture was installed on the esplanade in 1982 and speaks of a relationship between two kindred souls separated by centuries but not in spirit. This is the pure love of Pygmalion and Galatea. An idealized woman on a pedestal, nearly immortalized, almost realized.

Here in Lyon, they make a beautiful pair.

# 62

## Where the Poor Were Loved

### HOSPICES DE BEAUNE, BEAUNE

Descending into the two-acre cellars of Joseph Drouhin, one of the finest and most prolific wine producers in Burgundy, I entered the veins and arteries of the city of Beaune, and they course with wine. In this palatial cave, where some 30,000 bottles are stored, there are Greco-Roman walls from the 4th century and a 15th-century trapdoor leading up to the residence of the Dukes of Burgundy, who in their golden age of treachery and might, sported names like John the Fearless, Charles the Bold and Philip the Good—the latter of whose troops turned Joan of Arc over to the English to be burned at the stake. These were powerful men, and they cared about their wine, so much so that Philip the Bold outlawed the cultivation of the gamay grape (which he deemed a "very bad and disloyal plant"), and made pinot noir the exclusive grape of Burgundy.

Unlike Bordeaux, the other great wine metropolis of France, which sprawls regally across wide boulevards and the Garonne River, Beaune exists in the tight enclosure of its medieval ramparts. There is a hint of mystery and glamour in  this small city, and I sensed the presence of a foreign agent or an Interpol detective at a café on the Place de la Halle or got a little giddy imagining I did. It's that kind of place: *film noir,* shadowy and old world. Sexy.

Beyond the nexus of wine and power in this city is God and charity, nowhere more than at the Hôtel-Dieu, also known as the Hospices de Beaune, a former hospital for the poor and the city's central landmark. How had I missed this in all my years in France?

I will forever be atoning for this slight to one of the most wondrous and unusual places in the country. Elizabeth Stribling, the founder of the eponymous Manhattan real estate brokerage firm, chairman of the French Heritage Society and part-time resident of France, was the first of many women to point me here, and I'm grateful she did. "The building is extraordinary," she tells me, "and its history even more so."

It was easy to miss the building on market day, as the exterior blends in rather too perfectly with the *tartiflette* vendors and columns of honey and warm bread that are spread out over the narrow streets and square. But once inside, the courtyard chants its own medieval glory. I was rapt by the sight of the richly gabled roof, covered with multicolored glazed tiles of gold, green, red and brown. Slim dormer windows pitch up sharply and are crested with detailed lead ornamentation. It's a festival of texture—stone, timber and slate—and the style was so popular it was copied throughout Burgundy in later years.

This "Palace of the Poor" was built as a charity hospital in 1443 by the Duke's Chancellor, Nicolas Rolin, who was the second most wealthy and influential man in Burgundy at the time, and one of Europe's most important diplomats. After the Hundred Years' War, Beaune was stricken with famine and disease, and nine-tenths of its citizens were in extreme poverty. Moved by such widespread misery, Rolin and his noble-born third wife Guigone de Salins decided to build the Hôtel-Dieu, funding the project with revenue from her family's salt mines. The Duke was sufficiently impressed to give the foundation that built the hospital tax-exempt status; thus began the Hospices de Beaune's mission to care for the area's orphans and its sick and impoverished citizens.

It was staffed by Sisters of the Hospices de Beaune, but by 1459, the charter was changed so that the nurses no longer were affiliated with any religious order. Still, they had to be pious and unmarried (although they were always free to leave). As caregivers, Rolin and his wife stipulated, in one of many moves considered progressive at the time, they also had to be treated well.

The couple hired some of the greatest artisans from Beaune and indeed all of Europe to build the hospital, but as austere as the exterior is, the interior is warm and inviting. Most impressive is the Salle des Pôvres (The Room of the Poor), 164 feet long with 52-foot ceilings, whose side walls are each lined with 14 beds, made up with crisp white linen and sumptuously draped in dense scarlet fabric. The paneled, vaulted ceiling is festooned with colorful dragons, whose teeth support the brightly painted crossbeams. The effect of this room is overwhelming, down to the floor tiles with Rolin's monogram and his wife's family name, and I can imagine the kindly nurses looking over their charges from behind the sick bed curtains, for privacy.

There are nine other chapels and rooms from later years in the building, a kitchen with a dual-hearth Gothic fireplace, stacked up with copper pans; there's also a pharmacy with mortars and pestles and a suppository mold with cocoa butter for lubrication. The drug dispensary contains glass apothecary bottles with faded labels containing an obscure slew of powders and remedies, from licorice to marshmallow plant to white fruit fungus to eyes of crayfish. At the entrance to the Saint Louis room is a rare Flemish polyptych, "The Last Judgement," commissioned by Chancellor Rolin, who is portrayed kneeling with his wife in prayer, followed by a set of 14th-century tapestries depicting parables from the Bible.

The most enduring story of the Hôtel-Dieu is revealed at the end of the tour, and once I learned about it, it began to resonate throughout my visit to Burgundy. Over the years, many vineyard owners have donated portions of their land to the Hospices de Beaune, which now maintains almost 150 acres of prime vines. Every year, on the third Sunday of November, the barrels of juice or very young wines from these vineyards are auctioned off to raise funds for the Hospices de Beaune. As part of a three-day celebration of the food and wine of Burgundy, it is the largest charity auction (since 2005, in collaboration with Christie's) in the world.

When I visited Drouhin, I was shown their Hospices de Beaune wine, and the *cave* at my chic guesthouse, La Maison Blanche, had several bottles as well. They are exclusive, expensive, quite desirable and very glamorous. If you trace the lines, they all begin and end within the walls of the city. The dukes, the power, the hospital, the wine, the philanthropy and the maze of cellars all unified eternally as the heritage and foundation of Beaune.

❧

# 63

## The First City of Chocolate

### BAYONNE, PAYS BASQUE

At Eastertime in Bayonne, chocolatiers burnish their creative credentials and spin the usual tropes of springtime bunnies, ducks and speckled eggs into awe-inducing displays of artistry behind their shops' windows. You will not see one of those stock rabbits in profile, and rarely is anything disguised behind gold foil wrapping. Instead the creatures are given mischief and personality, affixed with slivered almond buckteeth, coffee bean googly eyes, or caught in the act of stealing a carrot from a garden. This, plus the flavors, the crunches, pinches of spice, or soupçons of sea salt that will jolt you from chocolate ennui, both milk and dark.

Bayonne straddles the banks of the Nive and Adour Rivers, and in France, it is the cocoa bean's symbolic fountainhead. It is also the beginning and end of your chocolate odyssey, because this is where the story started in France and continues evolving today. It is a town of virtuosos, some old and many new, always innovating, yet grounded by tradition and geography in creating the one comfort on earth none among us could or should live without.

First the bad news: Chocolate arrived in Europe and then France at a considerable human cost. In Mexico, the conquistador Hernán Cortés saw the economic value of the drink the Aztecs called *xocolatl*, which energized Emperor Montezuma's troops for battle (and Montezuma for his harem). While annihilating the local population, Cortés also appropriated their cacao plantations, and in 1524 the first beans arrived in Spain. Soon the addition of sugar, vanilla and cinnamon rendered sweetness and flavor to the brew that had been considered medicinal. As Cortés conquered Mexico, so chocolate conquered the old continent, and Spain was Europe's center of production. Liquid chocolate made its way to France through royal marriage, as both Louis XIII and Louis XIV wed Spanish princesses. In Spain, the trade was run chiefly by Sephardic Jews, who were forced to flee for Portugal during the Inquisition. Again, they were swiftly pursued before finding refuge in the Saint-Esprit quarter of Bayonne, where they brought the tools and know-how of the cocoa trade to France. This story is artfully told in the Musée Basque in the Petit Bayonne quarter of the city, as is the next not-so-noble chapter. In 1761, an ordinance created by Catholic chocolatiers forbade Jews from working in any capacity in the industry—the industry they had themselves created. The parliament of Bordeaux annulled this decree in 1767, and by 1854, there were thirty-four chocolate makers in Bayonne.

If you are like me and have no willpower, I suggest taking two days to trace Bayonne's artisanal chocolate trail—otherwise the sugar and caffeine will turn the experience in your head from pleasing haze to jackhammer. Nor do you need a car—every one of these places has an outpost in Bayonne—but my little rented Citroën served me well, if only to begin at Puyodebat and its chocolate museum in the town of Cambo-les-Bains, about a half-hour inland. This Basque village was another stronghold of the trade, and young *maître chocolatier* Christophe Puyodebat thrives on local tradition. He has amassed a collection of old machines used to process the cocoa butter from the bean, antique labels and tin boxes, tools such as dipping forks and spreading knives, chocolate pots and china cups with mustache guards. He also runs a school, where you can create your own chocolates out of just about anything—light, dark, Spanish almonds, puffed rice, coffee, rum, raspberry—whatever you crave or nothing at all. From the shop, I procure a bag of praline ganache squares coated with dark chocolate and crispy *crêpes dentelles*. I snatch a bag of *fèves de cacao*, bean-shaped nuggets made with chocolate from the Dominican Republic. Lastly, I am handed a chocolate (and instructed to suck, not chew) spiked with espelette, the local pepper that almost imperceptibly heats up my mouth.

Next stop is on the outskirts of Bayonne to L'Atelier du Chocolat, where owner Serge Andrieu has his own entirely different museum and keeps headquarters for forty boutiques scattered throughout France. Here you see the gritty, labor- and time-intensive process of how cacao beans are cultivated and harvested from the colorful pod grown in the tropics, then soaked, fermented, dried, milled, crushed, liquefied and sweetened. There's also a display of vintage hand-operated mills, roasters, de-skinners and an 18th-century stone bean grinder.

Along the way, I sample some of the *grands crus* from their various origins—creamy Ecuadorian, bracing Venezuelan, and the slightly acidic one from Madagascar that feels like true, dark chocolate. I sample banana ganache, a square with a hint of prune and Armagnac, chocolate Florentine with caramel and toasted almonds, and the sweetest little Easter squirrel filled with hazelnut cream. Serge breaks hefty shards off big, scrolling plaques of every conceivable milk,  dark and white chocolate topped with dried fruit, caramelized nuts or flavored with lemon or sesame, and he loads them into a paper cone to make one of his signature *bouquets de chocolat*.

Nearly comatose, I am also deliriously happy. This could be due to high levels of mood-boosting serotonin, which is triggered by tryptophan in chocolate. I have one more stop today right in Bayonne at Chocolat Pascal, created by Pascal Moustirats. I sample his lighter-than-air ganache in his super modern shop that is hung with bright orange acrylic lamps. The hot chocolate served with a heap of whipped cream is perfection—sweet enough, thick enough—and I drink it outside on Quai Galuperie with a view of the impossibly slim houses that embellish the already perfect charm of the scenery.

On my second morning, I go directly to the rue du Port-Neuf, the rich chocolate center of this rich chocolate city. First stop is Daranatz, a mirrored 19th-century emporium graced with crystal chandeliers and lined in deep red carpet. From the street, it could be an exclusive Belle Époque parfumerie, and indeed, it has been on the same spot since 1890. Here, I buy bars of chocolate in plain, brightly colored paper, so chic I want to rest them on my mantle at home like minimalist artwork—candied ginger and dark chocolate in a deep violet wrapper, a bar of 88 percent African cacao called "Forestero" wrapped in fuchsia, and my favorite—dark chocolate with cocoa nibs in a deep brown wrapper.

Next stop is Pariès, another old-timer, started in 1904. I buy a box of *kanougas*, creamy chocolate caramels flavored with hazelnut, vanilla or coffee. Here I also develop a new obsession: the *mouchou* (Basque for "kiss"), a biggish macaron that is both sturdy and delicate, at once denser and chewier than the more familiar ones you see all over France. I get twelve of them in a very pretty illustrated box.

The last stop in the *tour de chocolat* is later that afternoon at the oldest house in Bayonne, the venerable Cazenave, pretty as an 1854 picture—the year it was founded. Here at the café behind the chocolate shop, I get—*everyone* gets, and has for centuries—*chocolat mousseux*, hot chocolate that is thick as molten frosting, topped with a header of foam, flavored with vanilla or cinnamon, served with a bowl of whipped cream, two thick slices of buttered toast and a pitcher of water. Cazenave is old-school in more ways than the lace tablecloths and silver trays on which your drink arrives. The house still grinds its own beans from South and Central America and creates its chocolate powder by hand (practically) in its own atelier.

Cazenave is a fitting end to a few days in Bayonne. If dark chocolate is full of antioxidant flavanols, *mousseux* is in a whole other category. It has almost the density of yogurt, is as hot as bisque, mouthy as custard. And when I stir in puffs of cream, and swallow sip by luscious sip, I need no more convincing: if chocolate is a superfood, this is the super-est of all.

❧

# 64 Queen for a While

## THE FRENCH GENERAL GETAWAY, MIDI-PYRÉNÉES

Grand stone manses by the thousands grace the countryside all over France, and their noble bearings linger for years, sometimes centuries, after the families who built them have gone to that great cotillion in the sky. I am forever drawn to châteaux, from the disheveled hillside beauties long past their glory days to the eternally radiant ones such as Chambord or Chantilly. *Sleeping Beauty* fantasies aside, who among us has not wondered what it would be like to actually *live* in a castle, even a very small one? Would I pad around in cashmere slippers? Could I still buy Pringles and eat them?

There are so few dukes to go around these days, and fortunately you don't have to marry one to take up residency in a château. Many hundreds of former estates have been converted to hotels or fancy chambres d'hôtes, some with 18th-century manicured gardens where you can sip your Kir Royale like a proper aristocrat. Also, the web abounds with all manner of spiritual retreats that take place amidst the sturdy bones of châteaux—meditation, yoga and wellness escapes—eased into efficacy by the venue's metaphoric backdrop. But for the sheer, immersive joy of it, one workshop retreat in the rich countryside of the Midi-Pyrénées stands alone.

Eleven years ago, Kaari Meng packed up her legendary Manhattan millinery shop French General and moved it and her family to Los Angeles. Her taste, reflected in the store as well as her many books, is singular as are her methods, which involve sweeping across France's flea markets and *vide-greniers* to buy discarded bits and pieces of treasure. With her distinctive eye, she collects French fabric, textiles, vintage ribbons and paper, buttons, tassels, jewels and all kinds of wondrous notions. And what's more, she can assemble them masterfully. Kaari does not craft with glue sticks and plastic flowers, but rather combines traditional techniques with an aesthetic that is utterly chic and French to the core.

Eight years ago, after a few steamy L.A. summers, she had an epiphany. "I needed to spend some time in a château," Kaari says. That June, she loaded up herself, her mother, a small team including her sister (also an artisan), twenty women and trunks full of supplies and headed for the sunflower fields and rippling hills near Toulouse. And so, the French General Getaway workshop was launched at the 14th-century Château Dumas.

The idea is simple: for women to spend a few weeks embracing a lifestyle that allows them to peek into the region's cultural heritage. They visit local farmers and flea markets, meet traditional artisans, and back at the château, eat delicious meals from local ingredients prepared by the chef. They visit a lavender plantation, a master weaver, and a mohair goat farm. Each day the women get busy in workshops and create original art atop crafting tables draped with antique linen, integrating vintage materials picked up locally that morning, for a song. Over the course of the retreat, they learn weaving, jewelry making, paper marbling, hand-lettering, and book binding. "Not everyone is a crafter or a paper or textile enthusiast," says Kaari. "But we all share the love of the hunt, and we all love to make beautiful things."

All the women anticipate the workshop with Denise Lambert, who has revived the ancient technique of woad, or pastel, dying that originated here near Toulouse, whereby the leaves of the yellow-flowered plant are crushed to make a brilliant dye—the famous French blue. The women buy lace, table runners, nightgowns and satin ribbons at the flea markets to dip into the woad vat. "It's a magical day," says Kaari. "We turn everything thirteen shades of blue."

What seems so effortless is the result of Kaari's careful planning, leading the women to balance the gentle pace of life in provincial France with the gratification of accomplishment at the end of a long day. "We create together, we eat together, we drink wine in the evenings outside together," says Meleen Dupré, a two-time attendee. "We're always busy but never exhausted. I still don't understand how Kaari does it."

Let's not forget that this all unfolds at a twenty-two-acre private estate in the sleepy green hills of Tarn-et-Garonne. With a large swimming pool, panoramic views, dramatically punctuated by the green spikes of cypress trees. In a château. A gloriously renovated, 700-year-old stone dwelling that, for a little while, you can call home.

❧

# 65 The Greatest Flea on Earth

## BRADERIE DE LILLE, LILLE

Some of the best European flea markets and antique fairs are in Belgium. So it stands to reason that the biggest, the pre-eminent, the *sans pareil* mecca for collectors and browsers in France takes place in Lille, the graceful former capital of Flanders, a short skip from the Belgian border. I've always wanted to use the word "brobdingnagian," and I've finally found the perfect context in the Braderie de Lille. It is massive, mind-blowing, a French Mardi Gras and thousand-ring circus served up with unbelievable bargains, God knows how many bottles of Stella Artois and mountains of *moules-frites*. Five hundred tons of mussels and easily that many *pommes frites* are consumed each year at the Braderie, which takes place the first weekend in September. Rather than throw out the dark gray mussel shells, Lille restaurateurs pile them up outside on the sidewalk in an informal competition, leaving the city full of makeshift glossy towers that resemble hills of anthracite coal you'd see outside a mine.

The Braderie is visited by roughly two million people each year—no one knows for sure how many, and really what's the difference when you are talking about such swarms of humanity? They travel in for the day on the speedy Eurostar from London, on the train from Paris, and more broadly from all around the planet that late-summer weekend to hunt for deals, surprises, or just that longed-for set of ruby glass tumblers. I'm not saying that everyone will love the Braderie. Whether you do or don't, though, it is unforgettable, especially when you leave with the perfect little treasure.

I didn't think I was much for the carnivalesque cluster—umm... *jam*—either. I love to browse for antiques in France, but usually prefer the saner outdoor *brocantes* that one can stumble upon weekend mornings. Where does this stuff come from, and how does it wind up on tables and stalls at markets that take place nearly every weekend, in nearly every town in France? I'll never know, but it is one of the indisputably great characteristics of this country and one I never tire of appreciating. My house is full, truthfully too full, of picture frames and tart pans and Bakelite-handled pie servers that inexplicably caught my eye some morning. Once on a reporting trip to Toulouse, it was the first weekend of the month, when the huge flea market unfolds along the allées Jules Guesde. Behold, I had a lovely set of blonde boxwood chemist's bottles.

At Éspace Mosson in beautiful Mediterranean Montpellier, I bought a few dozen mismatched linen cocktail napkins, one embroidered with a trio of olives, another with a straw hat. I am committed to ironing them by hand for life. And then there are the *vide-greniers*—hit or miss yard sales on any city street, where you can plow through crates of vintage key rings or find a claw-foot soap dish for one euro. I picked up an old porcelain yogurt pot for a song and now keep my makeup brushes in it. I love it, but even more I love the memory of wandering that Sunday in Cannes, of how this perfect vessel found me in the crowd. And similarly, I love the industrial chrome lampshade that hangs in my kitchen, which I carried back on the train from Lille, then all the way home to Connecticut.

The Braderie de Lille dates back to the 12th century, but it really got going in the 1500s, when domestics were granted permission to sell household items discarded by their employers. The event gathered steam, and today, there are sixty-two miles of vendors throughout the city and its environs. The event kicks off with a half-marathon on Saturday morning, and the selling begins when the last runner has finished the race around 2 P.M. (though you are allowed to peruse the goods before then). Then it's thirty-three hours of non-stop Braderie-mania. Ten thousand vendors line the streets of Lille—luxury antique dealers, lower key sellers with good-quality *brocante*, and purveyors of new ethnic clothing and artwork. The Lille Tourist Office now has an app, but off the bat, I would recommend you make haste on Saturday for the Façade de l'Esplanade, along the Canal de la Deûle for the best finds—dishes, silver, linen, copper pots, décor, furniture, costume jewelry, perfume bottles—anything—where you will find that pearl you had no idea you were looking for. The cobblestone streets of Old Lille and rue de la Clef are packed, of course, but strollworthy for the elegant stalls and picture of old-Europe perfection. Or, you can skip Saturday entirely and come instead for the Sunday morning market in Wazemmes, which absorbs the celebration and is hyped-up and extra festive.

But do bring something home, even if it is just a Ricard shot glass or a fifty-cent antique postcard to tack on your wall. Carry cash in small bills, and if you love something, buy it on the spot (after bargaining, of course), because if you wander off to think about it, it won't be there when you return. Merchandise moves fast when people are on the hunt for good deals and that, too, is a tradition in Lille.

❧

# 66 *Clear Water*

## SNORKEL ON THE ÎLES D'OR, PROVENCE

I am partial to islands and sunny ones most of all. It is my long-standing belief that they are actually good for us, to risk the ground beneath us and feel our extrahuman buoyancy. But there are islands and then, there are the Îles d'Or, just off the coast of Hyères, about thirty miles south of Saint Tropez. Here, you could imagine being in the most intimate spot in the Caribbean or the Indian Ocean, with the significant advantage being that you are in France. But from another time, without snackbars or schlock shops, only the fragrance of Aleppo pine, eucalyptus and island lavender.

Everything here reinforces the intangible allure of an island where, floating in splendid isolation on sand and water, a person is almost weightless. A burden of any kind is anathema to an island's airy, watery grace, which is why we sometimes call them paradise. On Porquerolles, I love the sensation of lightness and of having almost no barrier, physical or otherwise, between the jade shallows and me, of being both protected and unfettered. On the Plage Notre Dame, I go from sand as white and fine as talcum powder to a dip in the warm sea and back again, effortlessly, all day. I'll wade in and slip on my flippers, mask and snorkel, then shoot off into the water to knock around the coves to explore the circus of submarine life. There are bright orange sea tomatoes, spiny scorpionfish, two different wrasse fish, one with glossy stripes, the other a psychedelic sky blue, olive green and rust. I see a grouper as big as a lap dog, butter-colored anemone, and radiant purple sea slugs crawling about the reefs. I feel lithe and nimble.

When I emerge, the songs of cicadas and native pheasants mix with the citrusy scent of Macrocarpa cypress and flowering strawberry trees—the arbutus. Here, everything feels airborne, waterborne. Even time. I came here at 19 and again thirty years later, and the only difference is that now I am diligent about sunscreen. The sun on your back is the sun on your back, as eternal a sensation as a cool drink in summer. This is why snorkeling is good for our species. It erases the years.

Porquerolles is a short boat ride from La Tour Fondue in Hyères and the other two islands—Port-Cros and Île du Levant—from Port St. Pierre. Because *naturism*—nudity—on Île du Levant is de rigueur, even required, I will skip that one here, it not being my thing...although if it is yours, there is no prettier place to sunbathe in the altogether.

In 1912, François-Joseph Fournier, a Belgian who owed his great wealth to gold and silver mines in Mexico, bought Porquerolles as a wedding present for his third wife. I know, it beats a waffle iron. He planted 500 acres of still-thriving vineyards and thousands of trees, but the stretches of sand beside the immaculate water were already there, as were a string of ancient forts, a windmill and the legacy of brigands who hid their booty in an underground cave beneath one of the island's *calanques*.

Snorkeling here is casual, and because Porquerolles and Port-Cros are part of a National Park, they are protected marine and wildlife preserves. Port-Cros is a desert island—no vehicles of any kind, and an easy water taxi from Porquerolles. It too has its colorful history of pirates, convicts and centuries of conflict, but now it's an idyll draped in honey-scented myrtle trees and green oaks. Several shipwrecks rest in the waters of the Îles d'Or, and in the Bay of

Port-Cros, divers can explore the remains of *The Whale*, one of Louis
XIV's ships that went down in 1710. But I prefer to skim the water at
the speed of a fish, popping briefly below the surface.

The snorkeling trail off Port-Cros is one of the marvels of the
Côte d'Azur. Plage la Palud is a forty-five-minute walk from the

port, past overgrown flax-leaf broom, tree
heath and wild olive trees. And it's isolated:
there are no equipment rentals; you must
carry snorkeling gear with you. The under-
water nature trail will take you through virgin
seascape, handily marked by buoys describing
the area's marine life—the fragile great purple
gorgonian coral, that can appear neon blue or electric red. Sea
sponges, crimson cardinal fish, the noble pen shell—the giant saltwater clam—that sticks straight up from the sea floor, and sweeping
meadows of Neptune grass.

Parenthetically, the home offices of Port-Cros National Park
are in Hyères, at the former villa belonging to Edith Wharton,
one of many illustrious writers who settled there. Hyères, long an
object of obsession for the cultural and political elite, is the sun-
swept unRiviera, the cut flower capital of France, a city of narcissus
and viola, orange orchards, and lemon groves. One of the jewels
in Hyères's crown of flowers is Wharton's Castle Sainte-Claire,
where she wintered from 1927 to her death at 1937—France was her
home; she had abandoned America forever. This most American of
women planted the most exotic of gardens—70,000 square feet of
subtropical species, such as yucca, lantana, aloe, salvia and bird of
paradise. I wonder if she ever ran across Mr. Fournier or his wife,
invited them to tea on their way to their island utopia, maybe to
chat about their latest horticultural projects. I wonder, too, if she
loved to paddle around the clear pool of a cove with the sun on her
back. I like to think she did.

# 67 *Picasso, with a Bonus*

## MUSÉE PICASSO AND GERMAINE RICHIER, ANTIBES

Pablo Picasso cut a spectacular path through the Riviera, parts of which still gleam with the memory of his unrivaled greatness. By the time he died in 1973 at his villa in Mougins, five miles inland from Cannes, Picasso had lived in Provence for nearly three decades after relocating semipermanently from Paris, where he moved from his native Spain in 1904. The Côte d'Azur, with its mimosa blossoms, olive groves and sun-drenched hills, was closer geographically and perhaps spiritually to his mother country, from which he had been in exile after his stance against the fascist dictator Francisco Franco.

Picasso fell under the Riviera's spell on his first visit to Avignon in 1912 (his masterpiece *Les Demoiselles d'Avignon*, painted in 1907, refers to a street with the same name in Barcelona), and he visited frequently during the 1920s and 1930s. In 1945, already in his sixties, with Paris liberated but hardly recovered from the war, he began to voyage there more regularly. Always restless, he passed through Ménerbes, where he had bought a home for his former lover Dora Maar, and Golfe-Juan, where he bunked at a friend's villa. He spent time in Arles, Aix-en-Provence, Cannes, Vallauris and Antibes, the latter two of which have dedicated Picasso museums, as of course, does Paris.

The Musée Picasso in Antibes sits ablaze in white-hot sunlight on the edge of the Mediterranean, housed in a 17th-century château with ramparts that plunge right into the rocks below. The time he spent there in the autumn of 1946 represents a tiny but pivotal sliver in the artist's life. As is frequently the case with Picasso, it was buoyed by energy from a new muse and love, the painter Françoise Gilot, whom he had met three years earlier in occupied Paris.

In her 1964 memoir *Life with Picasso,* Gilot writes of her first visit to what was then known as Château Grimaldi in Antibes. "You're going to swear here that you love me forever," she recalls him saying, and she duly obeyed, though Gilot would leave him in 1953. But her presence in Antibes was vital to the sense of regeneration as a man and as an artist that Picasso felt during his stay. While there, she learned she was pregnant, and her son, Claude, was born the following May.

The château was at the time a struggling museum of Napoleon-era collectibles, and Picasso had coincidentally tried to buy the building two decades earlier. In 1946, with plenty of empty space to fill, the curator agreed to let Picasso use the second floor as his atelier. Still as prolific as he had been in his youth, Picasso began painting with astonishing vigor and excitement, on—and with—any of the scarce materials available in postwar Antibes: plywood, fiber cement panels, boat paint and Ripolin—cheap, and ready-mixed. When he left the château in late November (when its name was officially changed to the Musée Picasso), he donated twenty-three paintings and forty-four drawings from his stay there and later, an extraordinary collection of unique ceramics he made in nearby Vallauris, in which Françoise's curvaceous body is often transformed into pots that evoke an ancient heritage. The museum, filled with the work Picasso made there and soon after, represents an almost perfect time capsule.

The Antibes period shows a palpable sense of renewal, marked by a profound visual response to the light, atmosphere and rituals of the Mediterranean setting (sea urchins, fish, fisherman); it's also bursting with ardor for Françoise, the woman with whom he would share the next years. It is most masterfully embodied in *Joie de Vivre (1946)*, the largest painting in the collection. "This conveys Picasso's joy after World War II at being on the shores of the Mediterranean, in the company of Gilot," says Marilyn McCully, leading Picasso specialist who has most recently written about his visits to the Côte d'Azur in the 1920s and 1930s. "The mixture of her presence—the dancing nymph in the center—and creatures drawn from mythology who dance around her in the composition clearly demonstrates how Picasso brought personal and ancient associations together in his work."

Outside on the Museum's terrace, the lapis watery backdrop makes an ideal setting for the sculptures of Germaine Richier, which evoke both the antiquity associated with the Mediterranean region and the modern that Picasso so boldly represents indoors. Given his unfortunate reputation with women, chronicled so forcefully by Gilot herself, it's a bit of karmic irony to have these bronzes here, standing tall above the water like sentries. Even more delicious to have them immortalized by Graham Greene, who lived in Antibes for twenty-five years—the confluence of art, literature and history that is a matter of course on the Côte d'Azur. "Gusts of rain blew along the ramparts, and the emaciated statues on the terrace of the Château Grimaldi dripped with wet," he writes in the opening lines of *Chagrin in Three Parts*, "and there was a sound absent during the flat blue days of summer, the continual rustle below the ramparts of the small surf."

Germaine Richier, born in 1902, came of age in the arts at a time when they were affected, scarred and molded by the devastation of two world wars. She was also of a generation where the artistic talents of women such as Camille Claudel were largely ignored and sculpture still presented itself mostly in figures that were heroic, macho renderings of the permanence of man.

As a sculptural apprentice, she learned techniques but also a way of thinking that would lead to her own unique style and interpretations of the figure, which evolved with world events. Like Claudel, she stood alone among her early peers of mostly men, such as the surrealists Giacometti and Max Ernst.

As sculptural figures metamorphosed alongside the horrific events of the mid 20th century, Richier stepped up the changes in her own work creating hybrids—part human, part man, part woman, part animal—as well as figures depicting action and events. She died in 1959 while setting up an exhibition at the Musée Picasso; the pieces here are both the largest in scale and biggest grouping of her work. They embody a time where a heroic self-perception of man (and woman) has been marred and questioned by the horrible deeds perpetrated in World War II. They portray Mankind as a reduced vulnerable hybrid shell—here, in front of a deep blue Mediterranean background. Nothing is more French: existential questioning, violent history, in front of a beautiful cultivated setting, on the ramparts of a onetime fortress, outside of a former atelier where love, life and creation took hold.

❧

# 68

## The Dreamscape of Genius

### DÉSERT DE RETZ, CHAMBOURCY

One September day in 1786, the painter Maria Cosway accompanied Thomas Jefferson, the U.S. Ambassador to France, on an outing to the Désert de Retz, an estate about fifteen miles west from the center of Paris. It was well-known at the time and at the height of its glory. Marie Antoinette was a frequent visitor, perusing botanical books in the library and drawing inspiration for the pastoral village she would build at Versailles. The Désert's wealthy owner, designer and architect François Racine de Monville, was a generally remarkable man who was also an accomplished musician (flute and harp), athlete, archer, epicurean and popular figure in Parisian society.

Jefferson and Cosway arrived in their carriage to this landscape fantasy, a neverland of mysterious follies, ruins and curious buildings representing different cultures of the world. Upon entering, they would have had to duck under a man-made rock entrance. It was a sort of initiation, designed for the visitor to pass through the darkness of the boulder and leave the world they came from before arriving at the light—and enlightenment—of the Désert.

There were lakes, glowing meadows on which elm, linden, beech and chestnut trees swayed, greenhouses, orchards, a working farm and an orangery with citrus, oleander and jasmine. Winding pathways with unforeseen surprises around each turn added drama to the terrain. Montville created all of it—conceived it, designed every building, imported every tree, ordered every plant, most of them exotic and all of them looted during the Revolution, after Monville sold the Désert and the grand vision it represented in 1792 (he was imprisoned during the Revolution, but was spared the guillotine and died of infection in 1797).

In Jefferson's time, as now, the Désert de Retz was not some ho-hum rich man's vanity project. It was the flowering of a bizarre, bold imagination. *"What the heck was he thinking?"* you ask in stunned silence upon seeing the insane brilliance of the Broken Column, the centerpiece of the Désert, the master's residence. The house was constructed as a false ruin, with deliberate cracks and fissures, shaped like a Doric column that was truncated or chopped off. It stands four stories high, with windows recessed in the flutes, and suggests the Tower of Babel while integrating the symbolism of the Freemasons, which was considered throughout the Désert in its many pyramids and triangles. Inside the Column, a clever arrangement of oval rooms surrounds a spiral staircase rising up to a skylight ceiling, one of the features that is said to have most delighted Jefferson.

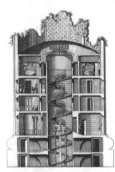

The Broken Column, surely one of the most imaginative buildings ever constructed, is also pure genius. It is the visual touchstone through which you first and most powerfully experience the enchantment of the Désert, a place infused with just enough spookiness to feel like a landscape you might drift through alone in a dream.

Perhaps Monville in his time was not so much an enigma as he is today. He left few writings, produced no heirs, and though he was friendly with all the great artists of the day, no portrait or other likeness of him is known to exist. But if the Désert de Retz is his only legacy, it is a brilliant one and singles his as one of the quintessential minds of the Enlightenment, when ideals based on science, reason and intellectual progress swept away a worldview based on faith and tradition.

The *jardin pittoresque*—picturesque garden—movement started in England in the early 18th century, and for those with resources and land, it became the rage in Europe. Monville's aim was to create an Anglo-Chinese garden, which are characterized by studiously informal, rather than formal, landscaping studded with architectural follies or *fabriques*. There were seventeen follies in the Désert de Retz, representing different civilizations—an Egyptian obelisk and pyramid that was the property's ice house, the Tartar Tent on the Island of Happiness, the Temple of Pan representing ancient Greece, and a teakwood Chinese House, now lost, which was Monville's residence before the Broken Column was complete. He built all of them, except the 14th-century Gothic church, representing Christianity, already a ruin when he purchased the property.

Today when you arrive at the Désert de Retz, you cross over into his once-exuberant realm. Until recently, time had run a little roughshod on Monville's triumph, the layers of age creating a second masterpiece. As the follies and grounds fell into disrepair, they became increasingly draped in greenery—ivy, moss and foliage gone wild. Nature had taken over in its own thrilling and untamed way, causing Monville's false ruins to become actual ones. Sporadic efforts at restoration prevented the estate from going entirely to seed, and today, it remains the best-preserved example of an 18th-century folly garden in France.

Only a few of the follies are still standing, and even that is fortunate—it was almost razed for a housing development. Here, you are swept by the calm of the landscape, the rustle of foliage and soft curtains of ivy; all you see are birds and the gorgeous trees around you. What's awe-inspiring and yet also tragic is how untouched the grounds are since the 18th century. In engravings from the period, they appear virtually identical. Fortunately, the property was bought by the city of Chambourcy in 2007 (for the token sum of one euro), and there is a master plan underway to fully restore and rebuild the Désert de Retz according to Monville's original design.

Colette, one of many writers and artists inspired over the years by the decaying folly garden, marveled at the crumbling, overgrown remains. "The abundance at Retz is that of a dream, a fairy tale, an imaginary island," she wrote. This remains the essence of Monville's magical domain.

❧

# 69

## The Walls Are Alive with Color

SAINT PIERRE CHAPEL, VILLEFRANCHE-
SUR-MER AND VILLA SANTO SOSPIR,
SAINT-JEAN-CAP-FERRAT

The Hotel Welcome sits at the edge of the curved amphitheater of
pastel buildings that rim the Port de la Santé in Villefranche-sur-
Mer. The young and stylish manager, Catherine Galbois-Sigwalt,
whose family has owned this low-key but elegant corner of heaven
since 1943, shows me to my quarters, Room 22, the most famous
in the house. This is where, from 1925-1926, Jean Cocteau hun-
kered down for a year-long opium bender and phase of artistic
introspection. He had mentored a brilliant young writer, Raymond
Radiguet, who, following a trip to Africa together, caught typhoid
and died at age twenty. Cocteau was inconsolable, and the Welcome
was his refuge.

Room 22 is a serene palette of pale blues and grays, and there
is a puddle of afternoon sunlight on the floor. I bring my bottle of
Badoit and a hunk of *fougasse à la fleur d'oranger*, a Provençal bread perfumed with orange water, to the trellised balcony that overlooks the
sea and Saint Pierre Chapel. This small church inspired Cocteau
to return to Villefranche frequently, and in 1956 he created a masterpiece there, one of several he gave to the Côte d'Azur, where he
was drawn so often throughout his life.

I thought I'd be consorting with ghosts of Rolling Stones past in Villefranche, where the band famously recorded *Exile on Main Street* at  Keith Richards's tax haven villa, Nellecôte, in the summer of 1971. But it's Cocteau who has left the deepest imprint here. It's hard to convey the magnitude of his acclaim in France and also to describe who and what he really was artistically, besides everything. He was a giant of the 20th century, a provocateur in art, literature, and film. Cocteau never seemed to stop working, crossing over disciplines, garnering the respect, and often collaboration, of the cool friends he made along the way: Marcel Proust, Igor Stravinsky, Sergei Diaghilev and Nijinsky from the Ballets Russes, Edith Piaf, Marlene Dietrich. He lived near his pal Colette overlooking the Palais-Royal gardens in Paris and attended bullfights in Nîmes and Arles with Pablo Picasso. The *New Yorker* correspondent Janet Flanner reviewed Cocteau's 1946 ballet *La Mort de l'Homme* in June 1946 and wrote about its creator: "The passage of time seems neither to wither nor even to interrupt the hothouse ripeness of his talent."

He wrote twenty-three books of poetry, five novels including *Les Enfants Terribles*, directed eleven films, at least three of which—*Orpheus*, the original *Beauty and the Beast*, and *The Blood of a Poet*—are classics of French avant-garde cinema. He wrote plays, screenplays, memoirs, did set design and ballet scenarios. He battled a recurrent drug addiction, about which he wrote a startling illustrated memoir: *Opium, the Diary of His Cure*, and when he went to rehab, Coco Chanel paid the bill.

As a visual artist he was equally, if not more prolific, creating paintings, drawings and portraits, the latter of which are instantly recognizable for their simplicity and refinement, using a minimum of lines to convey the waves in a subject's hair or surprise in an eyebrow. The largest collection of his work is ensconced in the 29,000 square foot seaside Musée Cocteau that opened in 2011 in Menton, the city that borders Italy and is known for its citrus orchards and mimosas. In that city's municipal marriage hall, the Salle des Mariages, he painted another triumphant homage to the Côte d'Azur, a mural of a couple under a big Provençal sun.

It took seven years of bureaucratic red tape to gain permission to decorate Saint Pierre, the 14th-century chapel that had enchanted him for decades and which he feared, as a storage place for fishing nets, would be destroyed by neglect. The Villefranche fishermen also opposed the project until Cocteau arranged to donate the entrance fee to their local fund. He succeeded at last, and was able to complete his work there in 1957 at the age of sixty-eight.

With all that resistance, he had to make it brilliant and he did. It's a wondrous achievement, with figures, watchful eyes, and delicate shapes covering every bit of wall space. The renderings are a mélange of biblical, figurative and decorative scenes that incorporate the quais, stairways, and medieval fortress of Villefranche as a backdrop. The simple but evocative drawings are colored with the washed ochre, blues, yellows and pinks of the seaside village. One panel is of local women bearing baskets of fish and sea urchins before bright waves under a swarm of faceless angels. On the ceiling too, figures float with the airy strength of Cocteau's uncomplicated lines. There are depictions of the life of Saint Peter, a servant handing him to Roman guards after the renunciation, and the rooster crowing; when he walks on water, the fishermen gawk and the fish leap in awe. All the scenes are crowned by flights of angels, in homage to the Baie des Anges in Nice. There is nothing to do but stare in reverence.

Villa Santo Sospir in Cap Ferrat is another story. Here, the joy practically jumps off the walls. In the spring of 1950, Cocteau was introduced to heiress Francine Weisweiller, one of the wealthiest and most stylish women in Paris. She was instantly besotted with Cocteau, and so began an intense period of friendship and patronage. Soon, she invited him to Santo Sospir, her flowering enclave that was one of the loveliest seaside villas in Cap Ferrat, which was a gift from her husband, Alex, who spent most of his time elsewhere with his mistress. Cocteau arrived for what was to be a few days, and wound up staying there on and off for twelve years while he completed other commissions, including St. Pierre Chapel.

The house was already a temple of sky-high but quirky Parisian style—think opium den meets tony beach cottage—but Cocteau was distressed by the sad white walls in such a riot of eclectic design, so he set to work. Francine was a devotee of the Parisian decorator Madeline Castaing, whose touches are everywhere from furniture and walls fashioned out of reeds to leopard print carpets all around the house. There is just enough whimsy to stay sophisticated, with fanciful accents throughout—a chair whose wooden frame is carved with lilies of the valley, a ceramic roast chicken and, most of all, Cocteau's drawings.

In Santo Sospir, there were no constraints to his creative genius, no fishermen to assuage or religion to pay deference to, so he let the muses fly. He painted with abandon—"tattooed" the place, he said—and the walls are a triumph of his signature line drawings, some of which have words attached in his tidy penmanship, giving the appearance of animated stories. The drawings are partially based on the Greek mythology that had obsessed him for so much of his career. Over the mantelpiece, Apollo glares with his hair fanned towards two hulking priests of the sun, who both wear the typical fishing berets of Villefranche. The Mediterranean, just outside the villa, was his other source of inspiration, and there are bright suns, the echo of a perched village and a simple fisherman's lunch. There are gods, satyrs, unicorns and in Francine's room, the story of the goddess Diana changing Actaeon into a stag when he happened upon her bathing.

The longtime caretaker, Eric, shows visitors around the house, filled with photographs of Francine, her daughter Carole, Picasso and other illustrious guests, who were served gin cocktails prepared from the mirrored bar cabinet still stocked with Angostura bitters and Aperol. He tells me that Cocteau was very inspired by two other artists who had painted their ways across the Côte d'Azur, Matisse and Picasso, and his drawings offered the occasional homage. The vignette of the fisherman's meal is of sea urchins and *fougasse*, which Cocteau coined "Picasso's hands" after a photograph by Robert Doisneau where the artist sits against a table set with fat doughy fingers of the cherished local bread. Picasso may have been a more categorizable genius, but Cocteau's mark is equally indelible in the south of France.

꒰꒱

# 70 The Salt Water Cure

## THALASSOTHERAPY, SAINT MALO

The practice of treating illnesses with seawater dates back to Roman times, when hot saltwater baths were prescribed for arthritis, tuberculosis and a host of other maladies. But it took a Frenchman to coin the phrase that is now part of the language, one Dr. La Bonnardière, a physician practicing in Arcachon. In 1865, he presented his clinical findings on the efficacy of what he called "thalassotherapy," from the Greek words *thalassa* (sea) and *therapeia* (healing), which extolled the benefits of the seaside as a holistic environment in the treatment of disease. In other words, not just the salt water but seaweed, sand and the climate by the shore.

These days, a thalassotherapy cure is not merely for medical reasons or to improve circulation, eliminate toxins, or increase muscle capacity—all of which are some of its proven benefits. In my case, I sought to soothe the demon stress, the beast that lurks at the root of so many afflictions.

Thalassotherapy spas line the coast from Biarritz and La Baule on the Atlantic up around to the northern shores of France. For my escapade, I went to Les Thermes Marins in Saint Malo on the English Channel, a town that occupies a point of land to the far east of Brittany just across from Britain. It's not compulsory to be a guest of the hotel, an expansion of an historic *belle époque* resort that seems to float above the beach, but I was, and so I delighted in riding the elevators in a clean white robe and slippers to the spa. Short on time, as always, I opted for à la carte treatments rather than one of the packages, of which there are many including some for *la jeune maman,* which offer a beautifully-appointed nursery with a cheerful minder who will watch and entertain your baby as you are soothed by the waters into postpartum well-being. Also, I declined the meeting with a physician, three of whom are on staff. No, I just wanted to see and feel the miracles the seawater could perform.

I was a rapid convert. Water from the bay is pumped into the spa, then heated, but undergoes no other process before being pumped back into the sea. There are over 2,500 species of algae in the waters off Saint Malo, and in one spa treatment, your body is ladled with gobs of thick green paste, wrapped and then hosed off. This must be what people mean when they say they feel like a goddess, when your skin is reinvented and supple and lightly scented from the sea. I loved the fog room, where you breathe briny mist, or the standing pool with 100 jets that give a powerful massage, even on the soles of your feet. The highlight of my hydrotherapy was a session in a bathtub of warmed sea water, scented with lavender and mint oils, with sprays of still warmer water focused on whatever parts of my body were most tired or sore. There are 80 treatment rooms in this spa, but I was meticulously attended to by my hydrotherapist at all times. Oh, and there was the food pyramid poster, suggesting one or two glasses of wine per day and a higher intake of pastries than red meat, for optimum health. The FDA would quake.

What really convinced me that this was someplace I'd like to return to with a passel of friends was Saint Malo itself. It has a colorful past of *corsaires*—pirates—who buckled their swash throughout the 17th and 18th centuries, amassing riches for the French kings as well as themselves and built lovely mansions outside of town.

It was one of France's busiest ports and, as such, was a perennial target for invaders. That's lucky for us because of all the handsome fortifications that were built to fend them off, all of which give the landscape of Saint Malo the aspect of an enormous sand castle.

I can recall no walk more ethereal than the one I took along the beach at sunrise in Saint Malo, following in the footsteps of the Grand Dukes of Russia, who holidayed at the hotel that is now Les Thermes. I descended from the esplanade to the sand in the direction of the walled city and tidal island where Fort National rises in a frothy expanse of water. I clambered across the rocks to the base of the fort, but it was too early to see the famous dungeons within. Beyond that was the tidal island, Grand Bé, smashed by rough waves for centuries, also only accessible at low tide. The grave of Saint Malo's famous local son, the writer and diplomat François-René Châteaubriand, lies gray and alone on Grand Bé. I found it rather humble, and the philosopher Jean-Paul Sartre did too—*too* humble. In her autobiography *The Prime of Life*, Simone de Beauvoir, the great feminist writer and Sartre's wife, relates that on a visit to Saint Malo, her husband found the tomb's fake simplicity so pompous, "that Sartre urinated on it as a mark of his contempt."

Within the granite citadel is a jumble of winding streets, fine little shops, and on the rue Jacques Cartier (a celebrated *corsaire*), a collection of crêperies, one after the other, impossible to choose. You can see it all and the vastness of the Channel from the wide promenade atop the ramparts, which this early in the morning is full of mostly solitary walkers. On the route back I marveled at the statuesque turreted villas with their cornices, bartisans and parapets, taller than they are wide, clad with dark slate roofs. I had to wonder: why don't I live here? And headed back to Les Thermes for another session in the womb of a warm, salty bath.

❧

# 71 *Remember the Fallen*

## BEACHES AND MEMORIALS OF
## THE BATTLE OF NORMANDY, NORMANDY

If you are inclined, as I was, to send "the boys" up to visit the historical areas of the Battle of Normandy while you hang back in Paris or Deauville, consider this gentle plea from someone who made (and regrets) this mistake. You really ought to go, too. War cemeteries are not just about men who sacrificed their lives on the bat-tlefield. They are about women: mothers, daughters, sisters and wives left behind. We imagine their grief as if it were our own, and humanize the remains beneath the crosses, transform them into our son, father, brother or husband. All of them died for something bigger than we can fathom seventy years later, and here we honor them, as well as the people who loved them.

There are thirty-nine official museums and commemorative sites, five landing beaches, and twenty-seven cemeteries in this slice of land that extends from Cherbourg to Dieppe, but you don't need an extended stay to visit and do so respectfully. Last time I passed through, it took just a little more than a day to revisit some of the highlights.

There is no other way to convey this. It is a very solemn journey. Wars have been fought for millennia all over this land we now know as France, and its history consists of one land grab and one occupying force after another. Romans, Visigoths, Saracens, Flemish have all had a foothold here, and Normandy, whose rugged shores were exposed and vulnerable to Viking and English invaders, has borne even more than its share of violence. The Nazis moved into France in 1940 and were well-installed in Normandy by 1944, when the Allies were ready to take it and the rest of the continent back by storm. "Operation Overlord" launched on D-Day, with one of the most ambitious amphibious assaults in the history of warfare: backed by 5,000 ships and 13,000 aircraft, over 150,000 troops—mostly American, British and Canadian—landed on a 60 mile stretch of Normandy coastline over 24 hours, starting in darkness on the morning of June 6, 1944.

Everyone will have her own personal and surely inexpressible reaction when confronted with the jarringly recent history here, whose tragedy, glory and sense of loss we share with France. Even for introverts, who may prefer to mourn or contemplate or pray in private, I recommend an organized trip, rather than winging it with a map. The guides are experienced and used to the emotions aroused here and have the discretion not to hustle or hassle you. In fact, it's important to have moments of solitude in which to visualize, absorb and process all you are seeing, and the guides understand this.

If you do go the adventurous route, a car is key. Either way, most people base themselves in Bayeux or Caen, which is where I met my guide Claire Lesourd. We drove my car along the N13 and exited at Formigny, where the last battle of the Hundred Years' War was fought in 1450. Our first stop was at Pointe du Hoq, where three companies of the 2nd Ranger Battalion landed that morning in seas so rough, many troops, with their 80-pound packs, drowned on the 200-foot walk to shore. They were sent in to remove six German cannons positioned there that might do serious damage to the Allied troops landing elsewhere. Because of weather and strong tides, their planned meet-up with another Ranger division was scrapped, and as they landed on the narrow beach they were fish in a barrel. They rigged ladders to scale the 100-foot cliffs to the German garrison. Within 24 hours, they had held off five counterattacks, but out of the 225 men who landed, only 90 survived. You walk through bomb craters lined with rocks and tufts of grass; yellow gorse and genet flowers seem incandescent in the flinty light. Claire is an encyclopedia, and answers questions if I ask them when we descend to the German command post.

We then drove along Omaha—one of the five landing beaches, which the Allies hoped to unify into one large beachhead—aside the stone village of Saint-Laurent-sur-Mer. I imagined townspeople rushing in every direction and soldiers from both sides concealing themselves among the hedgerows. On the wide sands of Omaha Beach there is nothing to do but stand silently and be moved. Its expanse is so vast and extends so far that at low tide, the water's edge disappears right into the sky. The battle here over a six-mile stretch was the hardest-fought and most costly of the war. In under an hour, 2,000 men of the 16th Regiment of the 1st Infantry Division and 116th Regiment of the 29th Infantry Division and two Battalions of U.S. Rangers were wounded or slaughtered.

What strikes me, and everyone I know who has walked on one of the landing beaches or through the ocean of crosses at a graveyard for the fallen, is the raw natural beauty of this place. Rain falls frequently and hard, as it did on D-Day, and the wind blows in gales one minute and gentle puffs the next. There is a hard shine to the sun when it emerges, that gives a silver sheen to the Channel waters and turns the vegetation electric acid green. It's an exercise in the limits of the human imagination to picture the bloodshed and chaos that unfolded here.

By the end of the day, 9,000 Allied troops were killed or wounded on the beaches, but they had a foothold in France and would use the pivotal momentum to advance across the continent towards ultimate victory: the defeat of Hitler.

I had been to the American Cemetery in Colleville-sur-Mer before, but this time it was winter, and the 9,387 white marble crosses seemed frozen in the cold. It is as the pictures portray it, a sea of graves whose symmetry of rows, like planted trees, play a game of geometry that multiplies the effect. There were many more dead than there are crosses. As bodies were identified, their families could opt to have them sent home to America. The ones buried here have found a resting place on the land they died trying to free.

Claire and I continue along the coast, past the charming fishing villages of Port-en-Bessin, and Commes and Longues-sur-Mer. We stop at Arromanches and see the remains of the Mulberry Harbors, giant artificial ports floating offshore that were constructed by the British, each of which unloaded a staggering 7,000 tons of cargo a day to supply Allied troops.

It is a long drive back to Caen, a city known more as the birthplace—and resting place—of William the Conqueror. The next morning I drive myself to the Mémorial de Caen, which some people call the Museum of Peace. I watch a film about Arromanches, and I know everyone in the auditorium feels the same pit in their stomach. Footage of boys young enough to still be in school, getting onto ships destined for the beaches of Normandy. Many of them would certainly die within hours.

There is a relentlessness about the wind in Normandy, and it is the first thing I notice behind the museum at the American Garden. The chilly gusts prompt me to adjust my jacket, snap the hood flaps under my throat. It is a two-tiered sanctuary, with granite stones that seem to float, surrounded by lawn, trees and birdsong, even in winter. There is a plaque that reads: *From the heart of our land flows the blood of our youth, given to you in the name of freedom.* On August 26, 1944, Generals Charles De Gaulle and Dwight Eisenhower marched down the Champs-Élysées to celebrate the liberation of Paris. Within nine months, Nazi Germany surrendered unconditionally to the Allied Forces.

New figures released for the 70th anniversary of the Battle of Normandy in 2014 indicate that there were over 209,000 Allied soldiers killed or wounded, 125,847 of them American. Mostly men. There are four women buried under white crosses in Coleville-sur-Mer, overlooking Omaha Beach. Sgt. Dolores Browne, PFC Mary J. Barlow, and Mary H. Bankston were members of the 6888th Central Postal Directory Battalion, all killed in a Jeep accident. As members of the first all-female, all-African-American battalion to serve overseas, their job was huge: to sort and forward the mail addressed to every soldier on the front. The last woman interred there is Elizabeth A. Richardson, a Red Cross volunteer from Indiana whose plane crashed near Rouen.

Four women, and four more reasons why this haunting countryside of spirits and memory is not just for military historians and men, but for all of us.

☙

# 72

## Sex on the Beach

### LA PLAGE DES JUMEAUX AND BRIGITTE BARDOT, SAINT TROPEZ

In summertime, Saint Tropez is crowded and loud, packed with nubile blondes in Dolce & Gabbana beachwear and gold stilettos who parade to and from yachts moored in the tiny port. It's true. Saint Tropez is all this, and it can stir up an unfortunate sense of, how do I say this?, uninvitedness, even if you've never been way up there on the guest list with Jay Z and Beyoncé anyway. It's tempting to dismiss this Mediterranean resort town as a blinged-out ruin from classier times on the Riviera or to avoid it because it feels buoyantly young and you feel decidedly less so.

But don't.

You should visit this fabled town once and, if possible, a whole lot more. Before you go, watch Roger Vadim's 1956 film *And God Created Woman,* which catapulted his twenty-two-year-old wife Brigitte Bardot—as well as Saint Tropez itself—into instant legend. The plot is forgettable, but not the scenes of the sleepy fishing village or the unprecedented sensuality of Bardot. Her first tease in the opening shots of the film, where she is seen lying facedown behind a white sheet that ripples in the sun, her nude, perfect curves displaying no tanline whatsoever, was the moment everything would change in the south of France. From then on, Saint Tropez would be synonymous with all things sultry and alluring, and Bardot would be a popular standard by which women, French or otherwise, would be measured. Now almost sixty years later, Bardot lives quietly in the house she bought in 1958, genuinely untouched by plastic surgery and active in animal rights as well as, at times, fringe politics. Somehow, her young and beautiful silhouette lingers here both in town and at the beaches, which are lined up along the Plage de Pampelonne in nearby Ramatuelle.

Through the years, though I have grown up and older, the bones in Saint Tropez have not changed at all, and I dare say they are more graceful than ever. Once, I reveled here doused in expensive champagne, young, silly and brown as a nutmeg (the Saint Tropez tan being the marketing gambit of the sunscreen brand Bain de Soleil). Several consecutive summers, I accompanied my new artist husband here while he worked on a sculptural installation at La Plage de Pampelonne. We still did the nightlife, but it was the jasmine-scented mornings I savored, and the low surf at the beach. Once, I came here at my all time nadir of glamour—with a toddler in tow, carrying baby weight under baggy, unflattering clothes. Much to my relief, I found an empathetic place where waiters at the Brasserie des Arts on the central Place des Lices were delighted to serve my son plain pasta and fill up his bottle with warmed milk. After dinner, we sat under hundred-year-old plane trees to watch the locals play boules. At the Plage des Jumeaux, where we spent our days, they would proffer a random plate of *frites* for him, just because.

When I returned years later with two teenagers in tow, I felt not at all as if I were leading my innocents into Sodom and Gomorrah, but rather delighted by how freely they could wander down to the port and stroll the Quai Jean-Jaurès together even after dark, take it all in, and get an artisanal ice cream at Barbarac. I bought my daughter a too-pricey-but-what-the-heck pair of K. Jacques sandals, made in Saint Tropez since the 1930s. I've been here, most wondrously, in winter when the light gets steely and the echo of your heels reverberates on the narrow streets. There isn't a Lamborghini in sight. My favorite store, Galleries Tropeziennes, is open all year. It is the oldest shop in town, selling fabric, clothes, and all kinds of unique and wondrous stuff that perfectly captures the essence of Saint Tropez. My friend Christy and I dreamed for years of trying to open up a branch in New York.

The beaches are just outside town, so a car is key there (as it is in most of Provence). As you drive the area's winding roads, you'll see them well-marked along the way. They all have parking, chaises, towels, cabanas and usually, great restaurants. My favorite, La Plage des Jumeaux, is a welcoming enclave that occupies an unnaturally high berth in my daydreams. It's not quite as buzzy as the equally beautiful Club 55. Cabane Bambou is lovely too, but is only open from April to October. La Plage des Jumeaux is open year round, but that is not the least of its charms.

The restaurant is draped in impeccable awnings of clean white and sea green stripes. The chairs and chaises are this color, too, which seems to be lifted straight from the Mediterranean a few yards away. It's a civilized place, where you can take an excellent three-hour lunch barefoot, when the sun is high and hot, sip on rosé, Badoit or Orangina, and nap away the afternoon on shimmering white sand.

There is nothing like that sleepy post-beach feeling when you drive back into town, sticky with sunscreen and salt water, hair stuffed under your straw hat. Bars bustle along the quai, the blondes are blonder, the bell tower of the church glows in a yellow pool of sun. There are, of course, less storied and more secret beaches to explore on the Mediterranean. At times my other big three—Sète, Hyères, and Cassis—better suit my state of mind. But there is only one Saint Tropez, and that's all there ever will be, and it makes no difference whose yacht is parked in the port. I don't really notice them anymore.

# The Ancient Place of Pilgrimage

## VÉZELAY

It's hard to know where to start with Vézelay, because so much converges there: history, architecture, two giant women of history—Eleanor of Aquitaine and Mary Magdalene—and religion, some of it fact and some, possibly fiction. Most powerfully, this town with its church and abbey high on a hill in Burgundy lends itself to some sort of personal mythmaking.

It could be magic, it could be its name, which contains no difficult French "r" to stumble upon and resonates like a scarf fluttering in the breeze. One anecdote does not make a trend, but several do, and it has become clear to me that any person who has been to the basilica at Vézelay really remembers it, and not with the explosiveness with which one recalls, say, Versailles, but quietly and with tenderness. Vézelay's church is not the most commanding in France nor is it as historically significant as some of her great cathedrals, but for someone who has been there, the snapshot lives indelibly as her own cherished memento. When Edith Wharton wrote about Vézelay in *A Motor-Flight Through France,* she remarked on the basilica's majesty in a way that might help us postulate a guess as to why a visit may be so haunting. The church, with its elevated detachment on the hilltop, bears over a thousand years of memories. "To have seen so much, and now to stand so far apart from life!" Wharton writes, as if the church were a patient witness whose wisdom, I am venturing a guess, is female.

I'm one of those people whose image of Vézelay, from my first visit there on my thirtieth birthday, is retouched to perfection. Upon return, I find it is slightly changed, still beautiful, but with renewed affinity to its history on a pilgrim's trail and the legacy of Mary Magdalene, after whom the Romanesque church is named.

I park at the bottom of the hill and walk up the road towards the Basilica Sainte-Marie-Madeleine. This sanctum is hers, the follower of Jesus who was a witness to his crucifixion and resurrection, possibly a prostitute and/or his lover, and for readers of *The Da Vinci Code*, the divinity of the sacred feminine and mother of his child. She is believed to have arrived by sea in France to live her last thirty years as a mystic and ascetic in a cave in Provence. It is also said that some of her remains were transferred to Vézelay from Provence in the 8th century to protect them from invading Saracens. In 1040, a PR-savvy abbot revealed the existence of the relics, ushering in a golden age of pilgrims for those seeking to repent before Saint Mary, who became her own breed of goddess. Thousands upon thousands of people made the trek to Vézelay until 1279, when the veracity of the relics was placed in doubt with the recognition of her tomb at Saint-Maximin-la-Sainte-Baume in Provence. And yet, fragments of what still may or may not be Mary remain in the 19th-century golden reliquary in the basilica's crypt. People embrace ancient mysteries according to their beliefs and believe what they need or want to—isn't that, after all, the definition of faith?

Vézelay was already associated with pilgrimages, and these days, I hear a lot around Paris dinner tables and travel blogs about those hardy souls who walk, fragment by fragment, the route of Saint James de Compostela, also known as the Way of Saint James, to Santiago de Compostela, Spain. It is one of Christendom's holiest cities, with a basilica housing the tomb of Saint James, who brought Christianity to Spain and was the patron saint against Islamic invaders. Since the 10th century, platoons of the pious have flocked to Vézelay—one of four starting points in France—to begin their 1,000 mile trek across Limousin, the Périgord, Aquitaine, Landes and the Pyrénées. On the day of my visit, the faithful, loaded down with packs, identifiable by the scallop shells dangling on their staffs, were just beginning to trickle up the hill.

Vézelay is one of France's Plus Beaux Villages, so it is unsullied by tacky souvenir shops; it's a quiet little town with one main street, dotted with a few bookstores and cafés. Like everywhere, it gets crowded in summer, and forget about Holy Week. When I arrive at the top of the Hill of Joy, as pilgrims of all kinds have called it for centuries, the church is strong and unmoving on the hillcrest. I circle the grounds to get situated and drink up the 360-degree gray-green vista of the massive Morvan forest and the valleys of the Cure and Yonne Rivers, with Burgundy's vineyards unfurling in the distance. From the fields below the basilica, Saint Bernard of Clairvaux preached the Second Crusade in 1146 to an overflow crowd. Legend has it that twenty-four-year-old Eleanor of Aquitaine, Queen of France and wife of King Louis VII, thundered on horseback decked out in warrior gear exhorting the crowds to wear the cross and follow her, her husband and 300 female servants to the Holy Land. While on this crusade, Eleanor had a political rift with her husband on the way to Jerusalem, which eventually led to the annulment of their marriage. By 1154 she was again a Queen—of England.

Which leads us back at last to the church of Saint Madeleine, peaceful on an early Sunday morning and everywhere doused in morning light. There are no colored glass windows to sully the blinding whiteness inside the basilica, which has emerged from fires, ransacking of every stripe, and mutilation during the God-averse Revolution to reach its current state of grace, aided by a do-over by the estimable architect Viollet-le-Duc in the mid 19th century. Here, the sturdy Romanesque narthex (the antechamber after the entrance) and nave (where the congregation sits) transition with the Gothic choir that surges towards heaven—two styles blended seamlessly into one. Yellow bands of sunlight are interspersed with shadows on the cool stone, from the pillars that rise to support the vaults. The side aisles, too, are flush with sunlight. Despite its age and the carvings of monsters on capitals and tympanums throughout the interior, the church's vitality packs a compact but subtle thrill, the kind, in Wharton's words, "such as the greatest art alone possesses."

I leave before the grounds get too crowded, walk down the hill to my car. It could be the light inside, or the poetic balance of the Roman with the Gothic, or the emerald green view of Burgundy, or just a conjuring up of Eleanor on a white horse riding up this very path on her way to Antioch that gives Vézelay its staying power in the minds of those who visit. Vézelay doesn't overwhelm as Beauvais or Chartres might, but rather, it rests gently on my shoulder. It's as if this quiet church on the hill remembers me now, too, and will for another thousand years.

As a final note, there are other, perhaps more powerful places in France to seek what some call the "sacred feminine" of Mary Magdalene, and these sites are massively important to Catholics and seekers of all faiths. One is in the Camargue in Saintes-Maries-de-la-Mer discussed in Chapter 30. Another is in remote Sainte-Baume, where the mountainside grotto Mary Magdalene spent her last three decades is now a candlelit sanctuary containing some of her relics. Pilgrims access the cave, maintained by Dominican monks, by a fragrant and often steep, rocky trail. About forty-five minutes away in Saint-Maximin-la-Sainte-Baume, inside the Basilica Sainte-Marie-Madeleine, is her crypt. This is near the small chapel where Charles II of Anjou discovered Mary Magdalene's sarcophagus in 1279, thus diminishing Vézelay's importance as a place of devotion. Inside the crypt are her relics, including her skull. It is not for the easily spooked, but for the faithful, it can be overpowering.

❧

# 74

## The Most Beautiful Garden in France

### VAUX-LE-VICOMTE, MAINCY

When you visit Paris, outings beyond the city are crucial, especially in summer when the pavement gets as hot as the tempers of tourists in line at the towers of Notre-Dame. One of the most glorious road trips imaginable is to the Baroque château and gardens at Vaux-le-Vicomte (pronounced vee-CONT), about an hour southeast of the city. Day, night, summer or Christmastime, you will strain to absorb both the splendor and dimensions of the place you have landed, more astonishing for its rich history and the fact that people—the Vogüé family—actually still live here.

"I love it because it's still a family-run château—and it feels that way!" says Heather Stimmler-Hall, the creator of the website *Secrets of Paris*, who shares my enthusiasm for Vaux-le-Vicomte, somewhat under-recognized on the typical grand tour, due possibly to the fact that it is more accessible by car than public transport. There is much to love, especially the sensation of being immersed in another, more regal era without getting tossed around by a crush of humanity as you might be in other, better-known châteaux.

A day here is distinctly and unmistakably French, with an immersion in history, art, style, classier-than-normal places to picnic, an excellent restaurant and a more casual cafeteria. And also, the somewhat cozy notion of being a guest of the family. "The dashing young sons who now run daily operations can be seen lending the staff a hand wherever needed, and there's even a gorgeous cookbook on sale in the gift shop with their mother's recipes and table decoration ideas," says Stimmler-Hall.

It's a warm touch that adds contemporary vitality to the glamour of the place. Vaux-le-Vicomte is often referred to as Little Versailles, but I know many people who believe the palace and garden actually surpass Louis XIV's forty-year royal masterstroke. If you are not in that camp, you still have to allow it has the better story.

It all began with the ambitious vision of Nicolas Fouquet, France's Superintendent of Finances under Louis XIV in 1653. Status-hungry and eager to impress his boss, Fouquet immediately started conceiving of a grand home and garden that befit his lofty position. He razed three villages to clear 100 acres for his château, and enlisted the genius of three of the glittering talents of France at the time: architect Louis Le Vau, painter Charles Le Brun, and horticulturist André Le Nôtre, who until then worked at the Tuileries, where he grew up and where his father managed the gardens.

Five years later, Vaux-le-Vicomte was complete, a spectacular estate of unprecedented magnificence inside and out. Le Vau situated the house on a moated platform, with large portals to the park; Le Brun painted figures on the ceilings and gilded angels on the walls. Le Nôtre, who was charged with creating a grand landscape surrounding the château, did just that, using decorative parterres, canals, waterfalls, hedges, sculptures and fountains. Most impressively, he combined them in a subversive *tour de force* of perspective using ingenious tricks to calculate visual illusions into the site's uneven topography, so the garden as viewed from the château was entirely different from how it actually was from inside the park. Then and now, these gardens are widely considered the towering achievement in French landscape design.

The story of Fouquet and his vanity project took an unfortunate turn on the evening of August 16, 1661. On that fateful night, he threw a lavish celebration to show off his new château to Louis XIV, complete with fireworks and the premier of a play by Molière, who was himself a guest. Louis was impressed— too impressed—by the display of no-holds-barred luxury, which confirmed suspicions he already harbored about his finance minister, who could scarcely have afforded such riches. Whether the monarch was outraged or threatened by Fouquet's extravagance, or he really believed Fouquet was guilty of financial malfeasance, in the eyes of the Sun King, Fouquet was a criminal. Three weeks later, Louis XIV sent D'Artagnan, the head of his Musketeers, to arrest Fouquet, who was charged with misappropriation of state funds. He spent the rest of his life in prison.

But if the night of August 16 was curtains for Fouquet, it was a great one for Le Nôtre. King Louis XIV was so impressed with the gardens at Vaux-le-Vicomte that he immediately enlisted Le Nôtre to work on Versailles, where his work reached stratospheric heights, and where he cemented his reputation—one that still holds true—as the most important landscape architect in the history of France.

Sad for Fouquet that his plan backfired, of course, but bygones are bygones, and now on summer evenings, we have the soft air, candles, a champagne bar, and the vivid memory of a man who paid dearly for his exquisite taste. "There's nothing more magical than dining on the garden terrace during the candlelight evenings in the summer, which end with a fireworks show," says Stimmler-Hall. "There's simply nowhere else like it."

❧

# 75 *When Pictures Tell the Story*

## MUSEUM OF THE TAPESTRIES OF
## BAYEUX, BAYEUX

 The Bayeux Tapestry is not a tapestry at all, but a 230-foot-long embroidered linen runner that is the greatest storyboard ever made, the world's most preeminent cartoon strip. I had long yawned at the thought of visiting some dank old wall hanging, but I felt morally bound to accompany a friend who considered such an outing a privilege and not a penance. What I discovered, as I crept the length of the narrative then walked it again, was an experience so powerful that I nearly wept. *Oh*, I thought, sufficiently humbled and a tad ashamed. *This explains it.*

Imagine if the Revolutionary War had happened in the 11th century, and human hands stitched the entire, detailed history of it with a needle and heavy wool thread down to blood in the battle scenes and provisions for the soldiers. Such is the scope of the Bayeux Tapestry. Now imagine that the 772-pound canvas then survived fires and natural disasters in the 12th century, was rolled up, moved all over creation, stored, used as a wagon cover, nearly cut to decorate a carnival float, tightly wound on two cylinders, and hidden in the belly of the Louvre to protect it from World War II

Allied bombs that decimated much of Normandy and then, the Nazi occupiers of France, who tried to get their hands on it anyway.

This was the incredible journey of the tapestry, and here it is today, not unscathed but nearly perfect, in a 17th-century former seminary in the historical center of Bayeux. This part of Normandy is William the Conqueror country, thirty minutes from his magnificent tomb in Caen and the two Romanesque abbeys—one for men and one for women—the ruler built to atone for the sin of marrying his cousin.

The canvas, averaging about twenty inches wide, is displayed under glass around the warmly-lit, U-shaped gallery and chronicles the two-year period leading up to the Norman Conquest in 1066. The storyline: King Edward the Confessor of England, who was childless, bequeathed his throne to his cousin William, the bastard Duke of Normandy who was descended from the Viking conquerors. (Normandy is derived from the Norse word "northman.") William was a big man and one of the toughest rulers in Christendom, brash and violent, who came to power in 1035 at eight years old. He defeated rebellions, revolts and survived aggressive challenges from all sides before emerging victorious and in control in 1060. In 1064, King Edward sent his brother-in-law Harold to Normandy to inform William that he was to be his heir to the throne. Harold swore allegiance, but upon Edward's death, he promptly seized the crown, rousing William to rally his forces and fight for what he had been promised. He and his men invaded England and defeated Harold at the Battle of Hastings on October 14, 1066. William became King of England, and this powerful cross-channel allegiance would endure until Normandy was absorbed back into the Kingdom of France in 1204.

The narrative unspools in chronological order, gathering urgency as the tension escalates, and this is why the tapestry is considered the definitive historical document of the Norman

Conquest. Besides the vivid scenes of bloodshed and mayhem, from the aesthetic point of view, I could only marvel at the precision in the needlework and the craft it required to turn this into high art.

The tale is told in five principle colors: terracotta, blue-green, gold, olive green and blue, with the sporadic addition of black, navy blue and sage green. Human faces and hands are stitched only in outline but with incredible precision and artistry. It's important here to get up close and to look at the facial expressions—the frowns, surprises, skepticism, anger and battle-hardened determination—as well as gestures and other exquisite detail rendered in the tapestry. Tête-à-têtes between men at a dinner feast seem nonchalant, and William, about to mount his charger, has a look of resolve with the most minimal of needlework. And the clothes! Chainmail, cloaks, tunics and robes are stitched to include shadow and movement.

There is excitement from the get-go, as Harold visits the ailing King Edward and soon sails to Normandy to swear his oath to William. The story, told in some seventy scenes, is always propelled forward, grips you and comes alive like a great action drama. Depictions of men dragging plows, riding horses or marching across the countryside, ships at sea, carts and wagons on the road, and soldiers who run wielding shields, swords and clubs all add to the growing momentum. The story approaches its bloody finale when William gathers his troops and boards his vessels to avenge the wrong done by Harold, the usurper. Along the length of the tapestry, the central tale is framed between borders depicting fables, animals, and countless other historical and seemingly ordinary scenes of everyday life, all of which add complexity to the composition. These border images become most dramatic at the conclusion of the tapestry, where archers point their arrows to the enemy, and dead or mutilated bodies lie in chainmail and armor on the battlefield.

Scholarly debate continues over the questions of who created the tapestry and when. However, it's widely believed that it was designed by men and stitched by a team of Anglo-Saxon embroideresses under the direction of a tapestry master. The delicate needlework of these women has left us with a magnificent artifact, but, sadly or fortunately, there are only three women (out of 626 human figures) featured in the main storyline: one is presumed to be Edith, the wife of King Edward, a second woman holds her child's hand as they flee a burning building at Hastings, and a third, known as the "mystery woman, Aelfgyva," is shown being touched—or struck—on the head by a cleric. (Or Harold. Or William?) The scene has mystified historians for centuries, more so because of the crouching naked man in the border below. It might have been a dirty joke on the part of the artisans, but it certainly gives innuendo to the interaction, and hints at a sexual scandal. On my second tour around the canvas, I saw two other women figures in the borders, both naked and in the presence of men from whom they seem to be recoiling. One of them appears below the scene where Harold rides towards William, the second one above the illustration of William as he reaches Hastings. However subtle and even tangential, they are not insignificant when considering the human cost of war, extracted to the extreme yet again in 1944, right here in this very corner of Normandy.

⚜

# 76 Rosé Vines

## DOMAINE DE TERREBRUNE, BANDOL

A region's signature wine can seem to take on the attributes of where it is produced. When you feel glamorous, uncork champagne from the sleek city of Reims. Bordeaux reds are rich and aristocratic, Burgundies are refined like the clean lines of the Côte d'Or. In the Var, the rosés are sunny and sexy, the summertime nectar of the south of France.

These crisp pinks served chilled are not the only wines of Provence, nor does Provence have the lock on producing them. There are marvelous rosés made in almost every region—among them Alsace, Languedoc and the Loire Valley. And although I consider those with the appellation Bandol the high priestesses of Provençal rosés, the area produces as many renowned reds and whites as it does the famous pinks. But still. For me, facts notwithstanding, Provence means rosé, and rosé means Bandol.

The town is on the coast between Cassis and Toulon, where the sea peeks between furrows of bright white cliffs, and meadows, vineyards and pine trees give texture to this southern-sensuous tableau. The Bandol seaside is scalloped with coves; behind it are the grapevines. The rosés are pressed with a combination of the Mourvèdre (at least 50 percent), Grenache and Cinsault grapes, which make a pale, salmon-hued wine. Despite their rosy complexion, these are not frilly or floral—far from it. Grapes that, by day, endure scorching heat are by night cooled by salty, maritime breezes, rendering a distinctive earthy freshness to the rosés and also enabling them to age or "cellar" well.

But I'm not thinking about long lifespan—mine or my wine's—in Provence. Bandol rosé's combination of complexity and airiness goes with life itself here. It can be drunk at lunch, at dinner or late at night under the stars. I drink it with fresh mussels or a plate of sliced tomatoes with olive oil, thyme and coarse salt from the Camargue. Bandol lightens the head without knocking you senseless; it slows you down just enough to heighten your perceptions of the cool trickle of sweat through the shoulder blades or the tartness of black cherries on the tongue. At home I'll drink a glass in the middle of the winter, during a polar freeze, when my only hope is the thought of a blue and white striped beach umbrella somewhere east of Marseille.

My friend and sometime-editor Lavinia Spalding, author of *Writing Away: A Creative Guide to Awakening the Journal-Writing Traveler*, shares my obsession with rosé but is besotted with one in particular: Domaine de Terrebrune Bandol. It's been a permanent fixation since her days as a server at a tony San Francisco restaurant where this was the only rosé important guests, movie stars and foodies would drink. "It became my favorite wine in the world," she says. "If I could, I would bathe in the stuff." When she left that job, the memory of it stayed with her, and ever since, she seeks it wherever she goes.

The wines from Domaine de Terrebrune—which means "brown earth"—are by several measures, anecdotal and otherwise, the finest Bandols in France. These entirely organic, storied rosés are dense and aromatic, made from grapes grown on terraced hillside vineyards, in soil that is thick with nutrients, especially limestone, that infuses a mineral-tinged magic on the fruit. On Lavinia's honeymoon, her new husband Dan, who of course knew about (and shared) his wife's predilection for one of the world's best rosés, drove her to the Terrebrune vineyard in Ollioulis in hopes of happening upon a tasting or a tour. What they received instead was a most fortuitous wedding gift: a spontaneous afternoon with the owner and caregiver to these seventy-four hallowed acres of vines, Reynald Delille, who proved to be as kind as his wines are sublime. When Lavinia, slightly overwhelmed by his generosity, asked him for his secret to this hauntingly good wine, he said simply, "No one could make a better rosé because no one tries harder or cares more than I do."

Through the course of their visit, they sampled bottle after bottle (most of them covered in cellar dust and without labels), whose identity only Delille could be sure of—a 2008 red, one from 2011, an old white to compare with the newest one, and then a vintage rosé, the Bandol of queens or at least of dreams. "I asked, 'How much would one of these bottles sell for?' relates Lavinia. He said, 'We would never sell this. It's only for friends and *very* special people.'"

The universe has a clever way of seizing the glow that emanates from a newly married couple like Dan and Lavinia, so it's natural that their journey to Bandol might have been enchanted. It's easier, of course, to make an appointment to tour the vineyard, which is open most every day. But for those of us whose weddings are decades behind us, "honeymoon" is just another word for something too perfect ever to end. Here, where life is colored with sunflowers and wild peaches, you can raise your glass of luscious pink wine to the joy in almost anything

※

# 77 The Virgin Warrior Saint

## IN THE FOOTSTEPS OF JOAN OF ARC

If ever you despair of the teenagers of the world, consider Joan of Arc. For nearly 600 years, her mythic stature as a patron saint of France has endured, and no competitor has ever come close. In fact, it's almost not fair to tell our high-school-aged children about her, so unrivalled—so unrivalable—is the story of the Maid of Orléans's brief but monumental life. If not for the eyewitness accounts of her bravery, and transcripts from her 1431 trial, one would think she was not real at all but the product of some fabulist's imagination. Almost every aspect of her extraordinary life—an illiterate peasant called by God at 16 to save France, martyred at 19, and everything in between—defies credulity. Joan of Arc spoke to angels and the angels spoke back.

In 1412, the year she was born, the Hundred Years' War had been raging on French soil for seventy-five years. France was losing ground to the British, with which the Duchy of Burgundy was allied. With the death of King Charles VI of France in 1422, the infant Henry VI of England was declared King of France. Up in the village of Domrémy in the Vosges, an adolescent girl who heretofore spent her days spinning, sewing, praying, and running in the fields, began to hear divine voices of saints, angels and God. What she heard was unequivocal. She must meet the Dauphin Charles

VII, she must lead his armies to drive the British out of France, and set the crown upon his head. Joan of Arc would become the only seventeen-year-old in human history, of either sex, to command a nation's military forces.

Admist centuries of biographies, movies, and TV miniseries, Mark Twain's inspired book on Joan of Arc stands above the rest. He became fascinated with her when he was a teenager himself in Hannibal, Missouri, after picking up a sheet of paper in the street that turned out to be from a book about Joan of Arc. Many years later, he spent fourteen years researching and writing *Personal Recollections of Joan of Arc*, her life story as told to a fictitious childhood friend who traveled with her as page and secretary. The author of *Tom Sawyer* and *Huckleberry Finn* believed this to be his greatest work. His near-worship for her was boundless—for her magnanimity, convictions, faith in God, intellect and the sheer unbridled strength of body and purpose. "There is no blemish in that rounded and beautiful character," he writes in a later essay. "She is easily and by far the most extraordinary person the human race has ever produced."

Joan of Arc's memory is kept illuminated in France, especially in the places she passed through on her way to martyrdom and saint-hood. There will be some readers who wish to follow more tightly in her footsteps; this list is for the curious and the admiring, because whatever your faith, it's difficult to remain unmoved by Joan.

Her childhood home in Domrémy-la-Pucelle, a remote town in Lorraine on the bucolic banks of the Meuse River, is now a museum, where you can see her bedroom and the room where she was born in 1412. Close by is the Church of St.

Rémy, where she worshiped and which contains her stone baptismal font. There is a strong sense of her in the countryside, where her faith and spirituality began to blossom.

From here, the seventeen-year-old rode to the Loire, having never been on a horse, arriving in March 1429 at the Royal Fortress of Chinon, where she waited patiently to see Charles VII. Here, she relayed what God had told her: he was the lawful heir to the crown, God had sent her to deliver France from foreign bondage, and that she required an army to break the British siege of Orléans. If it fell, it would be curtains for France. In time, Charles was convinced and incredibly, named her General-in-Chief of the Armies of France.

While she was being vetted by church authorities in Poitiers, she dictated a letter to a clergyman for the King of England, the Duke of Bedford (his regent in France), and the English commanders at Orléans. It's hard to imagine the British reaction upon receiving her order to return immediately to their own land. "And if you will not do so, I am a *commander*, and wherever I shall come across your troops in France, I shall make them go," she writes, "and if they will not obey, I will have them wiped out. I am sent here by God the King of Heaven to drive you entirely out of France."

From Tours, where her iconic battle standard was designed, she marched to Blois to marshall troops, crossed the river and pressed on to Orléans. There she lifted the siege, accomplishing in nine days what the indolent almost-king had failed to do in seven months. Here you can celebrate her victory at the Sainte-Croix Cathedral of Orléans, where she gave thanks to God in front of an ecstatic crowd. Charles, the soon-to-be king, was off hunting, perhaps at the behest of his chief advisor, the notorious double-dealer La Trémoïlle, who was no fan of Joan's.

Joan continued her campaign, riding as a knight, under the banner, sheathed in white armor with her plumed cap, and continued to attack British strongholds in the Loire Valley. One by one, the enemy abandoned their garrisons: Jargeau, Meung-sur-Loire, Beaugency, Patay, all liberated by the middle of June 1429. Next stop, Château de Sully, a palace fortress of Disney-like perfection, then owned by La Trémoïlle, where Charles was making himself comfortable as Joan fought for him. She convinced him to ride with her to Reims to be crowned king, and successfully secured his promise of amnesty for all the French princes whose allegiances had faltered, once her mission was complete.

All of France was in a frenzy of support for the Maiden. She was considered an envoy from Heaven—"Daughter of God," "Victory's Sweetheart," and volunteers clamored to serve in her army. Leading the so-called Bloodless March, her charisma and power alone vanquished every town and fortress without a single casualty from Gien to Reims, escorting the Dauphin to Notre-Dame Cathedral, where every king since Clovis had been crowned. On July 17, 1429, the essential goal of her mission came to pass: he was anointed and crowned France's true and legitimate monarch, King Charles VII.

The Reims cathedral still wears battle wounds from shelling during World War I, and beside it is a great bronze statue of Joan on horseback, sword raised, shoulders back, looking up towards the heavens. Inside are kaleidoscopic stained glass windows by Marc Chagall and another figure of Joan, infinitely more serene in her countenance. Her tunic is yellow marble encrusted with lapis lazuli fleurs-de-lis, her face is carved from ivory, and gives the impression of great inner peace.

Compelled to march onward to Paris from Reims, her campaign was increasingly fraught with setbacks and opposition; unwavering, she made it to Compiègne, just fifty miles outside Paris. There, in May 1430, she was captured by Burgundian troops and imprisoned until she was turned over to the British (for a large sum of money) and sent to Rouen for trial. Black crepe bunting was hung all over the country in support of this invincible young soldier who had heroically saved France.

Today Rouen revels in her memory, even though it was here she was condemned and put to death. The tower where she was imprisoned is gone, but you may visit the Tour Jeanne d'Arc where she was threatened with torture, and the Place du Vieux Marché, where she was burned at the stake as a heretic. During her long trial, she was relentlessly interrogated by sixty-two judges who mocked her about the voices she heard, attempted to ensnare her into perjury, and showed nothing but contempt and ridicule towards her. Remarkably, she held her own and never broke. At one point, she was charged on sixty-six counts, including being a sorceress, false prophet, apostate, blasphemer, schismatic, a dealer in magic, a usurper of divine honors, and discarding decencies and proprieties of her sex. The latter was an object of obsession, as the inquisitors repeatedly questioned her about dressing in men's attire. She may, at the end, have been killed for dressing male, a fact that ups her proto-feminist credentials on top of being a great military commander and a supremely confident and capable young woman. At no time during her imprisonment or trial did King Charles VII intervene for her release or make any effort to save her.

After a thorough review twenty-five years later, the Pope declared her trial a sham and fully exonerated Joan of Arc, calling her a martyr. Another great woman and her contemporary, the poet Christine de Pizan, watched and wrote about Joan's exploits in 1429, the year they transpired. "Never was there such great strength, not in a hundred or a thousand men," she writes in *Le Ditié de Jehanne d'Arc*. "Before, one would not have believed it possible."

❧

# 78 Trailblazer on the Route du Champagne

## MAISON VEUVE CLICQUOT, REIMS

At home we call it the "good stuff," but the bottle says Veuve Clicquot. Its tangy yellow label is both a beacon and calling card, drawing you towards it while distinguishing itself from the bland masses at the wine store. This was exactly what Barbe-Nicole Clicquot Ponsardin, the widow—*veuve*—after whom the brand is named, had in mind when she first affixed yellow ribbons to bottles she exported to the United States in the early 1800s. How to make my product stand out? Accessorize it. Add a little flash. Today, the company owns the trademark on Pantone color 137C, also known as Veuve Clicquot yellow.

The blazing hue was everywhere when I had a tasting, toured the cellars and peeked behind the bottle in Reims. And I must say, I was utterly engulfed by the spirit of the place, where story threads of luxury, French history and a formidable female character entwine to form the nearly-perfect narrative. This, with a flute of champagne, and I could swear I was swimming in syrup under a cloudless, sunshiny sky.

It's an enlightening descent into the network of *caves*, where I get acquainted with the business chops behind the bubbles. At a time when upper class women kept busy wrangling their children's governesses or shopping for fine silk, Ponsardin's executive brain was clicking away as no woman's had ever done. While Napoleon's armies were advancing across Europe and wrecking the routes of trade, Veuve Clicquot was making inroads where it could under its highly competitive female namesake.

La Veuve Clicquot was born in Reims of wealthy parents and married a local man whose family was involved in many industries, including wine, to which her husband devoted himself. When he died in 1805, the twenty-seven-year-old widow was left with a little girl and his struggling business. Instead of packing it in, she shed the conventions of the time, took control, forged ahead and made history. "She smashed the glass ceiling before it was even invented," says writer Tilar J. Mazzeo, whose fascinating 2009 bestseller, *The Widow Clicquot*, details the story of the unstoppable Barbe-Nicole, who was "leaning in" before most women knew there was any role for them in the world besides domesticity and giving pleasure to men.

As the first woman in history to lead her own international business empire, La Veuve had a fly-or-die determination in its creation. One of her most notable coups was at the end of the Napoleonic Wars during the Emperor's demise, when Russia closed itself off to French imports. Ponsardin identified a port through which she could penetrate the blockade and get 10,550 bottles of her exceptional 1811 vintage to the imperial city of Saint Petersburg, where she was certain her brand would gain admirers among aristocratic circles and Czar Alexander himself. In a winner-take-all gamble that probably is still discussed in business school seminars on risk-taking, her audacity paid off. For the next fifty years in Russia, "Klitotskii" was literally the champagne of kings.

Echoes of this royal patronage reverberate, starting with the logo on the cork and label. An anchor (chosen by her husband as the company's signature in 1792) is set inside a drawing of the Great Comet of 1811, which readers of *War and Peace* will remember as a portent of Napoleon's march into Russia. That was also the year of the legendary "comet vintage" that Ponsardin managed to supply to Russia against all odds, winning her the lioness's share of the market there.

The *crayères*, or chalk caves, at Veuve Clicquot consist of over 400 softly undulating limestone quarries; once unconnected in ancient Roman times, they now extend unbroken for 26 kilometers beneath the streets of Reims. Walking under their sensuous white walls, I learn about the innovations La Veuve made in the production of champagne that are still in use. She perfected the industry-changing practice of riddling, collecting sediment that clouded up the bottle during fermentation, removing it, and recorking the bottle. She also invented the first rack to make this process easier—*un table de rémuage*—where bottles are set upside down into holes cut into the surface, allowing the sediment to settle in the neck of the bottle.

Because of La Veuve, our sparking wines today are crystal clear, but we also have her to thank for the current process of producing rosé champagne by *assemblage*. Until then, the dark skins of the pinot noir grapes were crushed and left to dye the clear juice during fermentation. Madame Ponsardin, unhappy with the taste, instead slow-pressed Bouzy rouge grapes to make a separate, red wine to blend with the white. The results are in the pinks, two of which I sample in the tasting room, including a Vintage 2004 rosé, luscious with hints of strawberry and red currant. There is nothing girly about this wine. It's a wine for women.

And in spite of its feminine connotations (yes, champagne is best when paired with flowers or diamonds), there is nothing girly about it, either. Champagne is the wine of kings, emperors and soldiers toasting victory. It's the drink of brides and their grooms, new parents, the recently promoted, of any joy worth celebrating. And here at Veuve Clicquot, we celebrate audacity itself, womanhood writ large and the tenacity of a young widow. We dress it up in yellow, and then we raise a chilled glass of the good stuff.

❧

# 79

## For All the Ships at Sea

### THE LIGHTHOUSES OF FINISTÈRE, BRITTANY

Life is relentless. Just ask a lighthouse. If we were born with a fraction of their resilience, we would never be undone by a really bad day. These immortal stone beings are like the best of humans, only better. They stand unwaveringly straight and tall, can withstand any degree of indignity that blows their way, and face each day with steadfastness and grace, no matter what happened the night before. What's more, a lighthouse offers indiscriminate comfort. Especially when the seas get rough, they are beacons in the dark or through a scrim of vapor. Frankly, we can learn a lot from them: about dependability and consistency, how to hang tough, and what a waste it is to do anything less than greet each day with a sense of optimism and purpose.

You could say, as well, that a lighthouse embodies a distinct and somewhat bygone poetry of the human spirit. It was a sense of adventure that made people take huge risks, leave terra firma, and begin to navigate the waters of earth, making it smaller in the process. Yes, I romanticize the lighthouse. So imagine my amazement to be in the presence of many of them, one after another, perched like watchmen on the *qui vive*. In Brittany's Finistère department, on the westernmost edge of France, the coast and rocky islets are dotted with twenty-nine lighthouses—*phares* in French. Many are working, some are dormant, and some are disintegrating from age and increasing irrelevance since the onset of GPS. But some, you can climb—in season, of course. It's rough on your knees, but great for your thighs and even better for the soul.

On the map, Finistère juts out like a dragon's head, its gaping maw breathing fire. The 750 miles of coastline has some of France's most dramatic landscapes—steep cliffs, sandy beaches, meadows, coves, rugged islands and granite outcrops battered by wind and water into fantastic shapes. Here, the English Channel clashes with the Atlantic Ocean, which creates some of the strongest currents and most dangerous conditions in the world, especially on the Iroise Sea, an Atlantic basin prone to particularly violent waves and weather. For hundreds of years, lighthouses have looked out on these turbulent waters and the fogbound wretches navigating them, witnessed too many shipwrecks, and prevented countless thousands more.

The station at Saint-Mathieu was established in 1692, and the 121-foot red, white and gray-trimmed tower was built in 1835 on the edge of a 60-foot cliff. It is set amongst the ruins of a 16th-century Benedictine abbey, which ramps up the sense of majesty here. At the top of a 163-step climb, the view from the unobstructed walkway is of dramatic headlands, the swirling sea, and the islands of Molène and Ouessant. The wind does battle with your hair, and there is a strong and familiar scent of salt and dampness that recalls my native New England shore.

You can't climb Kermorvan, a square-shaped tower that sits in regal isolation facing Le Conquet Harbor on a stretch of preserved coastal lands, but you can its inland partner Trézien, up the dizzying, narrow 182-step staircase (access is limited through the local tourist office). These lighthouses work in concert to guide safe passage through the strait connecting the Iroise and the English Channel.

From the ferry out of Le Conquet, it takes 75 minutes to reach the hilly Île d'Ouessant, which is a commitment, but a worthy one, if only to see Le Stiff. Roosted on a bluff at the northeast tip of Ouessant, this double-barreled 105-foot lighthouse was first active in 1699, under the reign of Louis XIV. One hundred four steps take you to the top for a gorgeous view of the island—including flocks of its small but wooly native breed of sheep—and the Celtic Sea. Also on Ouessant is the 180-foot Créac'h, whose interior is closed to tourists, but known to have one of the loveliest staircases in all of lighthouse-dom. It beams among the most powerful lights in the world, visible for almost 40 miles, signaling entrance to the English Channel. One day, perhaps they will restore and reopen the Kéréon Lighthouse, known as "The Palace" for its sumptuous interior of ebony and mahogany floors and Hungarian oak paneling. Built amidst the harsh Fromveur Passage and perilous stone reefs southeast of Ouessant, it is now said to be disintegrating from water damage and humidity.

The Phare Le Four is another forbidding structure two and a half miles offshore, built on a granite rock so beaten by angry breakers that it was known among lighthouse keepers as "hell." This, and the 1882 Phare de la Vieille, a stately castellated tower in the Raz de Sein, a bit farther south in Finistère, are two of the most iconic Breton lighthouses, both rising from the sea, slammed by waves and churning sea foam.

The Île Vièrge is the tallest traditional lighthouse in the world, and to ascend it requires a good deal of fitness and a healthy dose of courage: it is 270 feet high, the spiral staircase a vertiginous 397 steps, and the breezy open-air walkway at the top, narrow. You reach the island by a short trip from the tiny port town of Plouguerneau on the Aber Wrac'h, a granite-studded estuary on the English Channel. This giant is the undisputed master of its treacherous domain. The interior, too, is exceptional. Looking up, it resembles a many-chambered nautilus, as the spiral winds between walls coated with opaline glass the color of water and opens into a wood-paneled old lighthouse-keeper's watch. Breathtaking comes to mind in more ways than one when you gaze down at the sea from within the sea itself, especially to see the green-blue Aber and the reefs that make marine passage so fraught with danger.

Slightly to the east, a short ferry ride from the lovely town of Roscoff, is Île de Batz, a picturesque island of birds, butterflies, Breton horses, stone churches, hydrangea and a renowned exotic garden. The lighthouse is hewed from local granite and dates from 1836; only 198 steps to the top gives you a 360-degree view of the coast.

Lastly, an outlier, a one-off, but a can't-miss, way down in southern Finistère on the Pointe de Penmarc'h, where the Phare d'Eckmühl towers over two neighbors in a cluster of lighthouses. It was built with a bequest by the daughter of a decorated Napoleonic marshal and named in his honor, to make up for all the lives lost in the wars he fought. Sadly, the opaline walls are crumbling along the helicoidal 272-step staircase, which rises up to a gorgeous wood-paneled room with a gray marble ceiling and a bronze bust of the marshal. The panorama is tremendous—the bay, the chop and the jagged shore, as is the saltwater breeze.

It's stirring to look over these mythical waters from this lofty, windblown vantage point. From here, light beams over the water, beckoning the sea-weary home, steering their ships into safety. We should all be so patient and so tirelessly good.

⁂

# 80

## Châteaux and Fresh Air

### THE LOIRE VALLEY OF
### CATHERINE DE' MEDICI BY BIKE

The fact that there is but one chapter in this book on the gilded Loire Valley should be taken to mean an emphatic, "Make haste." There is not a single château there whose history—whose *story*—could not fill volumes. To say nothing of the fact that these are some of the most knee-weakeningly gorgeous buildings on earth, so beautiful in fact that to take them in all at once can be like upending a five-pound bag of sugar straight into your mouth. Ah, but how delicious to overdose on splendor. In fact, I'm already exhausting my supply of synonyms for "beautiful," and I've barely begun to write. The thesaurus offers "nice." Oh, help me, language fairies. This is the Loire Valley, and understatement need not apply.

Before I get to Catherine de' Medici, Queen of France, châtelaine of several of the Loire's most sumptuous turreted properties and one of the most intriguing women ever to grace this earth, a note on how to best tour her enchanted kingdom. My answer is unequivocal: by bicycle. This is a far cry from the Tour de France, so if you crave a workout, be warned you'll only warm up when the thermometer spikes. This is flat-roading, languor pure and simple, along riverbanks, through drowsy villages with cobbled streets and animated markets, the subtle counterpoint to the regal excess at the châteaux.

There are lots of expensive ways to do it, and that may be your preference and within your means. Private, dedicated guides, abundant meals and cushy lodgings arranged by someone else. But the Loire Valley Tourist Board and specifically Loire à Vélo makes it so simple to do it yourself you think there's a catch. There isn't. If you start at Orléans and plan to ride the ninety miles to Tours, you can easily finish it in four days, arranging your hotels in advance with stops—at minimum—at Domaine National de Chambord, Château de Cheverny, Château Royal de Blois, Domaine de Chaumont-sur-Loire, Château Royal d'Amboise, Château du Clos Lucé and Château de Chenonceau. Seven out of twenty-one châteaux, whose towers and forests are reflected in the rivers of central France, all major historical monuments, cultural icons bearing the marks of bygone royal favor. You can always come back and see the rest.

Within this itinerary, the objective is to pace yourself, absorb the scenery, and if you wish, engage with what fascinates you through your stunned meanderings. The gardens, such as the one that inspired Leonardo Da Vinci at Clos Lucé, where he spent his final years. The architecture—Amboise's collection of spiral turrets. The details—Chambord's unforgettable double-helix staircase. Extravagance. Blois's 564 rooms. The idea that these palaces were built, inhabited, maintained in the first place. The intrigue. The women.

What moves me is the lady whose memory floats through the gleaming corridors of Blois, Chenonceau and Chaumont-sur-Loire: Catherine de' Medici. Mother of three kings. Humiliated wife. Savior of the French crown. Renowned poisoner? Though her shadow lingers elsewhere—her ballroom at Fontainebleau, the Tuileries (one of many noble buildings she erected), and the Basilica at Saint-Denis where she was entombed, it is here in the Val du Loire where she is most vividly present.

So let's get this poisoning thing out of the way. Was Catherine de' Medici or was she not a vile murderess, plotting treachery on all her enemies? Or is that a smear invented by male historians to besmirch a powerful woman, especially an ambitious one whose ten-children legacy needed protection and oversight? They were all heirs to crowns and future consorts of kings whose every move could affect the destiny of Europe. Kathleen Wellman, Professor and Chair of the Department of History at Southern Methodist University and author  of *Queens and Mistresses of Renaissance France*, believes the latter. "I'm convinced you can't win the war of history if you're a mother," she says. Wellman points to Alexandre Dumas's juicy novel *Queen Margot* for ginning up Catherine's bad reputation. He portrayed her as a crazed villainess and dark magician, plotting alliances while employing poison gloves, lamp oil and even the pages of a book as lethal weapons as she schemed to install another son, Henry III, as king. At Blois, however, the guides are trained historians, skilled in dispelling some of these lurid myths. Her so-called poisoner's apothecary, the "secret chamber" containing 237 small cupboards, is an engineering curiosity with hidden locks and pedals more likely to have been built by King Francis I, who refurbished the château in 1515, for jewels or other precious *objets d'art*.

The backdrop of *Queen Margot* was the Saint Bartholomew's Day Massacre. On that day in 1572, the pent-up hostility between Catholics and Huguenot Protestants exploded in Paris just days after the marriage of Catherine's daughter Marguerite de Valois (Margot) to Huguenot Henry of Navarre (the future King Henry IV, who would renounce his Protestantism)—a political move if ever there was one. Matchmaking for royal expedience was for centuries an extreme sport.

Catherine, a Catholic but an even more passionate politician, held sway over her son King Charles IX, and either she, Charles, or someone else at the top ordered the assassination of a Huguenot leader and the targeted killings of others who were in Paris for the wedding. Tens of thousands of Protestants were slaughtered in the aftermath, and it's safe to say her role—whatever it may have been—in the massacre has been a major blot on Catherine's record. But Professor Wellman believes she was no wanton citizen-killer, either. "I believe that if Catherine did order the massacre, she likely believed expedient assassination of leaders would lead to peace," she says. After all, that kind of measure was in keeping with the political behavior of kings of the day, and no one could have predicted the fervor the killings exacerbated. "History has treated her poorly, in large part, because it was deemed inappropriate for any woman to be a true political force."

The struggles of Catherine the person, mother and wife are crystallized at Chenonceau, known as the "women's castle." It was built by Katherine Briçonnet in 1513 and maintained by a Madame Dupin during the Revolution, and in between it was embellished by Catherine and Diane de Poitiers. Diane was the mistress of the king, the woman he loved, the woman with whom he interlocked initials on his royal monogram. Mistresses were common, but Catherine deserves our compassion for the flagrancy of her husband's disregard for her, matched only by his public ardor for his mistress.

Catherine de' Medici was the Florentine daughter of Lorenzo de' Medici, and in 1533, at fourteen, she was married to Henry II. By the time he became King in 1547, he was long in the thrall of Diane de Poitiers, a beautiful widow of high aristocracy who, when they fell in love, was thirty-six to his sixteen years. Though Henry never cared for Catherine, he still slept with her (they ultimately had ten children together) at the behest of Diane—she wanted a wife she could control, rather than see her replaced by a more desirable queen, so as to maintain power over Henry.

They served each other's interests until Henry's death in a jousting accident in 1559. He had given Chenonceau, the most luxurious castle with the most stunning grounds, to Diane, but Catherine took it back, as her son's regent. It belonged to the crown, but even those actions have been used to tar her as unrelentingly vindictive. In return, she gave Chaumont-sur-Loire to Diane. With its regal turrets and spectacular view of the river, it was hardly a consolation prize, though Catherine may have been happy to be rid of Chaumont. When it was her main residence, she had entertained all manner of soothsayers and astrologers there, including Nostradamus and the Italian Ruggieri brothers. Truth or another hokey myth, one fortune teller set her before a mirror wherein the faces of her children appeared, and she foresaw the deaths of her three sons and the accession of Henry IV, the Bourbon king. That was not to happen until thirty years later, by which time all of her son-kings and their courts had lived regally at Chenonceau.

But she deserves more credit than she has been given in the political realm, for managing to preserve the French monarchy in legitimate succession and for her indefatigable efforts in trying to negotiate with Huguenots and Catholics. Neither side really appreciated her deftness, as she tried to keep the balance that would allow her sons—Francis II, Charles IX and Henry III—to remain king. She had a civil war on her hands but kept the country together, and all her boys kept their heads. "To the student who digs deep into the history of the 16th century in France, the figure of Catherine de' Medici stands out as that of a great king," writes Honoré de Balzac in his glowing 1842 historical piece, *About Catherine de' Medici*. Surely she had better things to do than poison her enemies? Think about it.

❦

# 8 1 *The Master's Beginnings*

## THE CHILDHOOD HOME OF
## CHRISTIAN DIOR, GRANVILLE

Unless you shop in their boutiques, it's not easy to honor the giants of fashion in France. Coco Chanel's opulent apartment above her boutique on rue Cambon is not open to the public—occasionally a reporter will get a golden ticket and a tour. You may visit the gardens of Yves St. Laurent's cobalt blue villa in Marrakesh, but not his home in Paris. In fact, the only museum in the country dedicated to a fashion designer under the official "Musée de France" rubric is Christian Dior's childhood idyll on the weatherbeaten coast of Normandy. The couturier returned here frequently during his too-short but remarkable career. He would sit enveloped by flowers next to the reflecting pool he designed, in the breast of familiarity, comfort, beauty and home.

Christian Dior died of a heart attack in 1957 at fifty-two, only ten years after he showed his first collection in Paris. Over half a century later, the Dior name is more vibrant and relevant than ever, with Natalie Portman, Charlize Theron, Jennifer Lawrence and Marion Cotillard lending their faces to the brand that has been synonymous with luxury since its inception. When the designer debuted in 1947, he and his "New Look" received instant, worldwide acclaim. The collection's full skirts, wide shoulders and tiny cinched waists made a sweeping gesture that said unequivocally: the war is behind us, femininity and glamour are back, and nowhere matters more than Paris in the world of haute couture.

"Every woman should have pink in her wardrobe," Dior famously said. "It is the color of happiness." Probably no coincidence, then, that pastel pink is the color of Les Rhumbs, the villa bought by the Dior family in 1905, the year Christian was born. He was the child of a wealthy fertilizer magnate, and enjoyed a carefree boyhood in this pretty clifftop house in the seaside resort of Granville. The timing of my visit to this sun-soaked and wind-lashed oasis was optimal, which is less a statement about luck and planning than it is about the continually surprising history and cultural range of northern France. After several days touring this war-scarred region, from the trail of William the Conqueror to the beaches and villages of the Normandy Campaign, I was enroute to yet another monument of men, one of monks rather than soldiers: Mont-Saint-Michel, about thirty minutes down the coast from Granville. I decided that a stop at the Musée Christian Dior would be the perfect restorative breath. I parked my car outside the gate and passed the manicured hedge and lawns towards the museum. A steep climb from the beach via the coastal footpath can also lead you to the extensive gardens in back of the house that were mostly designed and planted by Dior's mother, Madeline, with the help of young Christian.

The gardens, more of a small-scale park, proved an irresistible distraction on my way to the exhibition. It is a classic English landscape with several distinct sections, some containing plum trees, hawthorn bushes, arched walkways and pergolas draped in roses, while others areas are thick with pink, purple and white hydrangeas, and around the pool, tangles of jasmine, camellia or honeysuckle. Most marvelous are the fragrance terminals set amidst the flowers, to reveal the scents that inspired Dior's perfumes, including the lily of the valley and rose de chêne of his first creation, Miss Dior, named for his sister who was imprisoned (and later released) in Ravensbrück concentration camp as a member of the Resistance.

Behind the cliff walk that leads to the beach, there is a screen of pine trees and a stone wall built by Dior *mère*, which buffet her flowers from the salty winds that blast up from the raging Channel. Most breathtaking of all is his mother's *roseraie*—the secret rose garden on the edge of the granite cliff.

The palette at Les Rhumbs was a constant throughout Dior's life. He often combined the grays of the Norman coast and stormy skies with floral pinks, both in his boutiques and in his designs, down to the packaging for his perfume Diorissimo, which was introduced in 1956.

With a rotating series of exhibitions, all integrating former collections and those of the couturiers who have taken the reins chez Dior since 1957 (including Yves Saint Laurent, Marc Bohan, Gianfranco Ferré and John Galliano), the museum inside the house is a celebration of his artistic taste and sensibility. It's hard to describe most of the haute couture on display at any given time as clothing. Rather, it is art, and there is a humbling sense of the quantity of labor by the teams of skilled artisans that contributes to each taffeta pleat and every hand-stitched paillette. An exhibit in 2010 was dedicated to the history of grand balls, which naturally included many of the House of Dior's most luxurious couture gowns. Another, in 2013, was centered on the Impressionists, whose inspiration Dior shared for the blooming gardens and changing light of Normandy. Dresses as lush as ripe blossoms were juxtaposed alongside a matching painting, and if you can ever get a copy of *Dior Impressions*, the book created to accompany the exhibit, you will be amazed by how closely Dior's heavenly creations echo those of the 19th-century painters. In early 2014, the exhibit "*Une maison, des collections,*" was dedicated to the sources of Dior's inspiration and a visual treat of haute couture in every shade of glorious, as well as accessories, sketches and lingerie.

Dior often cited Les Rhumbs as his greatest influence and even a metaphor for his own life. The house was as resilient as it could be, rising from Normandy's vapor and fog on a cliff that dropped straight down to the water's edge. "The garden was planted with young trees which grew with me against the winds and tides," he wrote. "But the walls were not enough to protect us from every tempest." The sun comes out too, in northern France as I saw the day of my visit. So one can imagine that a waft of heliotrope, mingled with the fresh scent of roses and the briny air, surely helped.

❧

# 82

## The Gem of the Sky

### THE MILLAU VIADUCT, MIDI-PYRÉNÉES

In writing about all these eye-popping places in France, I'm beginning to subscribe to the school of thought—*my* school of thought—that without personal gain, there is little point to travel. "Gain" meaning enrichment that can only come through memory, neither of bliss nor disaster but simply of place. Like everyone, my camera aids me greatly in my journey. It documents, jogs my spotty memory, records the sight for dinner parties and posterity and gives me something to moon over during winter ice storms in Connecticut. But what about the minutes and seconds before and after the snapshot? There are words if you can smith them, but no gadget so far that can record and preserve that holy communion, that "joy of the eye" as Edith Wharton called it, between viewer and vision. Just like the human mind cannot remember pain, we also strive to remember what our body did when we felt true astonishment, when we surrender ourselves to something beautiful. We know, however, that it accrues to our benefit somewhere in that infinite deep.

I knew all the facts about the Millau Viaduct, a grand feat of architecture completed in 2004 after three years, on highway A75 through the Midi-Pyrénées, to alleviate traffic jams on the road between France and Spain that caused havoc in this tranquil southwestern corner. It was designed by British rock star architect Sir

Norman Foster in collaboration with French engineer Michel Virlogeux, conceived like all the world's great structures from cathedrals to skyscrapers: to stun humanity with beauty and to push engineering ingenuity beyond its known limits.

But like Mount Fuji, the Pyramids at Giza, or other places constructed by man or  the divinity that render you speechless, you cannot prepare for the moment you catch that first glimpse of the Millau Viaduct. Driving northeast from Montpellier, it came into view, and we pulled over in Brunas. Seven radiant white spans, fine as angel wings, that rise and fall on the 8,100 foot expanse across the river. The bridge is made of 40,000 tons of steel and concrete, but it seems weightless, as if held aloft by air and wind. The rugged Tarn valley is sluiced with sunlight, and this ethereal thing floats right through the center of it. Its eminence was, for me, almost without precedent in France or anywhere else. We got obsessed, recalling a visit to the Grand Canyon, where we hopped on the free bus to take in the view from every corner and fold, at every time of day, and face another vista that couldn't possibly be as beautiful as the one before it, and yet surpassed it. Later that day, clouds rolled into the Aveyron and scattered across the spans, making it seem even more airborne and weightless than before.

The town of Millau can offer lots of suggestions and a list of nearby vantage points. You can take a bus to some of the lookouts, jump on a handy tour boat in the town of Creissels to sail under the structure and see the 700-ton pylons up close, or rent a kayak and do it yourself. You can also drive to the Plus Beau Village of Peyre for a long-shot view, or climb the 17th-century belfry in the town of Millau. The second most beautiful vista is in extreme closeup, a thirty-minute steep walk to the viewing point near the information center at the north side of the bridge. This closes at 7 P.M., which brings me to the dreamscape of the Millau Viaduct at night, when the 154 cable-stays melt into the darkness, leaving only the sky-high pylons and deck aglow. Try to name something more delicate, graceful and strong.

This bridge was orchestrated by people—teams of men and women. And just as we can't recall how we felt when moved by a great piece of music, nor can we reproduce the awe we feel looking out at this bridge at night with the stars peering down. What we can know for certain is that we have gained from it and that we are, as a result, enriched.

# 83 *Chasing Waterfalls*

## THE JURA AND THE QUEYRAS

When I lived in Paris, my colleagues at work enthused about weekend jaunts to places unknown (to me), where they ate slabs of Roquefort des Hautes-Alpes in an area called the Queyras, or sipped special yellow wine along the Route des Vins in the Jura, a four-hour car ride from Montparnasse. The assumption, as I saw it, may have been, *if you have to ask about these places, don't.* But I asked and am glad I did.

In writing about the feminine side of France, the beaches of three separate coastlines seem to take prominence in my brain, as do cathedrals and châteaux with their decorative skins and histories of formidable women. But I also have to remember the rest of our needs and how to meet them in this massive, magnificent country. Though a teeming morning market under Provençal sun is tops on my list, I realize we also seek to soothe our primal urgings, seek balm for the spirit, time and space for contemplation, and some uncluttered mountain air in which to find these things.

So, I give you the Queyras and the Jura, two areas of uncommon beauty separated by 250 alpine miles, which share one key attribute if it is seclusion you seek: remoteness.

My friend Melora Mennesson comes from Santa Fe, New Mexico, and though she lives near me in rural Connecticut, she had the good sense to marry a Frenchman, with ties to a hamlet in the Queyras, a secluded 160,000-acre park of mountains and valleys in the Alpes Provençales abutting Italy. Its isolation is its virtue—you'll not find many five-star hotels, but you will find hiking trails, spotless lakes and mountainside villages where you fill up your water bottle from a tap in the middle of town. The landscape is a primordial tableau of soaring peaks, larch forests and sloping pastures strewn with gentian, crocus, edelweiss, and wild strawberries.

One reason it is so untouched is that it can be hard to access unless you have a car, but that is also the point. Lyon, Avignon and Grenoble are the nearest airports in France, but they are all at least a three-hour drive, and the train hubs (where you may rent cars) are L'Argentière-la-Bessée, Briançon and slightly farther out, the regional capital of Gap.

French aviators call the Queyras the "trou bleu"—the blue hole— because the skies are pristine 300 days a year. "The main thing to know about the Queyras is that it is remote, wildly beautiful, and to be fully enjoyed one must love to hike, bike or raft," Melora tells me. It is a place to wander through pastures, past chamois and cows sporting bells, to the towns of Aiguille, Montbardon, Molines-en-Queyras and Saint-Véran, the highest inhabited village in all of Europe, which seems unchanged from centuries ago, with communal ovens and sundials. The latter, known as *cadrans solaires*, are ubiquitous in the Queyras and are usually painted plaques on the sides of churches, bearing snippets of fortune cookie-like sayings.

This is a place to feast simply on local cheese and *fromage blanc*, honey, sausages, and *argousier*, a vitamin-rich orange fruit that grows wild and is slightly more citrussy than an apricot. All that and *tarte aux myrtilles*, too, made from wild mountain blueberries, served with a glass of génépy, an herbal liqueur and popular digestif made from macerated Artemisia flowers.

Another friend, the writer and filmmaker Erin Byrne, is my go-to person on the Jura, an idyll of rushing rivers, drenched green forests, waterfalls and deep wooded gorges in the mountains of the Franche-Comté region near Switzerland. The Jurassic period is named for this place, where limestone rocks from the age were first studied in the early 19th century, and where Gustave Courbet grew up and invented the modern Realist painting. Byrne's experience of the Jura has been nothing short of life-altering. "It completely changed the way I travel," she says of the pure air and clear, starry nights. "The place is so beautiful that for the first time, I slowed down."

Her nesting place was in the 13th-century village of Nans-sous-Sainte-Anne, northeast of Lyon and south of Besançon, which is the nearest city (and the birthplace of Victor Hugo). The TGV from Paris or the train from Geneva takes you to Mouchard, and Nans is a forty-minute ride away. The village has its own dairy with cheese and fresh milk and a baker who toots his horn as he drives through town each morning. Nans is set among cliffs, with the sources of the Lison and Verneau Rivers—that tumble with cascades and roar with waterfalls—just a short distance away. "The hike to the Lison is possibly the most forest-fragrant, clear, greenly-pristine I have ever been on," says Byrne.

The ivy-draped Château Mirabeau, now privately owned, is the centerpiece of town. It is named after Honoré Gabriel Riqueti, Comte de Mirabeau, who was no stranger to ignominy. Early in his career, he ran away with Sophie, the young wife of the elderly Marquis de Monnier, and when he later was arrested (while on the lam for another infraction), she was sent to a convent. While in prison, the Comte wrote impassioned letters tinged with eroticism to his mistress, later published in book form as *Letters to Sophie*. Soon he would redeem himself with activism, and become one of the heroes of the Revolution until he was disgraced posthumously for allegedly being on the payroll of the enemies of France.

Besides hiking along chasms and exploring underground Verneau River caves, the Jura is also the best place for cross-country skiing in all of France. And crucially, one of the best for cheese and origin of some of the greats—earthy Morbier, tangy Comté, creamy Bleu-de-Gex and the inimitable Mont d'Or, the Vacherin whose winter season is far too brief. It is no coincidence that Louis Pasteur is a child of the Jura, and his home in Arbois is a museum

dedicated to his work developing the rabies vaccine and pasteurization methods. His early experiments, requested by Napoleon III, were not on milk but on wine, another of the Jura's abundant gifts. Erin Byrne adores the pale rosé called *vin gris*, and *vin jaune* (yellow wine) is an international cult favorite, with a distinctive mineral flavor from the limestone-rich soil, whose new vintage is celebrated every February in a lively wine festival that moves to a different village each year.

So there you have it. Away from the hordes. Exercise, fresh air, cheese, wine and wild blueberries by the kilo. Any—or all—of these will be tonic for the soul.

⁂

# 84

## Hike the Beautiful Border

### THE ROUTE DES VINS, ALSACE

There are a few benefits to centuries of Germany and France fighting over Alsace, one of them being cuisine that's a near perfect hybrid. Think German-style charcuterie, salty *moricette* bread, *kugelhopf*, *choucroute*, pale lager beer, white asparagus, and creamy soups chock-full of wild beasts from the *Schwarzwald*—the Black Forest—to the immediate east. In France, the borderlands (with Italy, Spain, Switzerland and Belgium as well as Germany) are always textured, complex areas, with not just food, but language, architecture, even politics contributing to a trans-frontier *je ne sais quoi*.

The walk along Alsace's Route des Vins is only fractionally about the wine. Here, the experience is equal parts earthy and exotic, of traveling historically significant tracts of road through some of the most stunning scenery anywhere in Europe. In fact, it's easy to see why this strip between the Vosges Mountains to the west and the Rhine River to the east has been a trophy for whichever King or Kaiser laid claim to it. Imagine: Germany lost the strategic and achingly beautiful villages of Colmar, Eguisheim and Riquewehr. They lost Château du Haut-Koenigsbourg, a fortress from the Middle Ages perched madly over the town of Sélestat and the Alsatian plain. It is all to France's gain. Alsace is a land that overflows with riches, man-made and otherwise, but you can't avoid the German flavor. Nor would you want to.

The whole Route des Vins extends north-south for 105 miles from Marlenheim west of Strasbourg, south to Thann, just adjacent to Mulhouse. Green and graceful, it passes by medieval castles, some—like Châteaux Landsberg, Ortenbourg and Haut-Andlau—in glorious ruins, and hamlets with flower-lined streets that seem detached from the modern grind. And this being France, there is the clamor of morning markets. Just imagine a basket full of sugary quetsche plums, ripe in September. They are larger than grapes, colored the deep royal purple of a Medieval gown. And they grow only one place in the world: right here.

The route encompasses some 1,000 producers of Alsatian wines. This is the land of intense, fresh whites, which are connected to their place of origin—Riesling, Pinot Gris, Gewurtztraminer, and effervescent Crémant d'Alsace. There are also 51 Grands Crus d'Alsace AOP—Appellation d'Origine Contrôlée, meaning they all must—and do—conform to set standards of *terroir*.

There are five distinct segments of the trail through the Haut-Rhin and the Bas-Rhin departments. As always, there are official wine tours and unofficial ones, too, or you may prefer to just keep driving, and take in the sweep of the land, the half-timbered houses with bright Crayola shutters, the village watchtowers and steep turrets. There are fifty mini wine trails along the route, most of them easy hikes of less than two hours through local vineyards, and you can visit as many wineries as you wish. But when touring on foot, especially on a longer haul, I prefer an organized trip for several reasons: I won't get lost (which often happens, even when trails are well-tracked, even close to home); someone will tell me where to go, and they will have a hotel room waiting for me at the end of the day. Best of all, when I relinquish myself to a guide, I have the freedom to observe and have a ball without the distraction of logistics.

Little could be better than to take this journey (or a part of it) with a group of friends, people who love to be together but can also cherish the scenery and the stretches of silence on the trail, as well as benefit from the well-calibrated physical exertion. When Carol Young Gallagher trekked for six days in Alsace with a group of her girlfriends from Greenville, South Carolina, she fell into a lulling routine, with purposeful days followed by evenings of camaraderie, laughter and rest. "The rhythm grounds you," she says of her early-autumn walking trip. Each day, saddled only with daypacks (their luggage would be dropped off by car ahead of them), they hiked seven to twelve miles, an ambitious pace even with fairly easy trails throughout. "You get up about the same time each morning, eat a healthy breakfast and set out. You walk, quietly sometimes, having fun talking other times, feeling the air and sun. You stop for lunch, maybe stretch out for a quick rest, then walk some more, arriving to your hotel by mid to late afternoon, where everyone looks forward to having a beer together." Oh yes, Alsatian lager. Yum. Then dinner, a book and deep, hard-earned sleep before starting out again in the morning.

Carol tacked a few days on either end of the trip, first to explore the cobblestoned, fairy tale wonderland of Colmar and on the other end, a fancy refurbished monastery in Sélestat. In between, her journey took her group from Kayserberg to Niedermorschwihr, where they stopped at a charming small winery. They hiked into the Vosges Mountains, diverted off the wine trail, and then circled back to Kayserberg. Along the way, they encountered some *vendanges*—the late grape harvest, it was autumn after all. At times they proceeded almost meditatively, and other times in lively conversation, usually with no other hikers in sight, staying at clean, comfortable hotels at every stop. "The countryside was incredibly lush and green," she recalls. "We often had beautiful vistas of little towns below us. The vineyards were already turning golden. The scenes were very pastoral, with cows, sheep and horses, even funny little donkeys. And storks, of course." The latter is somewhat of a local mascot, and through great efforts was rescued from extinction in the last twenty-five years. These amazing creatures have a distinct character, in flight or nesting way up on the roofs and in the treetops. They are a bit French, a tad German, but all Alsatian.

# 85

## The Shining White Mountain

### THE MER DE GLACE, MONT BLANC AND FRANKENSTEIN, CHAMONIX

Winter sports buffs already know that France is the most popular ski destination in the world, containing 30 percent of the planet's major snow resorts—368 in all, with 44,134 acres of slopes and 4,000 lifts—tucked into ravines and over mountains, most notably the Alps. In winter, the Savoie and Haute-Savoie glow with the rosy cheeks of the sporty and adventurous, whose days are spent making tracks in the snow and evenings in a rapture of gastronomic bliss. There is a high concentration of Michelin-starred restaurants in the French Alps, and though I've never been to La Bouitte in Saint Martin de Belleville in Les Trois Vallées, I could gaze longingly all day at a photo of its raw-wood paneled dining room, with its serene complexion of heather and gray.

Val d'Isère, widely considered France's most perfect winter sports destination, is world-class in every sense. Linked with Les Tignes to form one of the world's largest ski areas, there are literally hundreds of miles of piste and off-piste terrain. For the fearless, La Plagne has a legendary bobsled run built for the 1992 Olympics held in nearby Albertville. Luxurious Courchevel is the glamour puss of the Alps, directly linked with seven other resorts in the Trois Vallées area, including Val Thorens, Europe's highest-altitude resort. There are over 400 miles of slopes in the Trois Vallées domain alone. Only Megève can boast the opening scene of *Charade* with Audrey Hepburn eating lunch on an outdoor deck swathed in black fur over a chocolate brown, body-hugging Givenchy ski suit. Enter the witty stranger, Cary Grant, who says some kid is throwing snowballs at Baron Rothschild. Which refers to the fact that Megève was built by the Rothschilds, whose goal was to create the "St. Moritz of France," and it maintains that reputation to this day. These resorts are all equally alluring in summer, when the snow dissolves into flowering alpine fields blazing with butterflies, lined with recreational trails and farmers milking cows.

But Chamonix stands alone for its storied pedigree. The first Winter Olympics were held here in 1924, a little over a century after this glaciated valley was graced, in fiction at least, by Frankenstein and the monster. It was here that Mary Shelley conceived her Gothic masterpiece and based its most memorable scene. That is one of four reasons—hulking, beautiful reasons—why Chamonix is a must-see; summer, winter, under billows of snow or a tapestry of clover, blinding sunshine or blinding squalls. It is home to three other imposing giants: the Mer de Glace glacier, Mont Blanc—the highest peak in Western Europe at 15,781 feet, and the craggy Aiguille du Midi. As a bonus, there is no better route to Italy than the 7.2-mile Mont Blanc tunnel road that begins in Chamonix and ends in Courmayeur.

You reach the Mer de Glace and the heroic skyline that surrounds it via the 1908 fire engine red Montenvers Railway train, which climbs 6,275 feet from town, skirting up the sides of sharply-pointed, rocky Aiguilles ("needles"). From the overlook, you can see the ice blue Mer de Glace in all its noble fury. It is a spectacular vision, the largest glacier in France that covers 12.5 square miles and moves about 300 feet a year. Fixing your eyes, blinking, you swear it heaves an inch or two. From here, you can walk or board a gondola to the Ice Grotto—a man-made enclosure carved fresh each year into the glacier's frozen heart. In summertime, there is a hilly walk down into the valley and the Plan de l'Aiguille, the mid-station of the cable car from Chamonix to the summit of the Aiguille du Midi.

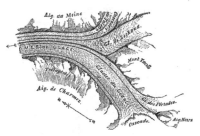

From a distance, this brooding promontory, crested with a communications spire, resembles a displaced Norman abbey, complete with mists hanging about the jagged flanks. The cable car takes you to the 12,605-foot summit, and though I wouldn't set a toe in the "Step into the Void" glass cage that was recently installed over a 3,000 foot precipice, I can still savor the view of Mont Blanc that looks close enough to kiss and the endless expanse of the French, Swiss and Italian Alps.

L'Aiguille du Midi is the launching area for one of Europe's most iconic off-piste ski runs, the 12.5 mile Vallée Blanche glacier along the Mont Blanc massif. With a vertical descent of 1.7 miles through stunning open scenery, it's challenging but doable even for moderate skiers. "I love to stop for fondue at the little chalet (the Requin Hut) about halfway down," says Katherine Johnstone, the press attaché for the French Tourist Office, who also advises you to reserve a spot on the cable car rather than leave it to chance.

Nothing today was even imagined when Mary Godwin, eighteen and pregnant, and her soon-to-be husband, Romantic poet Percy Bysshe Shelley, arrived by mule in what was then called Chamouni in July, 1816. That it profoundly impressed them is a matter of record. First, they recounted the excursion to the Mer de Glace in awestruck detail in letters published with their 1817 travelogue, *History of a Six Weeks' Tour*, which also included Shelley's ode *Mont Blanc: Lines Written in the Vale of Chamouni*. The desolate blue snows, the "palaces of death and frost," surging waves and precipices of ice that roared while constantly shifting—they were struck by the frightening beauty as they traversed the glacier's surface. "One would think that Mont Blanc," writes Mary, "was a vast animal and that the frozen blood for ever circulated through his stony veins."

It was 1816, the momentous "year without a summer," when the rains fell and sun barely penetrated the haze following the eruption of Mount Tambora volcano in Indonesia the prior year. Shelley and Godwin had been in Switzerland with their friend Lord Byron, keeping warm by fires against the alien chill, when one night, he said, "We will each write a ghost story."

"*Have you thought of a story?* I was asked each morning, and each morning I was forced to reply with a mortifying negative," she later recalled. But soon, Mary's dreams would be disrupted by visions of a scientist who animated a "hideous phantasm" out of, perhaps, parts of a corpse. Soon, Mary Godwin, who would turn nineteen in August, wrote *Frankenstein; or, The Modern Prometheus.* And lo, the terrifying, pivotal encounter between the scientist Frankenstein and the daemon of his own making takes place on the Mer de Glace, where the creature took refuge from the world that despised him. Here, the monster entreats his creator for compassion, begs to be heard, and asks him to bear responsibility for that which he wrought. "Seating myself by the fire which my odious companion had lighted, he thus began his tale," relates Dr. Frankenstein, after they cross the ice to the monster's hut. With this book and these words, Mary Shelley wrote herself and Chamonix into literary history.

❧

# 86

## The Waves Out the Empress's Window

### SURF BIARRITZ AND THE CÔTE BASQUE

The April day is mild, but the afternoon breeze picks up on the Plage des Cavaliers in Anglet, where Karine Labrouche, in a tangerine hoodie that sets off her healthy glow, runs Time to Surf school from a laid-back hut built right on the sand. Neoprene bodysuits—*combinaisons*—hang to dry alongside a selection of well-worn longboards and pointier shortboards. The beach is wide here; in the milky water I see a few figures rise and crouch in the distance and quickly come into clearer sight, riding towards shore on one of the Côte Basque's famous waves. The surf scene, bohemian buzz, temperate climate and physical oneness with the beach are why the coast from here to Biarritz to Hendaye on the Spanish border is called *la Californie française*. It's meant to be high praise, and it is, if only to point out the unique easygoing vibe and geographical kinship here on the southern Atlantic coast. But at the end of the day, in your exhausted euphoria, you get to see the pastel sunset over western France. That alone is perhaps the best reason why surf lessons should be *de rigueur* when traveling to the Côte Basque.

Today in Anglet, the waves are not exactly monsters. They are good surfing waves, excellent for beginners, somewhat gentle and foamy, but high enough to get some lift on your board. It doesn't take much for Karine to convince me that for women, there is no physical activity more gratifying, and that, as long as you don't have a serious joint injury preventing you from being able to squat on your board, anyone can do it. "The hardest part is putting on the wetsuit," she says.

Her lessons start with yoga, stretching and breathing on the beach, all to aid the *lâcher prise*, what the French call letting go. No one can control the swells that form way out in the ocean, or the waves they make, and that is a great lesson and rule number one in surfing. "There is no better feeling than to leave the earth behind you, and to go into the water in the morning when the sun is out and no one is around," Karine says. "You feel completely free."

Perhaps logically, the sport was introduced to the Côte Basque by a Los Angelino from Santa Monica. In 1956, the screenwriter Peter Viertel was in Biarritz during the filming of *The Sun Also Rises*, based on Ernest Hemingway's novel. The legend has many permutations, but the long story short is that he and his producer Darryl Zanuck noticed the gnarly waves below the balcony of their hotel and had their surfboards sent from California. Viertel first rode the breakers on Biarritz's Côte des Basques beach, and returned a year later with several more boards, generating widespread curiosity and interest in the sport. His name is legendary in Biarritz as the godfather of surfing in Europe.

Now, it's a regular stop for professionals. Every July the best female surfers in the world assemble here for the Roxy World Longboarding Championship, and the Oxbow, Rip Curl, Quiksilver and Billabong logos are ubiquitous on the twenty beaches in this stretch of coastline. But it almost never feels honky-tonk or seedy. After all, the snack shacks in the nearby surf villages of Guéthary and Bidart serve salmon tartare, *jamon ibérique*, *paté*

with guindilla peppers and Txakoli—the dry sparkling wine of the Basque region.

Biarritz has borne its evolution well, from royal getaway, to summer town of French aristocrats, to what it is today: hip, subdued, luxurious and athletic, all rolled into one irresistible package. It was Empress Eugénie who first put the town on the map in 1854, the year after her marriage to Emperor Napoleon III. That year, he built a palace for her (shaped like the letter "E"), that is now the magnificent Hôtel du Palais, which towers over the Grande Plage and the waves Peter Viertel made famous. She was known in France as Eugénie de Montijo and was a Paris-educated high-born Spanish countess who loved the familiar climate, customs and people in Biarritz, in such close proximity to her native land. In the memoirs of Augustin Filon, who served as her personal secretary when the family was forced into exile in 1870, he writes that of all her lavish residences, she loved her seaside existence here—which included picnics in Spain and walks in the Pyrénées—most of all. "Nobody thought of dressing for dinner," he writes, as if predicting today's casual elegance. "I think she was always most free and natural at Biarritz, more the Eugénie of the days of her youth," he writes, noting as well how much she loved the sea and everything about it. "I think [it] was the place she was most truly herself."

Who knows, maybe the Empress today would be a modern royal, at ease in public in her bikini, who could grab a board and paddle out beyond the froth, seeking her own Endless Summer. Or maybe she would take a private lesson with Emmanuelle Joly, a personal surf coach and six-time European champion. Like Karina, she's a goddess of the waves whose exuberant and visible good health and fitness is reason enough to give it a go. "When a woman succeeds for the first time, she is so happy," she says. "That's why we surf. It's an amazing feeling."

And just think. At the end of the day with the sun sinking low, you are bone-weary and gratified from a day charging the waves. And, you're eating dinner on the beach, watching the sunset. In *France*. Tell me it gets any better, and I probably won't believe you.

❧

# 87 Town from another Time

## AIX-EN-PROVENCE

In 1954, the American writer and on-again off-again expat Mary Frances Kennedy—M.F.K.—Fisher, who had moved with her two young daughters to Aix-en-Provence, was gently chastised by a friend while they strolled the Rue Cardinale. "Oh no!" the man cried. "Not you too! Not another tiny poetical masterpiece on the trees, the flowing waters, the many-hued effluvia of Aix!" Yikes. If there was little left to say sixty years ago about this gentle city, pray, what remains today for us poor scribes? But there was no stopping M.F.K. In fact, the anecdote appears in one of her most observant books, *Map of Another Town*, a soulful memoir of Aix-en-Provence, and yes, its gurgling waters and soft southern light, as well as the eccentric, the generous, the down-on-their-luck, the war-ravaged and sometimes, the American-averse Aixois.

Even today, the allure of Aix-en-Provence is its timelessness. So we soldier on, stay on cliché alert, and still convince ourselves that no one has experienced the sensate bliss quite as profoundly here as we have. Authenticity is the point, and why we keep coming back. Aix contains that kernel of truth we seek in escape, a place whose qualities feel familiar even as they are being revealed. It arouses our feminine sensibilities of comfort and appeals to the voluptuary in all of us. If it were human, Aix would be kind, and if it had a soundtrack, it would be a breezy riff on the piano. Here, the sweetness of the world returns to you better than it ever was before, in the juice of a nectarine from the market that drips down your chin, and on the shady Cours Mirabeau, often dubbed "the most beautiful main street in the world," framed on either side by double rows of plane trees. In the lilac furrows of Mont Sainte-Victoire, ever the fresh-faced muse so many years after Paul Cézanne painted her more than sixty times. In the sounds of the city's many fountains that are famous in their own right—the elegant Four Dolphins, the Fontaine d'Espeluque with its sea green pool of water, or the formal basin on Place d'Albertas.

Aix was founded in 123 B.C. by the Roman consul Sextius Calvinus, who believed in the healing power of the thermal springs that bubbled up from 260 feet below ground. The original baths are still visible in what is now a modern spa housed in an 18th-century ochre building, and the waters are as they were: 90° F, loaded with magnesium and calcium. For centuries, aching luminaries stopped here for the cure, including Thomas Jefferson, who sought physical therapy for the wrist he busted when he tried to jump a fence in Paris. He found his four days and forty thermal treatments quite useless, but Aix was another story. "If I should happen to die at Paris, I will beg of you to send me here and have me exposed to the sun," he wrote in March 1787. "I am sure it will bring me to life again."

These layers of history are what give Aix the permanence that allows you to walk in whatever time strata you choose. Gallo-Roman ruins give way to narrow medieval streets, not far from the graceful architecture built to herald Aix's former position as the political and cultural capital of Provence. Nearby is the ultramodern Fondation Victor Vasarely, highlighting works by the 20th-century op artist who gets much reconsideration in the postdigital era. Even the Saint-Sauveur Cathedral, constructed with stone quarried from nearby Rognes, active since Roman times, is a time capsule. The Romanesque cloister contains carved columns, some of which seem to wrap around each other, which meld into the Gothic supports and a gleaming Renaissance dome.

The beautiful architecture of the Quartier Mazarin dates from the 17th century, and it all makes space for Paul Cézanne, who was born here and died here, and while he lived, preserved Aix's luminosity for all eternity. At the Bastide du Jas de Bouffon, situated at the end of an allée of chestnut trees, you recognize the inspiration of many of his works. He painted the walls of the oval salon in what was the family country house, feverishly trying to convince his father he could be an artist. Those twelve monumental paintings were removed in 1912 (and transferred onto twenty-two canvasses), but now you sit inside the lovely salon and view an astonishing slide show, which superimposes them upon the wall. Also in Aix is Cézanne's studio, L'Atelier des Lauves, exactly as he left it when he died in 1906, with his coat and hat hanging on the rack and easel set up near the window. You can feel the painter's spirit here and imagine bowls of apples posed for a still life that would change the way we look at things.

All the historical threads lead to the Cours Mirabeau, and M.F.K. Fisher's favorite restaurant, Les Deux Garçons, known as the 2Gs, still humming after all these years. But the Glacier, another place she dined often with her two little girls, is no longer around, though its menu is recorded for eternity. "Fresh asparagus, tepid and not chilled, with a vinaigrette made at the table; plain boiled chicken with rice and a good sauce, all called Poulet Suprême or something like that; a bottle of *blanc-de-blanc* from back of Cassis...." This simple sentence is vintage M.F.K. Fisher, whose route along her private, internal map of Provence has seeped into her readers' consciousness, if not necessarily that of Aix itself. "The odd thing is that in Aix, they don't really know who she is," says her biographer Anne Zimmerman, author of *An Extravagant Hunger: The Passionate Years of M.F.K. Fisher*. And yet her cultural relevance could not be more important in 2014. Her tagline tends to be "food writer"—she was, after all, the author of *How to Cook a Wolf* and *The Gastronomical Me*—but that understates her contribution to literature and even her cultural prescience.

Zimmerman says it would not be a stretch to call her the first modern writer, whose thematically loose narratives have a lot in common with contemporary blog posts. Until Fisher, no man or woman combined food and travel in their writing—what was memorable about the meal, how it tasted, how it smelled, how it made her feel. "Before her, no one cared where the chickens they ate were raised, or where their butter came from," says Zimmerman. "M.F.K. did from the very beginning." The thousands of us who have a travel or food blog owe her a debt of gratitude. She also did something remarkable in *Map of Another Town*: she turned a gentle memoir into more of a guidebook than she could ever know. What joy there is in following her inner map along the modern, antique streets of Aix-en-Provence.

❧

# 88

## *Savory Beauty*

### THE PAYS D'AUGE, NORMANDY

I must praise the white-light beach towns that illuminate La Côte Fleurie—Deauville, Trouville, Honfleur, Cabourg—as well as the cheesemakers and cider houses in the area of Normandy called Pays d'Auge. Many of these people and places deserve their own story—starting with Marie Harel, who first created Camembert—and some of them, their own book. Marcel Proust was inspired enough to base Balbec, the fictional town in *Remembrance of Things Past*, on Cabourg. But I've put them together in one humble listing because we all love efficiency, and a day traversing the Pays d'Auge is more satisfying and culturally complete than a week in most countries.

I've mentioned before how complicated France can be in the specificity of its geography, and the locals are unwavering sticklers. It took a circuitous car trek for me to figure out the Pays d'Auge, which unites the departments of Calvados and Orne in Lower Normandy (which was split into upper and lower regions in 1956). Perhaps the area's rare diversity is what confounded me in the first place. In the span of an afternoon, you can travel from sexy beachside promenades to vistas thick with orchards, to dairies with some of the best cheese in the world.

The Pays d'Auge is a vertical rectangle (or close enough to one) whose top edge is the coast, and capital Lisieux is its midpoint. Just a few miles inland from the Promenade des Planches at the beach in Deauville, where bathing *cabines* are mostly named for movie stars who have attended the American film festival there, the landscape changes. You begin to encounter the seeping richness of pasture-land and grazing cows, most of which are different colored varieties of a local breed called the Normande, developed over centuries by Norman farmers. These cows may be blond, brown, or mostly white, but all of them have distinctive eye rings or "lunettes," and all of them produce sweet milk for Normandy's famous cream, cheese and butter.

At first the place seems thematically disparate. There are pinnacle-of-style parts and down-to-earth ones, coast, littoral and farmland, mansions and modest half-timbered houses. But a unifying harmony emerges from the fastidious sense of local pride here, and people put forth the regional identity as a genuine matter of course. This is visible, for example, in the center of Honfleur. Handsome green bottles of Cidre Bouché Brut from the Cider Route, shellfish from the fishing boats off Trouville, and raw-milk Pont l'Évêque cheese are all for sale at the markets that line the stone streets in town. The ad campaign could read: Together, we are all Pays d'Auge.

This medieval port town of Honfleur, the birthplace of Eugène Boudin, the artist who inspired the Impressionists to paint out-doors, is a good place to start for a round-trip. Sunlight is sharp and piercing here, and it's easy to see why creative types were drawn to this impossibly perfect village, with its narrow streets and quais around the Vieux Bassin, a picturesque tableau of moored boats and a rainbow of café awnings. Writers, too. Charles Baudelaire settled here for a while and famously declared, "My time in Honfleur has always been my fondest dream." The town's greatest landmark is the Church of Sainte-Catherine, built by sailors and shipbuilders out of the only material they knew: wood.

It's about an hour's drive down to Camembert, to pay homage to Marie Harel, whose legend looms large around these parts. She was a dairy farmer working in the Manoir de Beaumoncel, and in 1791 she concealed a fugitive priest from the region of Brie who was on a journey to safety after the Revolution. At that time, clergy were asked to renounce their faith, and when they refused, they became outlaws. While he was in hiding, the priest showed her how to produce the white rind that could enrobe the region's creamy (but very runny) traditional cheese. And so, Camembert, as we know it today, was born. Sadly, a statue to Marie Harel was beheaded by Allied bombs in 1944, but a second one, a gift from Ohio cheesemakers in 1953, stands—whole—by the marketplace. There is a sweet museum in Vimoutiers and you may visit La Ferme Durand, which is the only town in Camembert still making cheese the Marie Harel way.

A ramble through the Fromagerie Graindorge is a fascinating way to spend an hour, watching the raw-milk Livarot and Pont l'Évêque get strained and ultimately molded into their familiar forms. The mature cheeses are stacked onto racks like hundreds of miniature yellow cakes. A group of women in the binding room prepare the Livarot for market by wrapping a bulrush five times around the finished cheese.

Here the credos of hormone and antibiotic-free cows, free-range dairy and farm-to-table are nothing new, but the way it's always been done, even though milkmaids have given way to the efficiencies of the factory. Behind the exceptional cheese is exceptional milk, produced by cows who grass feed on the clovered pastures that carpet the Norman countryside, which the farmers claim makes the milk super creamy and rich in fat and protein.

Drive along the Cider Route, studded with apple orchards that sprawl behind ancient hedgerows. Calvados (apple brandy) is the headiest of the *eaux-de-vie*, my particular favorite for a very-late nightcap, and I visit Etienne Dupont at Domaine Dupont in Victot-Pontfol. It is refreshing to walk along the green allées where

his cider apples proliferate and are harvested, to see the presses and the distillery, and I marvel at the refined splendor of it all. The air is moist and fresh, and he hands me a snifter of really strong stuff straight from the barrel.

It is an incongruous thirty minutes back to La Côte Fleurie and the resort of Deauville, built for the gilded set in the 1860s, who had begun to discover the beauty of a beach holiday, especially one with horses and gambling. It is here on the rue Gontaut-Biron that Coco Chanel opened her first shop in 1913 and shocked the leisure class by wearing masculine clothes and open-necked shirts. Deauville remains as streamlined as one of the couturier's suits that launched right here, and the wide beach below the boardwalk is a marvel of simplicity, marked with orderly rows of red, blue and yellow umbrellas that flare as brightly as Balinese flags.

Trouville-sur-Mer, just up the road from Deauville, was made famous by Claude Monet's paintings (as were so many places in Normandy). He honeymooned here and mixed grains of beach sand into his paint. You can sense the light, the wispy clouds and the muffled wind in Monet's Trouville, and it is the same today. The beach seems endless in both directions, and in the evening few people remain, giving the feeling of dreamy isolation. When the tide is out, the water's edge seems to be in another world.

Finally, it's dinnertime, and there are two choices: Les Vapeurs or its next-door twin, Les Voiles. My friends from Paris make a point to come here occasionally on a weekend for *moules* and little gray shrimp that practically leap from the sea onto your plate.

The paradigmatic bistro, Les Vapeurs is crowded and joyous, with a menu that touts "traditional," "copious" and "pure butter." In truth, however, I've been waiting all day for dessert: Tarte Tatin, caramelized apples topped with raw Normandy cream. I try to savor it, local style, and think of the cider farms and dairy cows that roam the pastoral landscape just a few miles from here. I end the day back in Honfleur, and in the morning, I will give a wave to the Pays d'Auge's most famous/infamous woman, Charlotte Corday, as I pass Le Ronceray, the typical Norman farmhouse where she was born. Her story is worth telling because although you might not be aware of it, you certainly know her. Corday was a murderess and folk hero, the woman behind Jacques-Louis David's painting *Death of Marat*—sent up by the Simpsons, emulated by Lady Gaga, and generally one of the most recognizable artworks on earth.

Charlotte Corday was born into a family of noble lineage in 1768 in Les Champeaux en Auge, near Vimoutiers, and educated at a prestigious convent school in Caen. During the Revolution, her political sympathies aligned with the moderate Girondins, who were under attack by the more radical Jacobins. Jean-Paul Marat, intellectual revolutionist, led the Jacobin crusade to eliminate all political dissent, ordering the summary execution of anyone deemed "counterrevolutionary" for any reason whatsoever. Horrified by these excesses, Charlotte resolved to kill Marat, believing that taking his life would save hundreds of thousands of citizens.

Corday wrote letters explaining her actions and went to Paris. On the pretext of denouncing Girondins, she cleverly gained access to Marat's home and fatally stabbed him as he soaked in the bathtub. The day after the murder, the artist David, a great friend of Marat, was asked to paint the portrait of the assassinated man, whom he depicted holding Corday's letter of introduction, with the bloodied knife placed neatly on the floor beside the bathtub. She did not resist arrest and was guillotined four days later, ten days shy of her twenty-fifth birthday. Her sacrifice did not end the bloodshed, but she ultimately became a heroine of the French people. In her most famous posthumous portrait, painted by Tony Robert-Fleury in 1875, she is rendered as beautiful, her determined gaze lifted above her book, standing in the abundant landscape of her native Normandy.

# 89 *Little Paris*

NANCY

I often noticed that when people spoke of Nancy, the capital of Lorraine about 240 miles east of Paris, their voices tended to descend an octave. It was hard to discern if this was due to a inexpressible sense of awe for the place, or simply because anyone who was in on the secret preferred to gloss over it and hope that whatever they had to say would not actually be heard. I was intrigued, and it being France, getting there from Paris was *du gateau*. It takes all of ninety minutes on the TGV to travel to Nancy. This train has changed everything in France, not just in time. It has allowed us to follow up on every curiosity and taken away all of our excuses for not doing so.

Nancy seemed to exist in a different light, under a northern scrim. In *A Sport and a Pastime*, James Salter's short but nearly perfect erotic novel about an intense affair between a Yale dropout and a French shop worker, he writes of an assignation in Nancy—his lover's birthplace—in spare, polished prose. Outside the window, from the cocoon of their hotel room, he sees the stately 18th-century Place Stanislas and within it, the Opéra National de Lorraine. He notices a poster for *Lucie de Lammermoor* in "dark letters printed on violet." To me, the city seemed like the very essence of sensuality, full of secret but inviting niches.

To add additional luster, Nancy is a living, breathing design museum, the home of l'Ecole de Nancy where the Art Nouveau movement was incubated. It is also the turf on which Jean Prouvé, one of last century's most influential architects, perfected his signature minimalist style and where you can see many of his works, including a house built in 1954 in a leafy corner of the city. Sex and design. And food. Nancy is the birthplace of authentic quiche lorraine, *pain d'épices*, and Bergamotes candies. Even locals detour for the *véritable* one-layer macaron created by nuns in the 18th century and now made at Maison des Soeurs Macarons. This was a tip from Kim Massee, an American-born, Paris-raised feature film director, who is a very contented resident of Nancy, her husband's hometown. "It's like being in Paris," she laughs, "only better."

The big three, but nuance is what distinguishes Nancy from other great French cities. It glitters with sophistication without the prices, crowds and sometimes-overwrought intensity of the capital. It was once a provincial outpost but it is no more, and there is ease and a distinct lack of pretension with which it wears its glorious skin. Case in point: Kim and her husband love the seven euro Sunday afternoon performance at the opera (the same building seen from Salter's fictional eye), creamy and statuesque on the outside, with a sumptuous interior that could easily go mano-a-mano with Opéra Garnier in Paris.

Place Stanislas was envisioned, built, buffed, and gilded by the deposed Polish king Stanislas Leszczynski, whose son-in-law, Louis XV, gave him the duchy of Lorraine. The square was inaugurated in 1755 and today remains one of the most beautiful royal squares in Europe. The Grand Hôtel de la Reine is poised elegantly on the *place*. I've wondered if a room here could be the love nest of Salter's imagining? Either way, to wake up here with Place Stan at my feet is one of my reveries of European mornings, of the early sun reflected off the golden gates and incandescent buildings.

The Musée des Beaux-Arts is also on the Place Stan, and if you love midcentury design, the Jean Prouvé floor is an exceptional collection of his iconic pieces—wooden chairs and doors with round portals. Prouvé created high-style modular structures, and his work echoes in almost any edgy, cool, contemporary dwelling you'll see to this day.

It's a lovely walk from here to the Place André Maginot, on one of four itineraries on the tourist office's official Art Nouveau trail. On this route alone, there are nineteen sites, including Maison Houot with its turquoise, espaliered embellishments and the Graineterie Génin, a corner building ornamented with white ceramic poppies. Art Nouveau style flourished in the late nineteenth and early-twentieth centuries and integrated long, asymmetrical lines using insect wings, writhing vines, fruits, parts of flowers, and other organic details to create exaggerated, flowing forms in architecture and design. This included furniture, glassware, stained glass, wrought iron and ceramics fabricated for Nancy's newly wealthy patrons, who fuelled the local creative boom.

There are many big names to look for: Émile Gallé, the founder of the École de Nancy, the designer Louis Majorelle, architect Lucien Weissenburger, the Daum brothers—of the ornate, colorful glassworks that still exist today, Émile André, and others. All of them are represented in the Musée de l'École de Nancy, whose wonders when viewed collectively can at times verge on garish, but whose common roots in botany and expert craft depict a joyously unified artistic movement.

You will need a cab to visit two of the most famous Art Nouveau houses, Villa Majorelle, (or Villa Jika) and Villa Bergeret. The first is a riot of asymmetrical friezes, eaves and balconies, hugged on all sides by delicate branches, with a dark-paneled interior that blossoms in intricate renderings of plants. The imposing Villa Bergeret, built for a Nancéen postcard magnate, has brilliant stained glass windows that make me think of Louis Comfort Tiffany.

Of all the Art Nouveau riches in Nancy, there is nothing so preserved as L'Excelsior brasserie. The restaurant sparkles with more than three hundred lights reflected in omnipresent mirrors. Here, you can see Majorelle furniture, Daum lamps, Jean Prouvé banisters, graceful white ceilings with carved ferns, and stained glass windows created by another famous artisan of the day, Jacques Gruber. It's ideal for a desultory afternoon passing hours under the shimmer and glimmer. Crowds pour in all day, even for breakfast, and not just tourists. "For afternoon tea, or a tray of *fruits de mer* and a glass of white wine," says Kim Massee. "It's a little run-down, but oh, so spectacular."

Nancy is an ideal walking city, and when I overdose on the sweet pleasures of Art Nouveau, I get lost in the narrow streets and interweaving alleyways of the Old Town. The Grande Rue is the backbone of this medieval maze of shops, markets and slim houses with beautiful mullioned windows, and it seems to have changed little over the centuries. For my next trip to Nancy, Kim suggests the tiny Hôtel d'Haussonville here, a beautifully preserved 16th-century *hôtel particulier* close to the Ducal Palace, right off the Place St. Epvre and not far from the 18th-century expanse of the Place Stanislas.

This proximity of Renaissance to the Middle Ages to the earthy sensuality of Art Nouveau is a large part of Nancy's appeal. And then, there are the passionate lives one can imagine behind the hotel windows. This is the essence of what makes Nancy—sometimes—seem more Paris than Paris.

❧

# 90
# The City that Won't Let You Go

NICE

When I was younger, you know, a *lot* younger, Nice meant one thing: semi-nude sunbathing. Things have changed somewhat in France, but at one time, all of the Côte d'Azur was top-optional come summertime. On my first visit there, it was surprisingly easy to shed my bikini top and, with it, my Boston-bred inhibitions. For a while, Nice became my destination to drop my baggage, free my breasts and dive into a stack of turquoise waves. I connived a way to spend a few summers there, but I eventually cooled on Nice. Too many backpackers vying for space on the big-pebbled beach and a center that was choking on bad pizza joints. I discovered other seaside idylls where I could find some stillness and an actual slice of sand on which to rest my towel. And then, all grown up, I returned to Nice and was smitten once again.

It's strange to know a place so well and, in fact, not know it at all. That was Nice. About the time I came to my senses, I also fell back in love with the Russian writer Anton Chekhov, whose swoonworthy letters to his wife from his second long stay in Nice in the winter of 1900—"Take me and eat me with oil and vinegar. I kiss you fervently"—praise the town as a fragrant paradise where roses bloom in winter and the people are "jolly, noisy and laugh a lot." That stands to reason, as Nice (once known as Nizza) has lots of Italian blood from the centuries it was part of the House of Savoy. If it was good enough for the greatest short story writer ever, it better be good enough for me.

It was a favorite spot of Queen Victoria as well, who followed the lead of her countrymen who were so devoted to Nice that they built, at their own expense, the Promenade des Anglais, the walkway that stretches for miles along the Baie des Anges. Stairs lead down to the beaches, the free ones and the paying ones, with fancy chaises and restaurants that serve grilled fish and cool white wine.

This is where tourists tend to cluster, and I could avoid it, but why would I? Then I would have to forego the Hôtel le Negresco, a

 *belle époque* confection over 100 years old, with a pink dome in the shape of a breast, reputed to be inspired by the architect's mistress. Aside from its architectural charms and magnificent perch, it's also replete with five centuries of French art and antiquities, all blended with great original-ity and a good deal of flash by the hotel's longtime owner, Madame Augier. Her vision—down to the gold leaf moldings created by the hotel's own atelier and a 4-meter-tall chandelier made of more than 16,000 Baccarat crystals—was to immerse her guests in a wonderland of French art, culture and style. She pulled it off with flying—and unconventional—colors. The ground floor hideaway, Le Relais, is a jewel of old-world ele-gance, a wood-paneled cocktail bar whose velvet armchairs and dusky lighting make a secluded refuge for sleepy conversation and a snifter of Armagnac. "In Nice, you always have to get a drink at the Negresco," says Paris-based film director Antonia Dauphin. "I could happily spend hours there. It's such a classic."

Heaven, for me, is Old Nice and the Cours Saleya, the daily flower and produce market, *pissaladière* vendors, and the tiny

Merenda restaurant for *daube de boeuf à la provençale*. Bliss, too, is the weekend Marché Paysan farmers market for fresh cheese straight from the Alps, and a stop in the Maison Auer for a jar of candied ginger root in syrup (this being the confiserie where Queen Victoria came for her chocolate fix).

I love to walk past the vaulted porticoes of the Place Garibaldi and at night, see a movie at the Mercury Cinema. In my younger days, I never walked this far to the east, and certainly never ventured as far as the Colline du Château. I've climbed to the top in the past, but the elevator up is good for a jolt to the heart when the doors open to reveal the most remarkable view of the Côte d'Azur's sapphire waters. Ancient trees provide shade, and I explore the gardens and skirt a 19th-century waterfall that splashes on the slope once dominated by the medieval cathedral, whose fragmented ruins are here and there in the park. Most lovely is the vista down to the Old Port of Nice and the Basilica of Notre-Dame du Port. I will head in this direction next for *socca*, a pancake made of chickpea flour that the man at Chez Pipo scrapes from the shallow aluminum pan and serves piping hot, for me to douse with cracked pepper.

Clear across Nice, in the hills of Cimiez, is the Matisse Museum, and the trek uphill feels restorative on the back of my legs and bare shoulders. The painter's greatest legacy on the Riviera is not here, but at the resplendent Chapelle du Rosaire in Vence, about thirty minutes away. It was inspired by a friendship with his nurse who became a Dominican nun, Sister Jacques-Marie. Matisse began work on it at age seventy-seven and when complete, he considered it his career masterpiece. It is breathtaking in the sun, absolutely clean, white, sparkling and pure with the simple tiles and stained glass windows in the artist's distinctive blues and maize.

Nice was his home from 1918 until his death in 1954, and in 1938 he moved into the Hotel Regina, across the way from the pink

17th-century villa that houses the museum. Inside the airy rooms is an impressive collection, much of it donated by Matisse himself, of paintings, drawings, sculptures and his beloved paper cut-outs.

A woman gets more sure-footed the more she knows a place, and my feet know just where to take me in Nice, whether past 23, rue Gounod to stalk the ghost of Chekhov, or for an ice cream in the Old Town or a lemonade along the Promenade des Anglais. Nice is a sensuous little village within a city, alive with the smell of orange blossoms and onion tarts fresh from a hellfire oven. The palette is Matisse blue, peony pink, and sun-kissed yellow, best admired away from the churning crowds but alluring just the same, no matter where you stop to absorb the view.

# 91

## The Elegant Enclave

DINARD

During one midwinter road trip, even my loyal Citroën seemed to tire of the somber weather as we made our way through northern France. Both the car and I needed respite from the incessant lashings of horizontal rain and highway backwash. Instead of heading clear across Brittany as planned, I decided, upon recommendation of a friend, to stop for the day in Dinard, a seaside town of elaborate fairy tale mansions just west of Normandy. When I walked, hair matted, parka soaked, into Crêperie du Roy, an old-fashioned joint with a red painted storefront, I got that tingly rush of self-satisfaction. This was one of those smart things that happen when the itinerary gets junked.

This restaurant prepares crêpes in the traditionally Breton *sarrasin* style—with buckwheat flour. I savored every crumb of a *galette* that oozed with egg and Gruyère cheese, served with a glass of sparkling cider, which I had downed as well. When the waitress delivered a *crêpe au caramel au beurre salé*, my heart raced at the sight of this unfamiliar dish—a thick layer of melted gold swimming between the folds. Dinard had thoroughly seduced me and had done so the old-fashioned way: through my stomach. And then, you guessed it—bright sun beamed through the famously fickle Breton sky.

In all my years in France, Dinard had somehow eluded me. My friend, textile designer Keris Salmon (who spends part of every summer there) had often shown me captivating pictures that evoked the area's texture and grit. Of freshly caught langoustines and oysters still covered in kelp in the unpretentious market at Saint-Servan. Of fascinating *vide-greniers* (yard sales), candy-hued sailboats that dot the bay, and haunting granite formations and pounding surf in nearby Ploumanac'h, Locquirec and Plouezoc'h. Dinard is a great jumping-off point to explore the rest of Brittany, from Finistère to Rennes to Saint-Brieuc. "We love the dramatic landscape and rocky coastline, which is a lot like Maine," she says. "It's kind of the anti-Provence and not at all ostentatious."

I drove from Saint Malo via the Barrage de la Rance, a stunning piece of engineering and the world's first tidal power station that harnesses the impressive tides of the bay, the highest in Europe, for electricity. You can also walk across the dam from Saint Malo and back via the eight-mile coastal path. The Plage de l'Écluse in the center of town is a setpiece, down to the blue and white striped cabanas and meticulously groomed sand. There are two circuits on either side of the beach to explore the architecture and vistas of Brittany's shores and beyond. First, to the rocky promontory at La Pointe du Moulinet, with a dramatic view of the Barrage de la Rance and Saint Malo, where the spire of Saint Vincent Cathedral seems to pull the fortress straight up from the sea. The real eye candy on the route is the succession of stone neo-Gothic mansions, built by industrialists, noblemen, Russian princes and local luminaries, with gabled slate roofs, parapets, and façades draped in ivy. The second walk, to La Pointe de la Malouine, offers still more views and cliffside mansions with zillion dollar views. The most jaw-dropping of all is the towering brick Les Roches Brunes, built between 1893-1896, that despite its grandeur and proportions has sweetness about it, like a giant playhouse for the most spoiled French dolls. The villa's bay windows seem to hang directly over the waves.

The sun dips behind the clouds, and soon the rain starts again, and with that the aspect of the mansions shifts from girlish and graceful to rather forbidding. I head down the hill for salt caramels that you can buy any number of places in Dinard, but which tend to be made elsewhere in Brittany, in towns such as Cancale or Quiberon. Historically, Bretons salted their butter, while Normans did not. Salt from the marshes has been harvested for centuries in the medieval town of Guérande, traditionally part of Brittany, so it was always cheap and plentiful. Next door in Normandy, salt was expensive, so the farms churned out that lovely sweet butter without the addition of *fleur de sel*. Salt caramels might be a trend in Brooklyn and San Francisco, but they've been doing it that way in Brittany for decades. Sweet and creamy and a tiny bit salty, each wrapped in cellophane, I buy half a kilo and dig right in.

On the way back to Saint Malo, I stop at Armox-Lux, one of the main brands of the iconic striped Breton sailor shirts, which no one in France seems to wear, but which come in all kinds of colors schemes—light blue and chocolate brown, pink and ecru. I can't resist a top in classic blue and white, crisp and tidy as the beach awnings in Dinard. I knew I would be back, and I was, on a day so clear and fine I hardly even needed to be rescued by lunch. But it was Brittany, and who am I to pass up a perfect crêpe or two?

※

# 92

## Blue Water, White Cliffs

### ÉTRETAT, NORMANDY

Everyone is a poet, often a struggling one, when gazing at the chalky cliffs, known as the *falaises*, of Étretat, whose sheer faces rise straight up like a wall from the whitecaps of the English Channel between Le Havre and Dieppe. I pause to observe the timeless scene, search for an original turn of phrase to describe the arches that plunge into the water and seem hewn into the cliffs by a stone carver. When that fails, I simply focus on what it feels like to stand here under the sky that blends into the ocean, whose currents nuzzle the stone curves and spires as if they are conscious beings.

Speechlessness can take over when confronted with this degree of beauty, especially natural rock formations, whether in Arizona's Grand Canyon, or Port Campbell, Australia. I'm giddy, buzzed. The mind spins, duly blown. But here on Normandy's Alabaster Coast, the sight and the hollow song of the seagulls may lead a witness down other avenues, towards insight, the shadowy recesses of the human heart, and something bigger than mere awe. The 19th-century Boston poet Louise Chandler Moulton, friend of Mark Twain and Julia Ward Howe, wrote not about Étretat's splendor as viewed from the pebbled beach, but about love slipping away:

We two, with lives no star of hope makes bright,—
Whom bliss forgets, and joy no longer mocks,—
Hark to the wind's wild cry, the sea's complaint,
And break with wind and sea against the rocks.

As a muse, Étretat's powers are potent as well as eternal. The archways, or gates, were rendered by Eugène Delacroix, Eugène Boudin, Gustave Courbet and most prolifically by Claude Monet, who voraciously documented the luminosity and colors here as inspiration for over fifty of his paintings. He traveled to Étretat frequently and hung out with the local celebrity, writer Guy de Maupassant, who had built a posh villa there. (Some of Maupassant's short stories feature the beach at Étretat as a contained stage where the drama unfolds between the limestone portals on either side.)

In February of 1883, Monet painted twenty views from the beach, and when they evolved from studies into paintings, they would become some of Impressionism's most quintessential images. He climbed the cliffs with his easel, struggled with Normandy's wet winter weather, billowing mists and changing tides, and sketched the fluctuations in atmospheric conditions and shifting light. In *The Cliff, Étretat, Sunset*, the Porte d'Aval and the Aiguille (the "Needle"), a 230-foot rock spire that juts straight up from the sea, are almost black before the setting sun. Monet also battled rushing waters to study the massive arch called Manneporte, and from there, painted east towards the monumental Porte d'Amont, dabbing his canvas with slashes of orange or deep violet. His *falaises* appear dappled in sunlight in a gentle sea, or mired in clouds while the waters whirl. You sense the awe Monet had for his subjects and how these forms were so much more than statuesque objects worthy of his paintbrush. Rarely does the ghost of genius feel more within reach than it does here in Étretat.

When you stand at the center of the beach on the stone carpet of opalescent geodes, the kind formed from sedimentary rocks, you feel them, rounded and softened by the sea, rolling under your feet. In sunlight, the reflections from quartz crystals set the expanse between the arches ablaze, and it's pleasant to imagine the gatherings Maupassant wrote about in his fiction, the ladies in bathing attire gasping as they enter the chilly water.

Walking left along the beach, when the tide is out, I'll venture underneath the arches to peek into the black cave in the Falaise d'Aval and through the gate towards the pointy pinnacle of the Aiguille. Nearby are stairs that lead to the well-marked path up the cliff, and at the top, I cross over to the precipice, a bit too close for comfort, to see the chop, leaden and opaque, through the keyhole of the Manneporte. The trail laced with wildflowers leads to the top of the formation, which Maupassant described in his story "The Penguins' Rock" as "an enormous arch through which a ship could pass." From there, the vista is framed by the pale bluffs that roll evenly up and down the coast.

The path continues for miles, but instead I descend to the seaside promenade, then head towards the Falaise d'Amont at the other end of the beach. Eighty-three steps to the top of the cliff, the path widens to a flat grassy area, past a sweet stone chapel, Notre-Dame-de-la-Garde, built in 1854 to protect seafarers. Behind the chapel is a monument to a pair of aviators who vanished here in 1927. A soft rain falls, so I take caution on the edge and then climb down the chalk steps of the arch, which is almost vertical and is slippery even on a dry day. I land at the bottom, on a beach beside Porte d'Amont. The cliffs up the coast are colossal walls, topped with grass that resembles a soft green coverlet. There's a blustery rain this February day, and the fact that I can empathize with Claude Monet as he fought the elements strikes me as absurd, but it is also true. I'm soaked, out of breath and—as most of us tend to be in Étretat—overwhelmed. I've been battered by wind here in winter and baked by summer sun, and all I can ever do is gawk with respect and amazement. I still cannot find words for these heavenly cliffs, but they seem so patient. They will wait for me and for every other poor fool who was rendered speechless here on the beach at Étretat.

❧

# 93

## The Strange and Wonderful Land

### VOLCANOES AND CHEESE, THE AUVERGNE

When I lived in Paris and was having a bad day, I would drag my boyfriend to l'Ambassade d'Auvergne, a restaurant near our apartment in the Marais, for a warm dish of *aligot*. To state it inelegantly, *aligot* is cheesy mashed potatoes with a hint of garlic served with Auvergnat *saucisse*, that—cholesterol be damned—is one of the world's most dreamy concoctions. With a base of Cantal cheese (one of several from the Auvergne), the dish originates in Laguiole (of the knife fame) and was first prepared for pilgrims stopping to rest on the trek to Santiago de Compostela. Like a bowl of rib-sticking oatmeal, *aligot* must have held the monks over for a rigorous day of walking and prayer. For me, those creamy, salty spoonfuls of heaven have frequently been the antidote to all that ailed me. The same could be said for the Auvergne itself, so fresh, inviting and unpretentious that it could be the geographic equivalent of comfort food—the best in France.

Those who know the Auvergne tend to be evangelical about it, for good reasons—cheese being a big one—so wild and brooding is the landscape, so unlike any other tract of wilderness in France. This central patch of the country, shaped rather like an animal-skin rug, is composed of a range of dormant volcanoes known as *puys* (from Provençal for "hill") with their attendant flat tops, hollow craters and violet lakes. At 302 feet, Lac Pavin, formed by lava flow and glacial erosion, is the deepest of all. In clear skies the water is almost indigo, and under clouds it becomes anthracite gray. The heart of the lake is as hushed as a painting when you stop and gaze at the reflection of the oars on your rented rowboat, or out at the fringe of spruce, birch and beech trees.

Nothing can dull the flawless spectacle of the highest volcano and icon of the Auvergne, Puy de Dôme (which you can hike or summit in an adorable little train) from the capital of Clermont-Ferrand, a city built out of black volcanic stone. Or Puy de Sancy, the highest point in the Massif Central, or the sharply pointed Puy Griou, or the gap of the Brèche de Roland—all part of the Chaîne des Puys that form a surging backdrop to the cheese route. As you drive, carpets of green vales and meadows separate you from the spent volcanoes that seem to tumble and roll in voluptuous crests, peaks and plateaus.

The Auvergne covers lots of territory, much of it through the Parc Naturel Régional des Volcans d'Auvergne. Here, the countryside still seems primordial, as the world was before man. This is what draws you in and keeps you snapping photos, mouth agape from one luxuriant panorama after another. But it is the cheese, the region's lifeblood and raison d'être, that will sustain you.

According to local officials, there are more cows than people in the Auvergne. Lots more. They feed on grass and flowers that extend to infinity along the rolling prairie and mountain slopes in the warmer months. Bright clumps of yellow Lady's Bedstraw, gentian, white hogweed blossoms, Alpine fennel, goat's rue, Bishop's wort, yarrow, wild thyme, and vanilla grass make up the sweetly perfumed diet for the spoiled Auvergnat dairy cows—the red and white Montbéliardes and the hardy Salers.

There are five PDO cheeses in the Auvergne—Protected Designation of Origin, meaning no one anywhere else can use the name—and together they round out Auvergne's earthy cuisine. They are the firm and chewy Cantal, produced for 2,000 years in  the department of the same name; creamy Saint-Nectaire, aged on a bed of rye straw; the mild blue-veined Fourme d'Ambert, made at high altitude in the areas around Puy de Dôme and Saint-Flour; the smooth and salty Bleu d'Auvergne; and Salers, made from the milk of grass-fed cows and produced on the volcanoes.

The Association de Fromages AOP de l'Auvergne has created a map with a whopping thirty-eight different producers to visit, most of them listed as *GAECs*—the official classification for local farmers—and will provide it, even mail it to you beforehand. The trail takes you through the central, south and west flanks of Auvergne, primarily through the Puy de Dôme and Cantal departments. Most of the farms are still family-owned, rooted in the Auvergne's agricultural traditions, now defiantly sustainable.

At Ferme des Supeyres, quite east of Clermont-Ferrand, cows graze at extremely high altitude and produce the fat-rich, perfumed milk for their exceptional Fourme d'Ambert. At Le Gaec de la Cime des Prés at Egliseneuve d'Entraigues, Stephanie Fau runs the cheese making operations at her family farm, producing velvety Saint-Nectaire from milk produced at an altitude of 3,500 feet near the Massif du Sancy. The Société Fromagère de Riom es Montagnes is a good-sized dairy where you can see one of the most important Cantal ripening cellars and taste the five Auvergnat cheeses. It is also the capital of Bleu d'Auvergne, fêted lavishly in the town each August.

The Cave de Salers is located in the picturesque fortified hamlet of Salers, one of the Plus Beaux Villages, located in the Monts du Cantal of the Parc Naturel Régional des Volcans. It is one of the

Auvergne's most beautiful settings, and you can see Salers ripening cellars and taste cheese from ten different producers. Sixty
Montbéliardes roam 172 acres of pasture at Anglards-le-Pommier
in Saint-Cernin, where they staunchly uphold their tradition
to produce raw-milk Salers when the cows are still in pasture.
Here you can also find luscious yogurt, butter, *faisselles* and then,
picnic nearby in the flowery fields. Lastly, the stately Chapelle
d'Albepierre Bredons looks over the Grange de la Haute Vallée, a
farm whose wildflowers and meadows provide nourishment for the
cows. The visit includes the gorgeous barn and a tour of the facili-
ties where they produce Cantal, Salers, and Bleu d'Auvergne.

While on a spin in the Auvergne, you can divert to some of
France's most under-visited treasures and medieval villages with
their attendant granite Romanesque churches. The Saint-Michel-
d'Aiguilhe Chapel in Le Puy-en-Velay, whose bell tower pierces the
sky from atop a volcanic outcrop; the powerfully aloof Forteresse
de Polignac and the dignified ruins of Château de Randon; the
privately-owned Château de Parentignat, a pristine reminder of
France at its most civilized, with a pure 18th-century English garden. There is Vichy, of course, with its famous thermal baths, and
the lesser-known Thermes de Bourbon-l'Archambault, which has
some of the loveliest mosaics and spa architecture in Europe; and
lastly, the noble Château de Murol, a fortress on a basalt outcrop-
ping, where the castle's flat roof is an aesthetic match to the trap-
ezoidal volcanoes beyond.

Or, you can just divert—reservation definitely necessary—due
south, where Auvergne meets Aubrac, to Laguiole and three-star
chef Michel Bras's knockout modern hotel and restaurant (Bras)
that he runs with his son Sébastien. The crisp architectural lines
would be daring even in Brentwood or Montecito, and here
its transparency and minimalist lines serve to blend the structure, almost discreetly, into the more dramatic landscape. The

mostly-glass building is boldly cantilevered over the expanse of wilderness and a broad vista of volcanoes and grassland on which cows munch pink and yellow blossoms. You can't imagine a better view. And at dinnertime, with fresh Cantal from the neighborhood, you can't imagine a better *aligot*.

❧

# 94 Les Plus Beaux Villages

## THE 157 MOST BEAUTIFUL VILLAGES IN FRANCE

If I had all the time in the world, plus bags full of money and not a lick of responsibility, I would rent a car and visit every last one of the Plus Beaux Villages de France and stay a week or so in each place. I would drive across the Auvergne and wind my way to Saint-Saturnin in Puy-de-Dôme and eat a peach by the Renaissance fountain in the center of town. I'd head towards Perpignan in the Eastern Pyrénées and find the medieval heart of Mosset, a tight assemblage of sunbaked buildings perched high above the Castellane Valley between the mountains and the Mediterranean. I'd do like my friend Natalie Randall, and rent a house in the flame-colored hilltop town of Roussillon in the Vaucluse, and buy ochre and sienna pigments from the markets to mix into my paint back home. One by one, I would cross them off my list: the rare, the radiant, the dramatic, the well-nurtured and beautifully maintained little towns in France.

By the time you have this book in hand, there may already be a cool new smartphone app that notifies you when you're within striking distance of one of the official most beautiful villages. In the meantime, Michelin has a special road map dedicated to all 157 of them, which are scattered on hilltops, lakeshores, river ravines and mountain crags throughout the countryside of France.

The French are serious about honoring their cultural treasures by designating the crème de la crème, and just a handful are anointed a Most Beautiful Village. This categorization began as a measure towards self-preservation and civic pride. In 1982, the mayor of tiny Collonges-la-Rouge, a village in the Limousin region, started a group consisting of other provincial mayors who were dedicated to promoting the historical legacies of their villages. They hoped their efforts would help stem flight from small towns to big cities, which posed a looming existential crisis to significant stretches of rural France. Today, this association is one of the most elite clubs of its kind. Membership is hard-won and involves a rigorous selection process that, name aside, is much more than a beauty contest.

Any town—even a geographically blessed or historically important one—that has relinquished its soul to a theme park does not stand a chance. Too many junk shops slinging too many gaudy souvenirs will doom a town from the get-go. That initial hurdle cleared, the town population cannot exceed 2,000 people, and it needs to house at least two significant historical landmarks that helped shape and define its heritage and which the village is committed to preserving. The town has to demonstrate proof of this municipal support. It is then evaluated in several other ways, while the mayor, the architecture, the commitment, and the plan all get a thorough screening.

The Plus Beaux Villages approach puts a particularly French spin on sustainable tourism. These towns want tourists, of course, but they don't want their visitors whizzing through only to leave their disorderly footprints behind. The whole endeavor is geared to promoting a respectful approach to tourism and raising the quality of what can be provided to these visitors. Mostly, they want to preserve what they have and share it with the rest of us in the best possible way.

I have yet to stay a week in one of the Plus Beaux Villages, but I have spent good hours in many, forever making notes, trying to stitch together a patchwork of memory—of the Mediterranean overlooks (Gassin), sleepy riverbanks (Montrésor), ancient ramparts (Rodemack) and places to stop for macarons (Beuvron-en-Auge). On the way to Cherbourg once, I had my GPS direct me to Barfleur (I could have used that app, actually), and I found a serene seaside town that was once the port of entry for Richard the Lionheart and other English kings, and the port of departure for William of Normandy when he launched his boats towards the Battle of Hastings. There was a rocky promontory to breathe the salt air, and a pleasant crêperie overlooking the cove. There was also a generous-spirited woman in the tourist office who sent me on a slew of side trips, which I would have done if only I'd had a week, or a lifetime. I love to imagine what I could learn and what I could see if I were to give myself up to exploring the most gorgeous places, in the most impressive settings, in the most lovingly tended-to towns in all of France.

❧

# 95 *Jewel of Picardie*

## THE FLOATING GARDENS AND
## CATHEDRAL OF AMIENS

Considering the French word for novel is *roman* as in "romance," it stands to reason that some of the most powerful love stories ever toiled upon and wept over are set in France. Amiens is not the first place I've been drawn to by fiction, but it was *Birdsong* by Sebastian Faulks that inspired me to go there. From the opening lines, I was hooked on his lyrical language, his description of Amiens, its lilacs, hedges, fishermen on the banks of the canals and floating gardens. *Birdsong* is a love story between the Englishman Stephen Wraysford and Madame Azaire, the wife of his employer. Soon, the story of their affair interweaves with Stephen's solo narrative, as he becomes a Lieutenant in the British Army, serving in the tunnels along the nearby Somme River. Here one of the bloodiest battles in history occurred from July to November 1916 during World War I. Love and war make the best, and usually the saddest, romances of all.

As you've noticed by now, there is no separating the past from the present in France, no mater how fast your wireless connection or how biodegradable the shower gel in your hotel room. A lot of this past is a downer, let's be honest, as much of the country's history happened over a continuum of wars won and lost. But viewed against the backdrop of the ages, omnipresent history is what always makes a trip to France important, no matter how many euros I spend shopping or how frivolous I may convince myself I want to be.

In travel, I like to seek context—fictional, real or otherwise—for my surroundings. I like to find a memory, even someone else's, to unearth, or a focus that prevents me from being a mere outsider, prone to losing out on the value of a place or worse, disappearing in the folds of a random city. And in Amiens, there is much more context beyond the beloved historical novel that imparts the memory of battles and war. There is great heritage as well—the cathedral and the *hortillonages*—and the rest is icing on a thick slice of *Gâteau Battu*, a heart-stopping cake made with ten pounds of butter and egg yolks.

Amiens is the capital of Picardie, ninety miles north of Paris and a unique iteration of the paradigmatic French city. Its timbered houses along the Quai Bélu in the Saint-Leu quarter, where the Somme splits into branches, have an almost tropical twist, with façades in pink, blue and canary yellow. From the Place du Don, you see the 367-foot black spire of Notre-Dame d'Amiens, whose slenderness is accentuated by the enormity of the cathedral on which it sits.

Beauvais, Rouen, and Notre-Dame d'Amiens form the three points in a magnificent triangle of 13th-century Gothic cathedrals in this corner of the country. Notre-Dame, at the northeast angle, deserves all the superlatives it gets. It is the largest cathedral in France, 476 feet long, significantly longer and wider than both Reims and Chartres. Inside, the scale comes to glorious life, as air, light and verticality envelope you in an elegant nave whose vault apex is 139 feet high (and which is three times taller than it is wide, due to a miraculous feat of cantilevering).

The cathedral is one of the best examples of High Gothic architecture in France by virtue of its unity—something that rarely happens with the strife, fires and other interruptions that can fell a stone church or fragment its construction. Most of it was built rapidly—from 1220 to 1270—and, for that reason, it is as harmonious a church as exists in Europe. During the Revolution and two wars that burned at its doorstep, Notre-Dame, though not unscathed, stood fast through it all. In 2000, during a highly advanced cleaning process, traces of the original paint used to decorate the three deep-set portals on the western façade were discovered. Every summer evening and at Christmastime, these exact colors are projected onto the cathedral in a brilliant laser light show, recreating its appearance in medieval times.

If the cathedral is the emblem of Amien's heart, the floating gardens—or *hortillonages*—represent its soul. It is an enchanted forest, a 741-acre jigsaw of canals and greenery right inside the city between the Somme and Avre Rivers. In the Middle Ages, the inhabitants of Amiens created a mosaic of raised, irrigated gardens within the ponds and canals that had begun to form as the Somme widened. Once, there were 950 family plots, passed down through generations, which grew fruits and vegetables for the entire city. Today, there are only 7 working *hortillons* (market gardeners), and over 1,000 privately owned and maintained gardens. On market morning, the *hortillons* fill up their punts with radishes, artichokes, leeks, melons and flowers and bring them to the growers market on Place Parmentier at the foot of the cathedral.

You can walk around the network of canals, called *rieux*, via a towpath, but I prefer the tranquil float under the willows and canopies of footbridges in a hired *barque à cornet*. The journey past low cottages through dense vegetation is one of the most unusual wanderings you can have in France. No cars, no electricity in these parts, only the rustle and cry of marshland birds—spoonbill, herons, coots, avocet, moorhens, ducks, and my favorite to say out loud: the great crested grebe. You will swoon at the savage tangle of flowers that changes from April to October: apple blossoms and weeping cherries, poppies, wild purple orchids and marigolds.

It's a joyful and contemplative backdrop for a city that, like so many others in France, has borne its share of sorrow. An estimated 1,200,000 soldiers were killed in the Battle of the Somme in 1916. The city remembers, and time glides on. Today, the *hortillons* still slip through their canals, and the cathedral spire stands tall over Amiens and no doubt always will.

᪥

# 96 The Little Dairy

## THE LAITERIE AND SHELL COTTAGE, RAMBOUILLET

Beyond its architecture, for a building to be truly great, the walls must also breathe a great story. The Sainte-Croix Cathedral in Orléans might be just another empyrean glory-dome had Joan of Arc never darkened its Gothic doorstep. The ballroom at Fontainebleau might be one of many gilded temples to royal amusement had it not been a locus of intrigue between Catherine de' Medici and her husband's mistress, Diane de Poitiers. And the Queen's Dairy, which celebrates palatially the virtues of milk, maternity and womanhood, as well as the Shell Cottage (*Chaumière*)—both at Château de Rambouillet—are shadowed by a narrative that owes its drama not to those who passed through but to those who did not.

Whatever your opinion of Marie Antoinette's reign and sense of entitlement, it is hard to dispute that she was a captive of her birth and her time. She was fourteen when she was married off to the future King Louis XVI, and they did not provide empathy training to the *haves*. This was no Kate Middleton—Marie Antoinette did not grow up with regular folks. Nor did her ferocious mother, Empress Maria Theresa of Austria, cut her much empathetic slack.

When Louis XVI overcame his sexual obstacles, he was the rare monarch not to maintain an official mistress. Unlike the Petit Trianon, which was built by Louis XV for his lover Madame de Pompadour, the Laiterie at Rambouillet was built by Louis XVI as a surprise for his own wife. He had bought the château and surrounding forests as a hunting lodge in 1783 and hoped that through the dairy, she would come to love Rambouillet, which she is said to have loathed, and want to spend more time there—with *him*—when he repaired there to hunt. She had already found Arcadian delight in her pleasure dairy at Versailles, and so he spared no expense and deprived himself of no luxury in an effort to surpass the Petit Trianon and entice her to Rambouillet.

Of course, the Revolution and the guillotine intervened before the dairy could get much, if any, use. "To me, maybe because of its spectacular beauty, it is a slightly melancholy place," says Elizabeth Stribling, luxury real estate specialist and chairman of the U.S.-based French Heritage Society. "It is an undiscovered jewel."

The Château de Rambouillet is now a French government building, where treaties are signed and visiting heads of state are housed, so it's good to call ahead to make sure the guided tours are still on schedule. To see the Laiterie and the Chaumière, you are required to tour the castle first and, as with all the grand royal properties, you should go prepared for lots of walking.

In the center of the royal menagerie and sheepfold sits the refined, neoclassical Laiterie. The salubrious effects of milk were much heralded at the time, especially among aristocratic women, who, influenced by thinkers like Rousseau, were encouraged not only to drink fresh milk but to breastfeed their children. It was all of a trend to return to the garden, as it were, and to promote healthful living. Marie Antoinette had in fact expressed the desire to breastfeed rather than use a wet nurse, but was denied.

As a thematic signpost, above the door of the sandstone building is a relief of a cow nursing a calf. The interior gleams with polished stone and impeccable detail, and the front, circular room is topped with a dome designed to welcome a cascade of sunlight. This is the Salle de Dégustation—the tasting room—where Marie Antoinette was to be offered milk, cream, a cottage cheese called *faisselle*, butter and even ice cream—all made on the château grounds by an expert team of milkmaids.

The second room, the Salle de Fraicheur, was where she and her guests would relax and digest. There are milky-white marble friezes by the artist Pierre Julien on both of the longer walls. The man-made grotto at the end of the room is a marvelous sight, coursing with fresh water, adorned with a Julien sculpture of Amalthea, the mythological foster mother of Zeus who nursed him to health with goat's milk. Medallions depict the milking of animals, and the highest one shows a mother delivering the freshest of all dairy: breast milk.

Sadly, little remains of the Etruscan-style china service, now the stuff of legend, commissioned by Louis XVI for the queen. One such remnant is a holy grail of the porcelain world, a flesh-colored drinking cup shaped like a full, nippled breast that rests on a tripod stand decorated with goat heads. Only one of the original four is known to exist and can be seen at the Musée National de Céramique in Sèvres.

The Shell Cottage, or Chaumière aux Coquillages, was commissioned by the Duc de Penthièvre (the richest man in France, who sold Château de Rambouillet to the king) for his daughter-in-law upon the death of her husband, his son. Surrounded by English gardens, the cottage's exterior resembles a simple peasant's hut with a thatched roof. The bones sticking out of the façade are ox femurs, thought to be porous enough to absorb the interior humidity. None of these features bear a hint of the splendor within.

Inside the salon, what first appears as intricate mosaic or marquetry is, upon closer inspection, a magnificent assemblage of thousands and thousands of seashells, all collected in Haute-Normandie. The rotunda, the pilasters, the walls and their four recessed niches designed to hold perfume burners, *everything* is elaborately and artistically covered in shells. Understandably, it took about three years to complete this room. The emerald green silk chairs and settee, decorated with shells and reed designs, are shaped to nest into the curved walls of the cottage.

The next room, the lovely boudoir, is decorated in girly pale blue, green and white with painted birds framed in gold. A beautiful place for a young widow to relax with her friends, right? Except the Duc de Penthièvre's daughter-in-law, for whom he created this treasure, was Princesse de Lamballe, the head of Marie Antoinette's household. She refused to denounce the monarchy and her dear friend the queen, and in 1792, was brutally killed by a mob outside La Force Prison. As for Marie Antoinette, it is uncertain if she ever even laid eyes on her husband's extravagant gift, let alone set her lips on one of her special porcelain cups.

✣

# 97 *And Offshore*

## ÎLE DE RÉ, ÎLE D'OLÉRON, ÎLE D'YEU, AND BELLE-ÎLE-EN-MER

France has its own antidotes to overpopulated seaside resorts, and the cleverest people already know it. Islands. Idylls of saltmarshes and sun-bleached fishing villages lulled by the hum of waves, luffing sails, and migrant birds. Lots of islands, rising from the waters off the Mediterranean, Channel and Atlantic coasts. These tend to be laid-back places where there is no gold-encrusted scene to keep pace with, only the meld of fresh air and the soothing routines of life offshore. Islands are for dedicated romantics who seek a certain breed of isolation, who don't wish to duke it out over parking spots and who like low-key cycling on low-voltage bikes with wicker baskets. By the time she boards the ferry, the islander has already weeded herself out.

Try getting a little insider skinny from someone who frequents Île de Ré in Poitou-Charentes, accessible by a narrow, 1.8-mile bridge from the handsome harbor of La Rochelle. They clam up, answer a fake phone call on the mobile, feign death. One can't blame them for not wanting to share. It is one of the most pristine experiences possible in France, tasteful, understated, refined but unpretentious. The island is a favorite with Paris's moneyed nobs, but it neither abides nor imparts any haughty airs. It does glamour its own way: barefoot in a pareo or a white linen sundress.

Take everything you love—fresh oysters and mussels at seaside cafés. Whitewashed villages—some on beaches, some on ports, with doors and shutters delicious shades of teal, green, and blue. Add sixty-two miles of bike paths that lead through forests, wheat fields, and salt marshland full of osprey and egret. And oh my, those beaches. Add vermilion hollyhocks that sprout from the cobblestones and shaggy brown donkeys in striped trousers. Add sea salt. *Fleur de sel* is harvested here and is mixed into the famed salt caramel ice cream at La Martinière in Saint-Martin-de-Ré, a hub edged with unsullied medieval ramparts. It's one of the most quintessentially French places you will ever see. But don't tell anyone.

Also in the Charente-Maritime is the wilder, less recherché Île d'Oléron. Its glories were first pointed out by my friend Merry Mullings, whose exquisite taste—she sells the highest-quality textiles in the world—does not mean she's not a regular girl who likes her relaxation to be casual, outdoorsy and of course, beautiful. "We love the western side, miles of pure white sand, rolling, surfable waves, warm water, and not a jellyfish in sight," she says. "Go out of season and there may be just four or five people on the beach."

It's true—off season is always best. Traffic can back up on the viaduct from Bourcefranc-le-Chapus on the way to Oléron's twenty-five beaches—those surfer-friendly ones on the west that Merry likes, surrounded by dunes and pine forest. The gentler ones are on the opposite east coast, separated from the rough Atlantic—stunning Gatseau, with its white-hot sands, and picturesque Boirie Beach, with a row of changing cabanas painted in bright stripes and solids, one of the most effortlessly chic sights you will ever see. And a few nude enclaves, if you don't like sand trapped in your bikini.

Mostly, Oléron has miles and miles of bike paths, waterways lined with washed-pastel fishing huts, clear skies and blue water, which conspire to usher in island euphoria. If that doesn't tempt you, imagine this. In Marennes-Oléron, a 24/7 vending machine dispenses chilled, meaty oysters from the Maison Gillardeau—the Hermès of shellfish in France. Have lemon will travel.

Up the Atlantic coast brings us to Île d'Yeu in Vendée department of the Pays de la Loire, reachable by a forty-five-minute ferry from Fromentine all year, and in summer, another one from Saint Gilles Croix de Vie. It's tiny, just 6.2 miles long and 2.5 miles wide, but there are 19 miles of perimeter coastline, all of it navigable by bike. And super mellow—Venice Beach to Île de Ré's Malibu. The island packs in the natural wonder: the north and northwest coastline is shallow granite cliffs, rocky inlets and breezy bays; east, across from the mainland, is a gorgeous strip of beach and dunes that stretches from bustling Port-Joinville to the Pointe des Corbeaux lighthouse. The south coast is a mixture of cliffs, swimmable coves, and an almost Celtic (or Breton) heathland scattered in springtime with wandering heather and asphodelus. Port de la Meule is a tiny gathering of civilization, flecked with the white of fishing boats bobbing in the harbor. Inland is the whietewashed village of Saint Saveur and an exceptional summertime market with several vendors selling chic, made-in-France hot weather fashion. The stalls are set up beneath wide umbrellas in primary colors to match the town's lollipop-hued shutters.

Île d'Yeu is about hiking the footpaths, cooling off in Gulf Stream waters, ducking into a 14th-century castle, getting waffles and artisanal ice cream at Tatie Bichon. Says Connaught Thomas, who works in the fashion industry in Paris, "The feeling is all about the uncomplicated pleasures of life. The island does that really well!"

Last stop on our island jaunt is due north to Belle-Île-en-Mer in Brittany. The photos in the brochure look like those exaggerated watercolors: ocean too blue, beaches too empty, mimosas too voluptuous, terrain too virgin. It's real. The ferry from Quiberon is its own sweet slice of pleasure with gulls swooping in the sea spray. Then you come upon the lighthouses of Le Palais lit up like Christmas candles and greet this dramatic granite outpost of craggy pinnacles and promontories, the softest green hills and those surprisingly barren beaches.

Bit by bit you feel its massive history that parallels that of France: ancient Celtic megaliths, fortresses erected by King Henry II to thwart pirate invasions, rebuilt as citadels by the great military engineer Vauban, on through British then German occupation. To the south is Bangor, a maze of rocky plateaus and surfing waves, the wildest part of the island. To the southeast is the 1,000 year-old town of Locmaria, with miles of towering cliffs and white beaches in which to bury your toes. Near Sauzon is Pointe des Poulains, where the actress Sarah Berhnardt came in 1894 at age fifty and fell desperately in love with the tempestuous landscape. She bought an abandoned fort set atop a seaside cliff and created a country house where she entertained illustrious Parisians as well as her family. "Belle-Île is a precious pearl, a delicate emerald, a rare diamond made iridescent from the blue reflections of the sky and the sea," she wrote. "I very much love this island."

All this and a tin of sardines. The fancy ones, dated like vintage wines, from the Belle Iloise cannery, producer of that brilliant paradox: stylishly packaged canned fish. I love the white tuna with extra virgin oil, the yellow container pretty enough to display on my coffee table. It's not a bad idea to stock up. This is an island, after all, an ocean away from terra firma.

❧

# 98

## Eat, Drink, Swashbuckle

GASCONY

Could even the French be unclear on the geography of Gascony? When I wrote one tourist official in the southwestern part of the country for information on the area, she wrote back, "Marcia, what do you understand Gascony to be?" It seems that Gascony—administratively and as a point on the map—is somewhat fluid, a vague green kingdom of perfumed fields and farms south of the Garonne River. But as a concept, Gascony is rock solid. Like Nirvana, it is a place of ideal happiness, an earthly Elysium, a land of milk, honey, duck confit and Armagnac as smooth as butterscotch. If anyone ever writes *A Year in Gascony*, watch out.

There is no hustle here, only flow—of rivers, of hills into ravines, and of life from one growing season into the next. Here, you marvel at the sheer abundance of everything except tourists. And noise. And traffic. It's not an area with any molten urban core but spread out softly like a fertile blanket over the Gers department in the Midi-Pyrénées. From there it moves west through the Lot-et-Garonne in lower Aquitaine over to the Atlantic, abutting portions of the Pyrénées south towards Spain.

Gascony is where small cities with honey-hued stone buildings cluster on the riverbanks. Northwest from Toulouse, there is Agen on the Garonne, where fat plums turn into sweet prunes, and Nérac on the Baïse, whose languid charms and old-style *chocolaterie* La Cigale inspired Joanne Harris's book *Chocolat*. There is Condom in the Gers, also on the Baïse, which has nothing to do with latex prophylactics, and everything to do with dark Armagnac brandy produced there and aged in oak barrels, served as the antidote to dinners where everything is steeped in pork or duck fat. There is Auch on the River Gers and a statue of Gascony's most famous prog-eny, the oft-portrayed Count d'Artag-nan, one of Alexandre Dumas's musketeers, who in real life, was involved in much derring-do for King Louis XIV. The area has a preponder-ance of 13th- and 14th-century forti-fied villages, or *bastides*, such as Larressingle and Montréal, and all throughout Gascony, there is a dense overlay of some 500 medieval châteaux and fortresses. Many are affixed with squared-off towers in the austere style unique to the area, built by the British over centuries of fighting against the French. The châteaux Busca-Maniban, Lavardens and Cassaigne are worthy of a detour and a morning. But even in the historical realm, cuisine has always been the coin of the realm, even a directive from on high. This is Henry IV country, the good king born in Pau, who first said—roughly translated—"A chicken in every pot." Now, it's foie gras on every plate.

There are stretches of sunflowers grown for oil and seeds, acres of fruit trees that heave with ripe peaches, figs and apricots, markets warmed by fresh peasant bread, Roquefort cheese. And there's Floc de Gascogne—a mixture of Armagnac and grape juice that will bring the roses to your cheeks. Yet it's true, duck fat is one of the major food groups here, along with cassoulet, dry-cured *magret*, thick rashers of bacon and every manner of sausage and terrine. But in Gascony, one gives in with abandon to these salty temptations.

Believe it or not, there's not even a downside for vegetarians, because the abundance of Gascon farms and orchards offers an almost wild sense of well-being for those who stay away from pig and fowl. "There is no soil like Gascon soil, no climate like Gascon climate," says Kate Hill. The exuberant American expat is the unrivaled master of all that is worth doing in Gascony—cooking, marketing, learning the palate, running your fingers through the dirt and discovering the chefs and producers of the region. "We are the California of France."

In short, Gascons are larger than life, the true *bon vivants* of France. There is one indispensable place in the area in which to learn one of life's key lessons—how to live it—and that is in Hill's kitchen and in her company. An itinerant Navy brat who grew up mostly in Hawaii, she procured a barge in Amsterdam twenty-five years ago and steered it into France. When it broke down in Gascony, she never left. Rooting herself in the rich local culinary tradition, she developed adroitness in preparing charcuterie, foie gras, confit, *rillettes*, among many other delicacies. Now Kate's expertise is sought after by professional chefs, amateur cooks and just regular men and women who wish to learn about the history and palate of Gascony. She gives courses and, sometimes, regional tours that last from four hours to four weeks, while her students stay at one of the darling hotels nearby. "I love to cover what people are interested in," she says about her shorter courses. "This is not a heavy duty cooking school, but my kitchen is always busy, and always our home base."

Kate's Kitchen-at-Camont is in Sainte-Colombe-en-Bruilhois, a four-hour train from Paris to the nearby town of Agen. In springtime, you might prepare a meal with fresh asparagus, artichokes, strawberries, spring lamb, duckling or rabbit. Summer, winter and fall offer other fresh market ingredients. And though the kitchen is well-equipped and bounteous as a 17th-century Flemish painting, where you could chop, eat, sauté and stuff all day, her other passion is to introduce guests to the vast and diverse dimensions of her Gascon neighborhood. "I love to peer down a beautiful alley, wander into a friend's garden, or visit one of the pig farmers who sources my charcuterie, she says. "To explore how food and history is all woven together, and how it ends up on our plate in this place called Gascony."

So voluptuaries, unite. And remember the French paradox? You may even lose weight, your cholesterol may well plummet. If, at the very least, you have just once tasted a *pruneau d'Agen* soaked in Armagnac, it will all have been worth it.

# 99

## The Food Center of the Universe

### LES HALLES DE LYON—PAUL BOCUSE, LYON

Let's not quibble over this. France is the gastronomic capital of the world and Lyon is the gastronomic capital of France. That makes Les Halles de Lyon the food center of the universe and the gold standard for covered markets in France. They are named after Paul Bocuse—one of the world's greatest chefs, widely credited as the inventor of Nouvelle Cuisine, and literally the poster boy of Lyon—who owes his career to a woman. It was women—the Mères Lyonnaises—who first defined the kitchens of Lyon and consequently changed culinary history.

At the end of the 19th century, as the silk trade began to decline, the prominent bourgeois families in Lyon were forced to dismiss their cooks. World War I and the economic collapse of 1929 also propelled many women into the kitchens of Lyon. They went to work in restaurants or even formed their own establishments where they served up hearty portions of perfectly prepared food, family style. Without consciously being part of any culinary movement, the Cuisine des Mères put Lyon on the gastronomic map.

At the time, there was a resurgence in regional cuisine, and the women knew instinctively how to refine it just enough to appeal to visitors beginning to travel through France in automobiles, following their *Guides Michelin*, which débuted in 1900. It was more than one-pot home cooking, and it far exceeded standardized hotel fare. Lyon's central location just west of the Alps and north of Provence, at the confluence of two major rivers, the Saône and Rhône, allows access to the freshest ingredients possible, which stream in daily.

The *mères* served limited menus, combining high bourgeois cooking with what the silk workers would find at the *bouchons*, the traditional Lyonnais restaurant where simple charcuterie could be eaten any time of day and washed down with carafes of Beaujolais.

Professor Rachel E. Black, who has been researching the *mères* and their part in the social history of France and the culinary world, points out why statistics are imprecise. "At the time, women couldn't have a bank account in France, and it's hard to run an official business without one," she says. She adds that no estimate can be made with certainty about how many female-owned restaurants there were in Lyon at the peak, but the trend continued until World War II.

Eugénie Brazier, the most famous *mère*, opened her restaurant in 1921 in the center of Lyon and later, a second in the hills outside town. In 1933, she was awarded three Michelin stars for both restaurants, making history as one of the first two women to earn three stars, and as the first chef to earn six stars in one year (a distinction she alone held until 1998). One day in 1946, a local boy, Paul Bocuse, rode his bike over to ask for a job and soon was an apprentice to Mère Brazier. He would become one of the world's first chef superstars. The original restaurant on rue Royale still serves some of her famous dishes—artichokes with foie gras, fricassée of veal sweetbreads and lobster, and of course, *quenelle*, the super-sized dumplings typical of Lyon. Mère Brazier perfected some of those recipes alongside Mère Fillioux at the restaurant belonging to the latter's husband on rue Duquesne. It was she who created some of the standards of Lyon gastronomy—pike *quenelle* casserole with crawfish butter, and *poularde de Bresse demi-deuil en vessie*—a chicken with black truffles under its skin (in "half-mourning"), poached in a pig bladder.

All of this history is beautifully, deliciously concentrated at Les Halles Bocuse. The marketplace has been the headquarters for Lyonnais gastronomy since 1859 and at its present location since 1971, where its exterior is deceivingly nondescript.

Inside, fifty-six merchants sell regional cheese, produce, *quenelles*, those plump Bresse chickens, pastry, bright red tarte aux pralines and charcuterie, charcuterie, charcuterie. The line is twenty deep at Sibilia (owned by Colette Sibilia) even at 9 A.M. on Easter morning, for pork sausage encrusted with pistachios, for *andouillette*—sausage made from tripe, and for *sabodet*—pig's head sausage. Lyonnais do love their organ meat. A few slices of spiced *saucisson sec* does me well for breakfast. Last night's dinner at Chabert & Fils, one of the city's iconic *bouchons*, had been delicious and seriously damaged my try-to-be vegetarian credentials. I couldn't eat *andouillete*, *fricassée de volaille*, beef snout and *quenelles* with shrimp sauce every day, but one must follow some gastronomic protocol when in Lyon.

It's hopping at the cheese counter at La Mère Richard, despite the death of the famed woman owner Renée Richard only weeks before my visit. Puffy rounds of Saint-Félicien are displayed with Picodon and Rigotte de Condrieu from the region, next to various flavors of Arôme de Lyon, a local cow's cheese infused with grape residue from wine production, as well as her specialty, Saint-Marcellin. There is a fragrant bowl of *cervelle des canuts* ("silk worker's brain"), a cheese spread made of *faisselle* and herbs, which mercifully contains no actual gray matter. A bag of bite-sized blocks of chèvre will do for a second course. Dessert is a slice of apple *galette* at a quiet table at Boulanger de l'Île Barbe.

Restaurants, seafood bars, wine bars complete the picture here at Les Halles, where a person can—and does—wander in bliss even on a Sunday, even on a holiday. One thing Lyon does brilliantly, even in the food realm, is to preserve its heritage without clinging to it, building upon that foundation to update and retell the city's narrative. That story is told to perfection at the modern, chic Les Halles. Mère Brazier hasn't wandered through here for almost forty years, but Paul Bocuse and the other great chefs of Lyon still do, knowing much of their magic starts right here.

# 100

## *Everything You Dream of*

### CORSICA

When she was growing up in Nice, my friend Françoise would sail over from the Côte d'Azur for summertime family jaunts to Corsica. No one is more passionate about her hometown than she, but when it comes to Corsica, she grows quiet, as if to introduce a solemn truth to follow. "It is ten times more beautiful than the most beautiful place in France," she declares and points to the cities on the map in front of us. Bonifacio, Calvi, Porto-Vecchio. "Every one of these places can fill an entire book."

And of course, there have been books—Boswell's famed 1768 travelogue of Corsica, and revered expatriate British writer Dorothy Carrington's many chronicles on her adopted home, especially the vivid portrayal of Corsican culture in *Granite Island: A Portrait of Corsica.* And lastly, an earlier one that reads like an advertorial for the tourist board, so lively is its prose, as colorful as the historical characters who have fleshed out the island's turbulent past. In *Corsica, in Its Picturesque, Social, and Historical Aspects: The Record of a Tour in the Summer of 1852,* the German historian Ferdinand Gregorovius writes, "... verily, I swear I have reached the magic shore of the lotus-eaters," upon entering the western seaside idyll of Isula Rossa. His infatuation was just beginning.

A little exaggeration can certainly sell a place, and this island—separated by a narrow strait from Sardinia due south—is the last refuge of the beach goddess or adventurer seeking the wildest geographical arrangements this earth can offer. If nothing on France's three coastlines can satisfy you, Corsica may well do you in.

In spite of Italian roots, from centuries belonging to Pisa and Genoa, Corsica has been a part of France since 1769—a link later reinforced by Napoleon Bonaparte, Corsica's most famous son, born that very same year in Ajaccio. Its position in the center of the Mediterranean has made it a plum bargaining chip for popes and the target of land-mad kings, overlords and pirates. But Corsica is and always was forbidding, its people not exactly unwelcoming, but relatively reserved in their hospitality compared to other sun-washed islands. In that way, it is often (though shouldn't be) overlooked.

You can fly to Corsica, but if you are a romantic, take a ferry from Marseille, Toulon or Nice, which can leave you at any one of six places. The northern part of the island, the Haute-Corse, has port towns of Calvi, Bastia and Isula Rossa. At the southern end, the Corse-du-Sud, are gleaming Bonifacio, Ajaccio and Porto-Vecchio. Once on the island, planning and patience are key. Bus service between the cities is infrequent, and you have to check schedules often. Driving can be hairy—narrow, often serpentine, roads that are jammed in August, distracting views and fast drivers who know the shortcuts better then you do. The way to see Corsica might best involve a base camp in the north or south from which to venture towards the Haute-Corse (which includes the wildly beachy and brambly Cap Corse, the little thumb extended towards Genoa) or the Corse-du-Sud, respectively.

Corsica is a mountain of granite plunked right into the sea, the most mountainous of all Mediterranean islands, with towns and beaches on the coast and all sorts of high-terrain activities packed into the green, river-and-lake-strewn interior spaces, as if baked into an already rich cake. Though many visitors opt for either seaside or inland adventure, it's definitely worthwhile to do both.

As one would expect from a Mediterranean island this stunning, the southern cities of Bonifacio and Porto-Vecchio play host to the glam set, whose yachts jostle around the harbor, one bigger than the next. Bonifacio is magnificent, with a bleached white citadel perched atop a stratified limestone promontory that hangs out perilously 230 feet above the harbor. The rampart walk is lovely, and if you have good legs and stamina, there is a steep climb down the King Aragon Steps, carved right into the rock face.

I recommend taking in the whole shining shore from a boat you can catch from town to further explore the nooks, crannies and caves along the coastline. If you want to swim, there are several options—a boat to the pristine Îles Lavezzi archipelago or a long hike to the joyfully secluded beach at Cala di Paraguano. Rondinara Beach, a white-sand enclave that is often dubbed the most beautiful in Europe, and Palombaggia Beach in Porto-Vecchio are not far off. When you come back to town, there are sturdy local wines and the freshest of fish. Food here is somewhat French, very Italian and all Mediterranean, a combination that lends itself to an enchanted, though typically rustic, cuisine. Corsican charcuterie is also legendary, with some visitors claiming they bring an extra suitcase to stock up on wild boar or pork sausages.

One unconventional way to see the natural beauty of the island is to take the train called U Trinighellu, or "the trembler," a moniker that in the past was no exaggeration. The main line runs north-south from Ajaccio traversing the heart of the island through Corte, a university town and the spiritual center of Corsica, then through Ponte Leccia to Bastia on the northeast coast. The train meanders along precipices past villages, chestnut groves, and many herds of livestock that regularly cross the tracks. A shorter spur runs east-west from the junction at Ponte Leccia to the coast at Calvi.

Before a recent upgrade to both the cars and tracks (which had been dogged with problems due to the rugged terrain), the old rickety trains were bone-rattling, terrifying and slow, but by all accounts more mythical. Now they are air-conditioned and designed with big glass windows so you can gather a wide vista. One can marvel at the engineering of the whole system, which took twenty-two years to build, much of the track being laid by hand over a century ago. The train goes from hill to hill over steep valleys on bridges of various ages and materials, the most famous of which, the Pont du Vecchio, just south of Ponte Leccia, was designed by Gustave Eiffel and completed in 1892.

If you are a hiker, you can do it, do it big, or do it really big here, with excursions lasting a few hours to two weeks. The island's interior is remote, wild and unspoiled. Parallel valleys are bounded by rivers that lash their way across the island and descend into capes, lagoons, coves and sloping maquis on the shore. The most extreme hike is the Grande Randonnée 20 (GR20), commonly regarded as the most difficult GR in Europe, which runs for 124 miles through the heart of Corsica at average altitudes of 3,500 to 6,500 feet. You can enter and exit the trail at any point, but another option is to hop off the train at any of the small towns on the route, bunk down at a little hotel, and make a day climb into the surrounding countryside. Col de Bavella is a good jumping-off-point for hiking excursions of every possible length, as well as rock climbing and canyoning, surrounded by some of the most striking high-altitude landscapes in Corsica.

There are over 200 beaches along Corsica's 620 miles of coastline—even small Cargèse on the western coast with its battling churches has the most adorable secluded beach with unisex topless volleyball. For pure beauty, I love the three-mile semicircular sweeping expanse of fine white sand at Calvi, where you can walk from the beach straight into forests of laricio pine, indigenous to Corsica. Calvi is a great base to explore the scenically and culturally rich Balagne region, and the coastline here is often described as one of the most dramatic cycling routes on the island. In fact, Corsica's appeal to cyclists is growing after the Tour de France started its 2013 race here to mark the event's 100th anniversary.

What is the most beautiful spot on this very beautiful island can spark a great deal of zealous debate. Some say it is the unspoiled Cap Corse, with its wild olive groves and dozens of abandoned towers the Genoans built to ward against pirates, that are still dignified, though crumbling, coastal sentries. A top contender is the magnificent Scandola Nature Reserve on the rugged west coast, accessible only by boat from Calvi or Porto. Here you find a combination of geologically eccentric cognac-colored rock formations and a deep blue clear sea. You might spot dolphins here, and a small boat can weave in and out of the coastal crevices. Equally spectacular are the nearby *calanques* of Piana and the Gulf of Porto, which are accessible by hike or car. The *calanques* (like their paler sisters in Marseille and Cassis) were formed by volcanic activity 250 million years ago and have been curiously shaped and eroded by the elements since. Some of the igneous rocks are infused with a bright porphyritic red, in jagged columns that extend hundreds of feet up into the sky. In the distance, through the *calanques*, at almost every turn, you see the sea, glimmering, blue and endless. This might be the most ideal of all the ideal places in Corsica to watch the sunset, with the flaming light of dusk setting the rock on fire as the sea kisses, then swallows, the sun.

გ%ა

# Books for Further Reading

Beauvoir, Simone de. *The Prime of Life: The Autobiography of Simone de Beauvoir.* Trans. Peter Green. New York: Paragon House, 1992.

Bruccoli, Matthew J. and Scottie Fitzgerald Smith. *Some Sort of Epic Grandeur: The Life of F. Scott Fitzgerald.* New York: Harcourt Brace Jovanovich, 1981.

Bruce, Evangeline. *Napoleon and Josephine: The Improbable Marriage.* New York: Scribner, 1995.

Colette. *Earthly Paradise: Colette's Autobiography Drawn from the Writings of Her Lifetime.* Ed. Robert Phelps. Trans. Herma Briffault and Derek Coltman. New York: Farrar, Straus & Giroux, 1966.

Faulks, Sebastian. *Birdsong.* New York: Random House, 1993.

Fisher, M.F.K. *Map of Another Town: a Memoir of Provence.* Boston: Little, Brown, 1964.

Fitzgerald, F. Scott. *Tender is the Night.* New York: Scribner, 1962.

Flanner, Janet (Genêt). *Paris Journal: Volume One: 1944-1955.* Ed. William Shawn. San Diego: Harcourt Brace Jovanovich, 1965.

Fraser, Antonia. *Marie Antoinette: The Journey.* New York: Nan A. Talese/ Doubleday, 2001.

Frieda, Leonie. *Catherine de' Medici: Renaissance Queen of France.* New York: Harper Perennial, 2006.

Frey, Julia. *Toulouse-Lautrec: A Life.* New York: Viking, 1994.

Hemingway, Ernest. *A Moveable Feast.* New York: Scribner, 1964.

Henry de Tessan, Christina. *Forever Paris: 25 Walks in the Footsteps of Chanel, Hemingway, Picasso, and More.* San Francisco: Chronicle Books, 2012.

James, Henry. *A Little Tour in France.* New York: Farrar, Straus & Giroux, 1983.

Moore, Roy and Alma Moore. *Thomas Jefferson's Journey to the South of France.* New York: Stewart, Tabori & Chang, 1999.

Jones, Ted. *The French Riviera: A Literary Guide for Travellers.* London: Tauris Parke Paperbacks, 2007.

Kenyon, Ronald W. *Monville: Forgotten Luminary of the French Enlightenment.* CreateSpace, 2013.

Lebovitz, David. *My Paris Kitchen.* Berkeley: Ten Speed Press, 2014.

Lovato, Kimberley. *Walnut Wine & Truffle Groves: Culinary Adventures in the Dordogne.* Philadelphia: Running Press, 2009.

Mazzeo, Tilar J. *The Widow Clicquot: The Story of a Champagne Empire and the Woman Who Ruled It.* New York: Harper Perennial, 2008.

Meyers, Jeffrey. *Scott Fitzgerald: A Biography.* New York: Harper Collins, 1994.

Napoleon Bonaparte, and Diana Reid Haig. *The Letters of Napoleon to Josephine.* Welwyn Garden City: Ravenhall, 2004.

O'Reilly, James, Larry Habegger, and Sean O'Reilly. *Travelers' Tales France.* San Francisco, CA: Travelers' Tales, Inc., 2002.

O'Reilly, James, Larry Habegger, and Sean O'Reilly. *Travelers' Tales Paris.* San Francisco, CA: Travelers' Tales, Inc., 2002.

O'Reilly, James and Tara Austen Weaver. *Travelers' Tales Provence.* San Francisco, CA: Travelers' Tales, Inc., 2003.

Pflaum, Rosalynd. *Grand Obsession: Madame Curie and Her World.* New York: Doubleday, 1989.

Sagan, Françoise. *Bonjour Tristesse.* Paris, 1954.

Salter, James. *A Sport and a Pastime.* New York: Modern Library, 1995.

Sand, George. *Story of My Life: The Autobiography of George Sand.* Ed. Thelma Jurgrau. Albany: State University of New York, 1991.

Sévigné, Madame de. *Selected Letters.* Trans. Leonard Tancock. London: Penguin Classics, 1982.

Shelley, Mary Wollstonecraft. *The Annotated Frankenstein.* Ed. Susan J. Wolfson, and Ronald Levao. Cambridge, MA: Belknap Press, 2012.

Stimmler-Hall, Heather and Kirsten Loop. *Naughty Paris: A Lady's Guide to the Sexy City.* Paris: Fleur de Lire Press, 2008.

Turner, Ralph V. *Eleanor of Aquitaine: Queen of France, Queen of England.* New Haven: Yale University Press, 2011.

Twain, Mark, Michael Meyer, and Leslie A. Fiedler. *The Innocents Abroad.* New York: Signet Classics, 2007.

Twain, Mark. *Personal Recollections of Joan of Arc.* Avenel, NJ: Gramercy Books, 1995.

Vaill, Amanda. *Everybody Was So Young: Gerald and Sara Murphy: A Lost Generation Love Story.* Boston: Houghton Mifflin Company, 1998.

Wellman, Kathleen. *Queens and Mistresses of Renaissance France.* New Haven: Yale University Press, 2013.

Wharton, Edith. *A Motor-Flight Through France.* Dekalb: Northern Illinois University Press, 1991.

Zimmerman, Anne. *An Extravagant Hunger: The Passionate Years of M.F.K. Fisher.* Berkeley: Counterpoint Press, 2012.

# Websites of Note

www.awomansparis.com
www.edible-paris.com
www.eleanorfootsteps.blogspot.com
www.elizabethmurray.com
www.frenchgeneral.com
www.kitchen-at-camont.com
www.lamomparis.com
www.onruetatin.com
www.plumlyon.com
www.secretsofparis.com
www.thegoodlifefrance.com
www.thepariskitchen.com

# *Index*

# Acknowledgments

By no means could I have written this book alone. I owe Renata Pepper my gratitude for her superb work in France, Kellie Duffy my thanks for her research assistance here at home, and Lydia DeSanctis the moon for her brilliant and tireless contribution to editing and researching this manuscript. Lavinia Spalding was and is endlessly supportive, the best friend, writer, and colleague I ever could imagine. I am grateful to Karen Lubeck for her research, and to Ray Mennin, who was a great help when I needed it most. I owe Beth Kseniak many thanks for her ideas and thoughtful reading of my manuscript. Abigail Pogrebin was incredibly giving of her time, friendship and editorial deftness—thank you. Thanks to Dolly Spalding, who smoothed out the countless rough spots in this book. There are no greater, smarter, saner, more patient, or more supportive gentlemen than my editors at Travelers' Tales, James O'Reilly and Larry Habegger, and I owe them my deepest admiration and gratitude.

When I first received this assignment, I was daunted by the task of whittling my initial list of about 100,000 places down to 100. The first people I contacted were Thérèse Verrat, Françoise Drotter, Antonia Dauphin, Ann Puderbaugh, Betsy Ennis, and Merry Mullings—I knew their ideas would be amazing, and they were. I loved Ava Mennin's fresh take on what women would love in France. Katherine Johnstone at ATOUT France was absolutely invaluable as a resource and support. Thanks, as well, to Marion Fourestier, who helped me greatly on the Côte d'Azur.

Over the course of writing this book, I learned how generous people are with their opinions, memories, and time. Some let me pick their brains, others I interviewed, and still others simply emailed me with the most brilliant idea ever. My fellow writer and traveler Kimberley Lovato was my very first interview on this book, and enormously helpful and wise. Likewise Erin Byrne, who shared her love and knowledge of France, and many ingenious ideas with me. So many others contributed greatly to this book, and showed me corners of France I might never have known about. I owe deep gratitude to Elizabeth Stribling, Heather Stimmler-Hall, Katrina Vanderlip, Sue Morris, Keris Salmon, Dana Thomas, Barbara Vaughn Hoimes, Professor Kathleen Wellman, Constance Hale, Carol Young Gallagher, Julia Frey, Lanie Goodman, Anna Kate Hipp, Sharon Kay Penman, Jean Davis, Jessica Stedman Guff, Isabelle Mathez, Nancy Evans, Melora Mennesson, Martha McCully, Natalie Randall, Wiz Lippincott, Merle Mullin, Maxine Rose Schur, Sophie Sutton, Kim Massee, Connaught Thomas, Janet Hulstrand, Christina Henry de Tessan, Rachel E. Black, Judith Williams, Kirsten Poitras, Carol Reid-Gaillard, François Gaillard, Susan Holmes, Christy Prunier, Maria Turgeon, Karen Robert, Anne Lepesant, Susanna Salk, and Valerie Cooper. I thank Judith Friedman for allowing me to interrupt her vacation in Paris to do some footwork for me, and Barbie Griffin Cole, too. My thanks to Ann Leary for all of her help all along the way.

I was repeatedly amazed by the organization and efficiency of the regional tourism offices and press officers throughout France. Florence Lecointre of the Côte d'Azur tourist office was a huge help and always responded within seconds to my many emails. Likewise her counterparts: Véronique Beigenger in Burgundy, Céline Boute in Aquitaine, Patricia de Pouzilhac in

Languedoc-Roussillon, Melody Raynaud in Provence Alpes-Côte d'Azur, Sandrine Pailloncy in Poitou-Charentes, and Jérôme Mercier-Papin in Normandy. I was frequently on the road in France and always alone, and I am so grateful to those who took such excellent care of me, especially Laura Brillon in Lyon, Nathalie Beau de Lomanie in the Pays Basque, Véronique Allen in Nîmes, Claire Lesourd in Normandy, Armelle le Goff in Calvados, Lauren Laval in the Camargue, Virginie Taupenot-Daniel in Burgundy, and Benjamin West in Reims.

Sarah Albee is a great friend, and she keeps me from getting done in when the going is tough. I owe countless thanks to Dani Shapiro for so many years of inspiration and guidance, and for being my bright light in our small town. Thank you, as well, all my dear hiking partners for keeping me sane and full of fresh air. Thank you Ann Hertberg for supporting me in countless ways, Liz Funk for the yummy sustenance, Sam Funk for research and technical help. My eternal gratitude to Maria daSilva for taking care of so much. A special thanks to my friends at the Oliver Wolcott Library in Litchfield, Connecticut, who dealt with my endless stream of book requests—always with great cheer.

My family, especially my parents Roman and Ruth, were awfully understanding as I disappeared from view. Thank you. As for my husband Mark Mennin. He is not only the most funny, patient, and brilliant man I have ever known, but he is a walking database on French art and architecture, and a repository of the details of our life and travels together in France. *Merci, mon amour.*

# About the Author

Marcia DeSanctis is a former television news producer who has worked for Barbara Walters, ABC, CBS, and NBC News. She is an award-winning essayist whose work has appeared in numerous publications including *Vogue, Marie Claire, Town & Country, O the Oprah Magazine, More, Tin House,* and *The New York Times*. Her travel essays have been widely anthologized and she is the recipient of three Lowell Thomas Awards for excellence in travel journalism, as well as a Solas Award for best travel writing. She holds a degree from Princeton University in Slavic Languages and Literature and a Masters in International Relations from the Fletcher School of Law and Diplomacy. She worked for several years in Paris, and today lives in northwest Connecticut with her husband and two children.